OECD Regions and Cities at a Glance 2022

OECD
BETTER POLICIES FOR BETTER LIVES

This document, as well as any data and map included herein, are without prejudice to the status of or sovereignty over any territory, to the delimitation of international frontiers and boundaries and to the name of any territory, city or area.

The statistical data for Israel are supplied by and under the responsibility of the relevant Israeli authorities. The use of such data by the OECD is without prejudice to the status of the Golan Heights, East Jerusalem and Israeli settlements in the West Bank under the terms of international law.

Note by the Republic of Türkiye
The information in this document with reference to "Cyprus" relates to the southern part of the Island. There is no single authority representing both Turkish and Greek Cypriot people on the Island. Türkiye recognises the Turkish Republic of Northern Cyprus (TRNC). Until a lasting and equitable solution is found within the context of the United Nations, Türkiye shall preserve its position concerning the "Cyprus issue".

Note by all the European Union Member States of the OECD and the European Union
The Republic of Cyprus is recognised by all members of the United Nations with the exception of Türkiye. The information in this document relates to the area under the effective control of the Government of the Republic of Cyprus.

Please cite this publication as:
OECD (2022), *OECD Regions and Cities at a Glance 2022*, OECD Publishing, Paris, *https://doi.org/10.1787/14108660-en*.

ISBN 978-92-64-77817-7 (print)
ISBN 978-92-64-73358-9 (pdf)
ISBN 978-92-64-78796-4 (HTML)
ISBN 978-92-64-93018-6 (epub)

OECD Regions and Cities at a Glance
ISSN 2617-3204 (print)
ISSN 2617-3212 (online)

Photo credits: Cover illustration: © Jeffrey Fisher. Chapter 1: © Corbis/Inmagine ltd. Page 35: © Artem Peretiatko/iStock/Getty Images Plus. Chapter 2: © Kiyoshi Hijiki. Chapter 3: © GlobalStock/iStock/Getty Images Plus. Chapter 4: © Pavel Vakhrushev/Shutterstock.com.

Corrigenda to publications may be found on line at: *www.oecd.org/about/publishing/corrigenda.htm*.

Foreword

Recent shocks to gas and energy supply and widespread increases in costs of living are challenging people's living standards in nearly all places in the OECD area. These shocks have put further pressure on cities and regions around the world, which, in the last few years, have been facing global megatrends and a global pandemic. Ageing, climate change and digital transformation, among others, were already challenging our economies and societies when the COVID-19 pandemic started at the beginning of 2020. All these developments have had unequal consequences within countries and the need to cope with them is increasing the demand for geographically granular evidence, indicators and statistics to support policy makers at all levels of government.

In this respect, *OECD Regions and Cities at a Glance* provides a comprehensive picture of past successes and likely challenges that regions and cities in OECD members and partner countries will face in their efforts to build stronger, more sustainable and more resilient economies. By relying on a combination of traditional and more innovative data sources, it describes the evolving nature of spatial disparities within countries from a multidimensional perspective.

The 2022 edition of *OECD Regions and Cities at a Glance* provides several new features. For example, it highlights how living expenses vary across cities and regions in terms of housing costs and energy needs (i.e. heating and cooling spaces), among others. The report also provides evidence of how regions and cities are adapting differently to a post-pandemic world, including in terms of the unequal uptake of remote working, the digital skills demanded in regional labour markets and the changing geography of housing demand. Other new features of this edition include measures of digital infrastructure quality across space, new subnational estimates of poverty rates, as well as a full set of subnational climate indicators.

The first chapter summarises how the economic impact of the pandemic spread across space and describes the regional patterns of the recovery with the most up-to-date available statistics. The chapter also includes subnational indicators on tourism, cultural industries and integration in global markets, which are new to this edition.

Another chapter covers the subnational dimension of climate change through a large set of new indicators on the environmental transition of regions and cities, including energy, industry, agriculture, transport and exposure to extreme climate events such as floods and wildfires. The indicators show that progress towards the goal of net-zero emissions is uneven between and within countries, with some regions still heavily relying on carbon-intensive energy sources like coal.

The final two chapters of the report include new insights on long-term demographic trends across regions, including regional population projections for a large number of OECD countries. One of these chapters presents recent trends of ageing, urbanisation and international migration. The other chapter focuses on housing affordability, health outcomes, digital infrastructure and inequality in income and services that affect the quality of life in OECD regions.

Taken together, the report provides a comprehensive and unique tool for decision makers at all levels of government who aim to account for specific assets and challenges of regions and cities when designing policy.

Acknowledgements

The *OECD Regions and Cities at a Glance 2022* report was produced by the OECD Centre for Entrepreneurship, SMEs, Regions and Cities, led by Director Lamia Kamal-Chaoui, as part of the Programme of Work of the Regional Development Policy Committee and its Working Party on Territorial Indicators. The report was managed and edited by Paolo Veneri, Deputy Head of the Economic Analysis, Data and Statistics Division, under the supervision of Rudiger Ahrend, Head of the Economic Analysis, Data and Statistics Division. Lead authors for each of the chapters are Alison Weingarden (Chapter 1), Alexandre Banquet (Chapter 2), Claire Hoffmann (Chapter 2), Cem Özgüzel (Chapter 3), and Marcos Díaz Ramírez (Chapter 4). Eric Gonnard and Claire Hoffman led the collection and statistical analysis of regional and metropolitan statistics respectively. The chapters of the publication benefitted from the contribution of Maria Paula Caldas, Nikos Patias, Ekaterina Travkina and Jan Domagalski. Alison Weingarden provided drafting contributions throughout the entire report. Maria Paula Caldas co-ordinated the design and implementation of the country pages complementing the report.

The report and country pages benefitted from comments by the delegates of the Working Party on Territorial Indicators and OECD colleagues, in particular Nadim Ahmad, David Burgalassi, Delphine Clavreul, Andres Fuentes Hutfilter, Mateo Ledesma Bohorquez, Alexander Lembcke, Maria Varinia Michalun, Ana Moreno-Monroy, Andrew Paterson, Wessel Vermeulen. Pilar Philip prepared the report for publication.

Table of contents

Follow OECD Publications on:

https://twitter.com/OECD

https://www.facebook.com/theOECD

https://www.linkedin.com/company/organisation-eco-cooperation-development-organisation-cooperation-developpement-eco/

https://www.youtube.com/user/OECDiLibrary

https://www.oecd.org/newsletters/

This book has...

StatLinks

A service that delivers Excel® files from the printed page!

Look for the *StatLink* at the bottom of the tables or graphs in this book. To download the matching Excel® spreadsheet, just type the link into your Internet browser or click on the link from the digital version.

Reader's guide

OECD Regions and Cities at a Glance 2022 provides a comprehensive assessment of how regions and cities across the OECD are progressing in their efforts to build stronger, more sustainable and more resilient economies and societies. The publication provides a unique comparative picture in a number of aspects connected to economic development, well-being, demographic change and environmental transition across regions and cities in OECD and selected non-OECD countries. The report assesses how regions and cities are adapting differently to the challenges of a strong recovery after the COVID-19 pandemic, the increasing pressure for energy transition and for ensuring affordable costs of living. The report focuses on the spatially heterogeneous effects of the COVID-19 pandemic as well as of those triggered by ongoing megatrends, such as urbanisation, digitalisation and demographic change.

The report is composed of four chapters, each with a specific thematic focus. Chapter 1 assesses economic performance across regions during the COVID-19 pandemic and subsequent recovery. It also describes longer-run trends in regional economic disparities within OECD countries. Indicators presented in the chapter include quarterly employment and unemployment, gross domestic product (GDP) per capita, productivity levels and growth, tourism, cultural industries, and trade and integration in global markets.

Chapter 2 examines progress on the environmental transition of regions through a wide range of indicators, including energy use, emissions by sector and exposure to extreme climate events. The chapter shows that, while most OECD countries aim for climate neutrality by 2050, progress is uneven between and within countries, with some regions still heavily relying on carbon-intensive energy sources.

Chapter 3 presents an overview of socio-demographic trends in regions and cities across OECD countries. It discusses how the projection of population trends, ageing and urbanisation are playing out in regions and cities. The chapter presents indicators on elderly dependency rate, within-country residential mobility, population growth and decline, as well as new evidence on the presence of migrants in OECD regions and their integration in regional labour markets.

Chapter 4 presents key aspects of inclusion and liveability in regions and cities, such as housing affordability, income inequalities and quality of the Internet connection. The chapter also assesses the health system's capacity, poverty and access to services. It highlights how regions and cities adapted differently from the shock of the COVID-19 pandemic with respect to remote working, digitalisation and housing demand.

Throughout the publication, regional disparities in different domains are looked at through the persistence of disparities across regions and cities over space and time. More precisely, the report proposes several approaches to measure regional disparities:

- A first, simple approach is the difference between the maximum and minimum regional values in a country (regional range).
- A second approach consists of ranking regions by the value of an indicator and taking the ratio (or the difference) between the highest value representing 20% of the population and the lowest value

of the regions representing 20% of the population. This approach assesses regional disparities less sensitive to possible outliers and cross-country differences in the size of regions.

- A third approach consists of using standard composite indexes, such as the Theil general entropy index,[1] or the Gini index, which reflect inequality among all regions. One advantage of the Theil index is that it allows to distinguish overall regional disparities in within-country and between-country components.
- A fourth approach consists of summarising spatial disparities by type of territory. This includes using the degree of urbanisation or the OECD classifications of small administrative regions (Territorial Level 3, TL3), such as distinguishing between metropolitan regions, regions close to a metropolitan area and regions far from a metropolitan area.

Geographic areas utilised

This publication features statistical indicators at three different scales, which are administrative regions, functional urban areas (FUAs) composed of local units and areas defined from grid cells of regular size. The table below summarises the different geographic areas for which the publication reports indicators.

Category	Description
Administrative subnational regions	Large region (Territorial Level 2) Small region (Territorial Level 3)
Functional aggregations of local units	Functional urban area (based on local units, OECD coverage) Cities (based on local units, OECD coverage)
Grid-cell areas	Grid-based functional urban area (world coverage) Cities (world coverage)

Administrative regions

Traditionally, regional analysis has used data collected for administrative regions, that is, the regional boundaries within a country as organised by governments. Data on administrative regions has also the advantage to refer to areas that are often under the responsibility of a certain subnational government or to the scale targeted by a specific policy implemented at the national or subnational level. Regions are classified in two scales: large regions (Territorial Level 2, TL2) and small regions (Territorial Level 3, TL3), which ensure comparability across countries.

FUAs composed of local administrative units

The places where people live, work and socialise may have little formal relation to the administrative units around them. For example, a person may inhabit one city or region but work in another and, on the weekends, practice a sport in a third. A broad set of linkages, such as job mobility, production systems or collaboration among firms, determines the interactions occurring between regions. Such interactions often cross local administrative boundaries.

In order to capture the above-mentioned interactions, the report uses the FUA definition, which was developed by the European Commission (EC) and the OECD[2] (see the section below or Dijkstra et al., 2019).[3] Boundaries of FUAs are available in practically all OECD countries. Being composed of a city and its commuting zone, FUAs encompass the economic and functional extent of cities, based on daily people's movements. Especially in the case of cities, the notion of FUA can better guide the way national and city governments plan infrastructure, transportation, housing, schools and space for culture and recreation. In summary, FUAs can trigger a change in the way policies are planned and implemented, better integrating and adapting them to local needs.

Areas defined from grid cells of regular size

Some sections of the publications, including land use, access to public transport and built-up areas, refer to geographic areas delineated from gridded data available at regularly sized cells rather than at local administrative units.

More specifically, grid cells of one km^2 are used to estimate the boundaries of cities and FUAs across the entire world. Cities are defined – according to the degree of urbanisation[4] – as clusters of contiguous cells with at least 1 500 inhabitants per km^2 and at least 50 000 inhabitants overall. Grid-based FUAs are composed of cities plus surrounding cells that are estimated to be in their commuting zones, based on a probabilistic model explained in Moreno-Monroy, Schiavina and Veneri (2020).[5] While this method is less direct than the use of commuting flow data to determine the areas of influence of cities, it can be consistently applied to the entire world while maximising international comparability.

Definition of metropolitan areas

In this report, the concept of FUAs is used to define metropolitan areas. The OECD-EU definition of FUAs consists of cities (local units where at least half of the population lives in clusters of densely populated grid cells with at least 50 000 inhabitants) and adjacent local units with high levels of commuting (travel-to-work flows) towards the cities. This definition overcomes previous limitations for international comparability of city and metropolitan statistics linked to administrative boundaries. A minimum threshold for the population size of the FUAs is set at 50 000 inhabitants. The definition is applied to nearly all OECD countries and it identifies about 1 200 FUAs of different sizes.[6]

The aim of this approach to FUAs is to create a methodology that can be applied across the whole OECD, thus increasing comparability across countries, unlike definitions and methodologies created within individual countries, which have been internally focused.[7] In order to establish this cross-country methodology, common thresholds and similar geographical units across countries were defined. These units and thresholds may not correspond to the ones chosen in the national definitions. Therefore, the resulting FUAs may differ from the ones derived from national definitions and the OECD functional urban delimitation may not capture all the local factors and dynamics in the same way as national definitions.

Classifications of regions and areas

Territorial level classification

Regions within the 38 OECD countries are classified on 2 territorial levels reflecting the administrative organisation of countries. The 433 OECD large (TL2) regions represent the first administrative tier of subnational government, for example, the Ontario Province in Canada. There are 2 414 OECD small (TL3) regions, with each TL3 being contained in a TL2 region (except for the United States). For example, the TL2 region of Aragon in Spain encompasses three TL3 regions: Huesca, Teruel and Zaragoza. TL3 regions correspond to administrative regions, with the exception of Australia, Canada, Germany and the United States.[8] All the regions are defined within national borders.

This classification – which, for European countries, is largely consistent with the Eurostat NUTS 2021 classification – facilitates greater comparability of geographic units at the same territorial level.[9] Indeed, these two levels, which are officially established and relatively stable in all member countries, are used as a framework for implementing regional policies in most countries.

Due to limited data availability, labour market indicators in Canada are presented for groups of TL3 regions.

For the non-OECD countries in this report, only TL2 regions have been identified for Brazil, the People's Republic of China, India, Peru, South Africa and Tunisia, whereas for Bulgaria and Romania, TL2 and TL3 are derived from the European NUTS.

Classification of small regions by access to metropolitan areas

The OECD metropolitan/non-metropolitan typology for small regions (TL3) helps to assess differences in socio-economic trends in regions – both within and across countries – by controlling for the presence/absence of metropolitan areas and the extent to which the latter is accessible by the population living in each region. According to such typology, TL3 regions are classified as "metropolitan" if more than half of their population lives in an FUA of at least 250 000 inhabitants and as "non-metropolitan" otherwise. A "metropolitan region" becomes a "large metropolitan region" if the FUA accounting for more than half of the regional population has over 1.5 million inhabitants.

In turn, the typology further classifies "non-metropolitan" regions based on the size of the FUA that is most accessible to the regional population. More specifically, "non-metropolitan" TL3 regions are sub-classified into three possible types:

- *With access to a metropolitan area*, if at least half of the regional population can reach an FUA of at least 250 000 inhabitants within a 60-minute car ride.
- *With access to a small/medium city*, if at least half of the regional population can reach an FUA of between 50 000 and 250 000 inhabitants within a 60-minute car ride.
- *Remote*, if reaching the closest FUA by car takes more than 60 minutes for more than half of the regional population.

The method relies on publicly available grid-level population data and localised information on driving conditions.[10]

In this report, the five types of regions identified are sometimes aggregated to three classes only, as indicated in the table below.

Acronym	Grouping	Reduced grouping
MR-L	Large metropolitan region	Metropolitan region
MR-M	Metropolitan region	
NM-M	Region near a metropolitan area	Region near a metropolitan area
NM-S	Region with/near a small-medium city	Region far from a metropolitan area
NM-R	Remote region	

Classification of small regions by degree of urbanisation

Traditionally the OECD has classified TL3 regions as predominantly urban (PU), intermediate (IN) or predominantly rural (PR) regions. This typology is mainly based on population density in each local unit, combined with the existence of urban centres where at least one-quarter of the regional population resides. An extended regional typology has been adopted to distinguish between rural regions that are located close to larger urban centres and those that are not. The result is a four-fold classification of TL3 regions: predominantly urban regions (PU), intermediate regions (IN), predominantly rural regions close to a city (PRC) and predominantly rural remote regions (PRR). The distance from urban centres is measured by the driving time necessary for a certain share of the regional population to reach an urban centre with at least 50 000 people (see Figure A.1 in Annex A for a detailed description of the criteria and the resulting classification of TL3 regions). Due to a lack of data, the extended typology has not yet been applied to Australia, Chile or Korea. In 2014, the European Union (EU) modified the rural-urban typology, using 1-km^2 population grids as building blocks to identify rural or urban communities, with the aim of improving international comparability; for the OECD-EU countries, this rural-urban typology is presented in the publication.

Sources of data for territorial statistics

OECD Regions and Cities at a Glance 2022 includes a selection of indicators from the OECD Regional Database, the OECD Metropolitan Areas Database and a number of indicators modelled by the OECD specifically for this publication. More specifically, some sections of the report provide, for the first time, comparable indicators on population, land use and quality of the Internet connection at both regional and metropolitan levels, among others.

The report also presents new, modelled indicators on the environmental transition, including on greenhouse gas (GHG) emission by sector, energy production and exposure to extreme climate events, for which various global geospatial data sources were used, as reported in the annexes of the publication.

Most of the indicators presented in the publication refer to TL2 and TL3 regions and come from official national sources, following internationally consistent methods for cross-country comparability. At the same time, regional and local data are increasingly available from a variety of sources: surveys, geo-coded data, administrative records, big data and data produced by users. While countries are making use of various sources to produce and analyse data at different geographic levels, significant methodological constraints still exist, making it a challenge to produce sound, internationally comparable statistics linked to a location. The trade-off between sound methodological estimations and international comparability should always be considered, as the latter depends on universally available information.

Most of the indicators for cities and FUAs are derived by integrating different sources of data, making use of geographic information system (GIS) techniques and adjusting existing regional data to non-administrative boundaries. Two types of methods to obtain estimates at the desired geographical level are applied, both requiring the use of GIS tools to disaggregate socio-economic data. The first method makes use of gridded data at different resolutions, which are always smaller than the considered regions. The statistics for one region are obtained by superimposing the source data onto regional boundaries. In these cases, the regional value is either the sum or the weighted average of the values observed in the source data within the (approximated) area delimited by the regional boundaries. For example, this method has been applied to estimate population projections in metropolitan areas.

The second method makes use of GIS tools to adjust or downscale data, available only at geographical levels that are similar or even larger than the geographical units of interest. In this case, the adopted method uses additional data (e.g. population) inputs that capture how the phenomenon under study is distributed across space.

Further resources

The different topics are visualised through interactive graphs and maps in the *OECD Regions and Cities Data Visualisation* platform (*https://regions-cities-atlas.oecd.org/*). Users can select from among all the indicators included in the OECD Regional and Metropolitan Areas databases and display them in different linked dynamic views such as maps, time trends and histograms. The website also provides access to the data underlying the indicators.

Another web tool (*https://www.oecd-local-sdgs.org/*) provides easy access to monitor the distance to the end values of the 17 United Nations Sustainable Development Goals (SDGs) for regions and cities in OECD and partner countries. The tool also compares the performance with other regions and cities in their respective country and helps identify peers in other countries.

The interactive web-based tool *www.oecdregionalwellbeing.org/* allows users to measure well-being in each region, compare it against over 400 other OECD regions and monitor progress over time. Each region is assessed in 11 areas central to quality of life: income, jobs, health, access to services, environment, education, safety, civic engagement, housing, social support network and life satisfaction.

Acronyms and abbreviations

	Description
Australia (TL2)	TL2 regions of Australia
Australia (TL3)	TL3 regions of Australia
GIS	Geographic information system
GDP	Gross domestic product
FUA	Functional urban area
IN	Intermediate (region)
LFS	Labour force survey
MA	Metropolitan area (functional urban area with a population of more than 500 000 inhabitants)
NEET	Adults neither employed nor in education or in training
NOG	Non-official grid
OECD#	The sum of all of the OECD regions where regional data are available (# number of countries included in the sum)
OECD# average	The weighted mean of the OECD regional values (# number of countries included in the average)
OECD#UWA	The unweighted mean of the country values (# number of countries included in the average)
PCT	Patent Co-operation Treaty
$PM_{2.5}$	Particulate matter (concentration of fine particles in the air)
PPP	Purchasing power parity
PR	Predominantly rural (region)
PRC	Predominantly rural (region) close to a city
PRR	Predominantly rural remote (region)
PU	Predominantly urban (region)
R&D	Research and development
SNG	Subnational government
TL2	Territorial level 2
TL3	Territorial level 3
Total # countries	The sum of all regions where regional data are available, including OECD and non-OECD countries

OECD country codes

Code	Country	Code	Country
AUS	Australia	ISL	Iceland
AUT	Austria	ISR	Israel
BEL	Belgium	ITA	Italy
CAN	Canada	JPN	Japan
CHE	Switzerland	KOR	Korea
CHL	Chile	LUX	Luxembourg
COL	Colombia	LVA	Latvia
CRI	Costa Rica	LTU	Lithuania
CZE	Czech Republic	MEX	Mexico
DEU	Germany	NLD	Netherlands
DNK	Denmark	NOR	Norway
ESP	Spain	NZL	New Zealand
EST	Estonia	POL	Poland

Code	Country	Code	Country
FIN	Finland	PRT	Portugal
FRA	France	SVK	Slovak Republic
GBR	United Kingdom	SVN	Slovenia
GRC	Greece	SWE	Sweden
HUN	Hungary	TUR	Türkiye
IRL	Ireland	USA	United States

Note on Israel: The statistical data for Israel are supplied by and under the responsibility of the relevant Israeli authorities. The use of such data by the OECD is without prejudice to the status of the Golan Heights, East Jerusalem and Israeli settlements in the West Bank under the terms of international law.

Notes

1. With the α coefficient equal to 1.
2. See Dijkstra, L., H. Poelman and P. Veneri (2019), "The EU-OECD definition of a functional urban area", *OECD Regional Development Working Papers*, No. 2019/11, OECD Publishing, Paris, *https://doi.org/10.1787/d58cb34d-en*. See also the "Definition of metropolitan areas" section.
3. See Dijkstra, Poelman and Veneri (2019).
4. For more details on the degree of urbanisation, see *https://ec.europa.eu/eurostat/web/degree-of-urbanisation/background*.
5. Moreno-Monroy, A., M. Schiavina and P. Veneri (2020), "Metropolitan areas in the world. Delineation and population trends", *Journal of Urban Economics*, Vol. 125, *http://dx.doi.org/10.1016/j.jue.2020.103242*.
6. For a detailed explanation, see Dijkstra, Poelman and Veneri (2019).
7. Some OECD countries have adopted a definition for their own metropolitan areas or urban systems that looks beyond the administrative approach. For example, Australia (Australian Bureau of Statistics, 2012), Canada (Statistics Canada, 2002) and United States (U.S. Office of Management and Budget, 2000) use a functional approach similar to the one adopted here, to identify metropolitan areas. Several independent research institutions and National Statistical Offices have identified metropolitan regions in Italy, Spain, Mexico and United Kingdom based on the functional approach.
8. The US TL3 regions are based on the Bureau of Economic Analysis' Economic Areas. For the latest information on the methodology, please refer to: *http://beagov.prod.acquia-sites.com/sites/default/files/newsreleases/general/2004/pdf/rea1104.pdf*.
9. For European countries, the Eurostat NUTS 2 and 3 classifications correspond to the OECD TL2 and 3, with the exception of Belgium, France, Germany and the United Kingdom where the NUTS 1 level corresponds to the OECD TL2.
10. Details on the method can be found in: Fadic, M., et al. (2019), "Classifying small (TL3) regions based on metropolitan population, low density and remoteness", *OECD Regional Development Working Papers*, No. 2019/06, OECD Publishing, Paris, *https://doi.org/10.1787/b902cc00-en*.

Executive summary

As regions and cities aim to recoup losses from the COVID-19 pandemic, sharply higher energy prices and shocks to gas supply pose new challenges for OECD economies. Despite the robust and widespread economic recovery in most OECD regions over the last two years, these shocks are affecting regions and cities differently. Many businesses now face higher costs of production, especially in energy-intensive industries and regions that rely on natural gas and fuel imports. For households, those living in cold regions will spend more on heating this winter and poorer households will experience relatively greater disruptions from rising energy prices. Finding affordable housing is also proving increasingly difficult in many places, but especially in large metropolitan areas, where housing demand is shifting towards more suburban locations. Policy makers need granular and timely evidence to understand patterns and trends in their regions and cities in order to respond effectively to people's needs.

This edition of *OECD Regions and Cities at a Glance* sheds light on the territorial impacts of recent economic developments across regions and cities in OECD members and partner countries. The COVID-19 pandemic had especially sizeable and widespread effects on economies, the health of people and their livelihoods. Some effects were transitory and their patterns reversed as regions recovered; others persisted well beyond the initial phases of the crisis. Between 2019 and 2020, the median region in the OECD saw a 5% decline in GDP per capita, but one-fifth of regions experienced declines of 10% or more. By combining official statistics with indicators from less conventional data sources, the report highlights territorial differences in economic growth and environmental progress along with social trends such as income inequality, housing affordability and demographic change at detailed geographical breakdowns.

Regional economic disparities remain large by historical standards. However, contrary to widespread belief, regional economic disparities did not increase in most countries during the first year of the crisis (2020); if anything, they slightly narrowed in a situation of widespread economic decline. Remote regions and those far from cities continue to lag behind metropolitan regions in terms of GDP per capita levels and growth. Foreign direct investment in OECD economies remains concentrated geographically, mostly favouring high-GDP regions. Similarly, cultural and creative sectors tend to concentrate in cities and capitals, with shares of creative jobs in some capital regions twice the country average. Moreover, productivity in the top regions remains nearly double that of the least productive regions within the same country.

Lockdowns and restrictions from the pandemic also led to unprecedented reductions in global greenhouse gas (GHG) emissions in 2020, although emissions rebounded strongly when these restraints were lifted. While most OECD countries aim for climate neutrality by 2050, progress is uneven and most regions and countries will need to do more to achieve their ambitious goals. Challenges in reducing the emissions from electricity production differ by region because energy sources and infrastructure for electricity generation vary substantially across places. For example, more than 50 regions across the OECD rely primarily on coal (a heavy pollutant) for electricity generation. Similarly, 50 European regions use mostly natural gas, a cleaner source, but one that depends on imports and eventually also needs to be phased out. Aside from coal-intensive regions, remote regions tend to use cleaner sources of power (e.g. renewables) than metropolitan regions.

Ongoing urbanisation and ageing trends also contributed to keep regional economic disparities stark and persistent over the last two decades. In OECD countries, the share of population living in cities has increased by 3 percentage points (pp) since 2000, reaching 49%, a trend expected to continue in the foreseeable future. Cities continue to attract most foreign-born people, as well as young migrants from other parts of the country. Even though ageing is ubiquitous, it typically is much stronger in rural and remote regions. This further challenges the provision of services. For example, adjusting for population, hospital bed rates are almost 50% lower in regions far from metropolitan areas compared to metropolitan areas and this gap has been increasing over time.

The growth of cities and metropolitan areas – as well as their advantages in terms of productivity and wages – typically comes with some costs, including lower housing affordability. For example, households in some regions of the Finland, Germany, Israel, the Netherlands and the United Kingdom spend on average 30% or more of their income on housing. Across metropolitan areas, buying a house in the city centre is 30% more expensive than in a suburban location, on average.

As noticeable from geographical changes in the housing demand, the sudden rise of remote working has changed the spatial reach of labour markets. While house prices in all locations have been rising over the last decade, prices in large metropolitan areas have started to grow faster in suburbs relative to central neighbourhoods after the start of the pandemic. Cities and metropolitan areas were also able to adapt faster to remote working due to the type of jobs located there, as well as generally better digital infrastructure. Across Europe, between 2019 and 2020, the share of remote workers increased by 70% in rural areas but it almost tripled in cities.

High-quality digital infrastructure is important for regions and cities to thrive in the current circumstances. Although the investment in digital infrastructure is contributing to closing some of the regional digital divides, many regions are still lagging. In some regions of Chile, Costa Rica, Israel, Japan, Mexico and the United States, one-fourth or more of the population lacks access to broadband Internet. Even when the Internet is available, its speed is still 40% lower outside metropolitan areas than within them. For example, two-thirds of OECD countries have Internet speed below the OECD average in regions far from metropolitan areas.

In 2021, a broad-based recovery followed the widespread economic decline of regions in the preceding year. By June 2022, half of the OECD regions had reached pre-pandemic employment levels. Still, women and youth struggle more in the labour market compared to other demographic groups, especially in regions with high unemployment rates. As of 2021, the median gap in unemployment rates between youth and the entire working-age population was approximately 11 pp across OECD regions, 2 pp higher than before the pandemic. Similarly, the employment rate among women was 12 pp lower than among men in the median region. Lower participation rates account for a significant share of the shortfall in women's employment, especially for female immigrants.

The pandemic has posed great societal challenges but it has also led to experimentation with digitalisation and new modes of working. Recent shocks to gas supply underscore the importance of pursuing an effective green transition, with regions and cities contributing according to their respective assets. Cities and regions that are balanced and diverse across economic sectors and demographics will likely be more resilient to future shocks, whether local or global.

1. REGIONAL ECONOMIC TRENDS AND SPATIAL DISPARITIES

Employment: Regional recovery and persistent demographic gaps

Economic growth and polarisation across regions

Productivity trends in regions

Regional attractiveness and integration: Tourism, trade and foreign direct investment (FDI)

Cultural and creative sectors

This chapter presents key facts about economic performance across regions during the COVID-19 pandemic and subsequent recovery. It also describes longer-run trends in economic activity across regions and sectors. Indicators presented in the chapter include employment and unemployment, gross domestic product (GDP) per capita, productivity levels and growth, tourism, cultural industries, trade and integration in global markets.

Employment: Regional recovery and persistent demographic gaps

Unemployment rates rose in nearly all OECD regions in the wake of the COVID-19 pandemic and containment measures but, as restrictions were relaxed in many places, employment started recovering. By early 2022, nearly half of regions had rebounded to pre-crisis levels. However, gender and age disparities in employment remain wide in most regions.

The COVID-19 pandemic and related containment measures led to substantial falls in employment and rises in unemployment rates in nearly all OECD countries and regions in 2020, even in countries that initially managed to contain the number of infections. The median unemployment rate across regions rose by more than 2 percentage points (pp) in the initial phase of the pandemic, from late 2019 to the middle of 2020 (Figure 1.1). The median decline in labour force participation exceeded 2 pp across regions during the initial phase of the pandemic. Even in the least-affected regions (lowest 25% of employment rates in mid-2020), unemployment rates rose by 1 pp while unemployment rates in the most-affected regions (highest 25% in mid-2020) rose by more than 5 pp. Because the rise in unemployment was greater for regions with high (8% or higher) pre-pandemic unemployment rates, regional disparities in unemployment increased. This was not the case when comparing across countries: for example, some of the countries with high pre-pandemic unemployment rates had relatively small unemployment changes in 2020 (e.g. Greece and Italy) while others had very large increases in 2020 (e.g. Colombia and Costa Rica), also reflecting differences in the statistical treatment of furloughed workers (Arnaud, 2021).

Indeed, labour survey data in many countries do not capture the full extent of disruption to employment because most OECD countries provided unprecedented job retention schemes for the pandemic (OECD, 2020). At the peak of the crisis, job retention schemes in OECD countries provided support to roughly 20% of workers who were employed before the pandemic started; support measures have receded substantially since then (OECD, 2021a).

Two years after the peak in unemployment rates, many regions still experienced shortfalls in employment relative to pre-pandemic. As of Q2 2022, employment rates had recovered in nearly half of OECD regions (based on 33 OECD countries), where recovery is defined as employment rates equal to or above pre-pandemic rates. The majority of countries have a mix of regions that have recovered and those that have not (Figure 1.2). Within countries, Chile, Colombia and Costa Rica had the widest range of outcomes across regions. Greece also had widely disparate outcomes, with some regions achieving more-than-complete recovery (e.g. Western Greece) and others with substantial shortfalls in employment rates relative to pre-pandemic (e.g. tourist-exposed regions such as the Ionian Islands).

Although many countries had high rates of COVID-19 in early 2022, the economic recovery has continued and the OECD-wide unemployment rate recently reached 5%, better than its pre-pandemic average (OECD, 2022). While youth unemployment spiked in 2020, over the last two years, it has nearly returned to its pre-pandemic levels. Youth unemployment typically rises more than overall unemployment in downturns and falls more in recovery periods (An, Bluedorn and Ciminelli, 2022) and in this case, a third of OECD countries implemented subsidies to encourage employers to hire young people during the COVID-19 crisis (OECD, 2021b).

Nevertheless, women and youth continue to have substantially lower employment rates than other demographic groups in nearly all OECD regions. Excluding Finland, where female and male employment rates are similar, in all other regions the gap is greater than 3 pp and the median gap between male and female employment rates is 12 pp (Figure 1.3). In most OECD regions, differences in labour force participation account for a sizeable portion of the gender gap in employment. This gender gap is not necessarily reflected in unemployment rates because many women report being out of the labour force – neither working nor unemployed. While additional childcare burdens for parents during the COVID-19 pandemic held down female labour force participation in many OECD countries (Djankov and Zhang, 2020), the gap between female and male employment actually narrowed in 2019-21 in approximately half of regions (and 60% of the 28 OECD countries) with available data.

In all 60 regions (of the 7 OECD countries with regional data), youth unemployment rates are higher than those of other working-age adults; in 2021, the median gap was 11 pp across OECD regions. Within countries, the difference between youth and overall unemployment is generally larger in regions with higher overall unemployment rates. In Hungary, overall unemployment rates range from below 2% to 6% across regions while the lowest regional youth unemployment rate is 8% (Budapest, 2% overall) and the highest is 14% (Northern Hungary, 6% overall). During business cycle downturns, young people appear to face greater disadvantages relative to older, experienced workers – especially in weak local labour markets.

Source

An, Z., J. Bluedorn and G. Ciminelli (2022), "Okun's Law, development, and demographics: differences in the cyclical sensitivities of unemployment across economy and worker groups", *IMF Working Paper WP/21/270.*

Arnaud, B. (2021), "Has COVID-19 distorted international comparability of unemployment rates?", The OECD Statistics Newsletter, Issue 73, *https://issuu.com/oecd-stat-newsletter/docs/oecd-stats-newsletter-12-2020.*

Djankov, S. and E. Zhang (2020), "COVID-19 widens gender gap in some but not other advanced economies", *https://www.piie.com/blogs/realtime-economic-issues-watch/covid-19-widens-gender-gap-labor-force-participation-some-not.*

OECD (2022), *OECD Employment Outlook 2022: Building Back More Inclusive Labour Markets*, OECD Publishing, Paris, *https://doi.org/10.1787/1bb305a6-en.*

OECD (2021a), *OECD Employment Outlook 2021: Navigating the COVID-19 Crisis and Recovery*, OECD Publishing, Paris, *https://dx.doi.org/10.1787/5a700c4b-en.*

OECD (2021b), "What have countries done to support young people in the COVID-19 crisis?", *OECD Policy Responses to Coronavirus (COVID-19)*, OECD, Paris, *https://www.oecd.org/coronavirus/policy-responses/what-have-countries-done-to-support-young-people-in-the-covid-19-crisis-ac9f056c/.*

OECD (2020), "Job retention schemes during the COVID-19 lockdown and beyond", *OECD Policy Responses to Coronavirus (COVID-19)*, OECD Publishing, Paris, *https://dx.doi.org/10.1787/0853ba1d-en.*

Figure notes

1.1: Median and quartiles are calculated on a quarterly basis for 355 regions over 33 OECD countries. Unemployment rates in TL2 regions are based on the population 15 years of age and older.

1.2: Ratio of quarterly employment rates in TL2 regions, based on population ages 15 and older. The employment rate in 2022 Q2 is divided by the pre-pandemic employment rate (2019 Q2). Countries sorted by national average.

1.3: Quarterly employment rate gaps (male minus female employment rate) in TL2 regions, based on population ages 15 and older. Countries sorted by national average.

1.1. Unemployment rates in large (TL2) regions, 2019 Q1-2022 Q2

Percentage of labour force

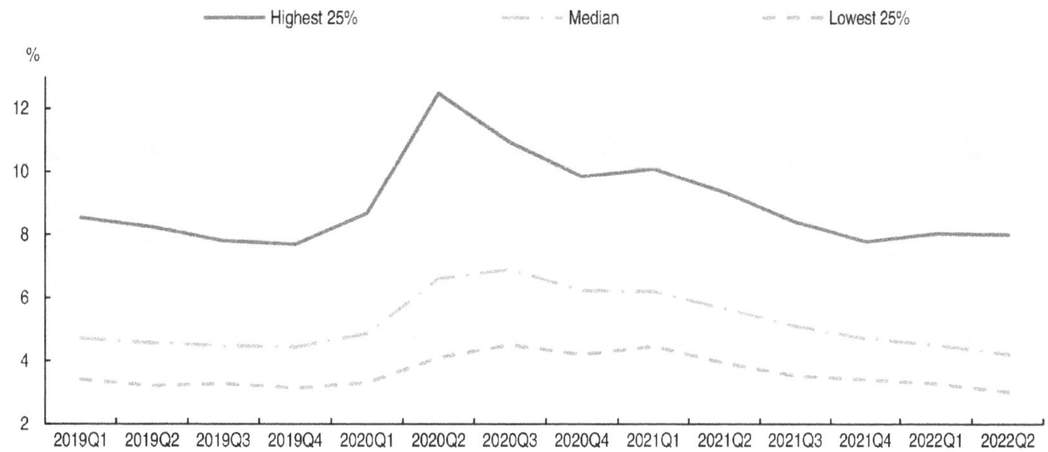

StatLink https://stat.link/1l90ur

1.2. Employment rates in 2022 relative to 2019 in large regions (TL2)

Employed as a percentage of the population: Ratio of 2022 Q2 over 2019 Q2 values

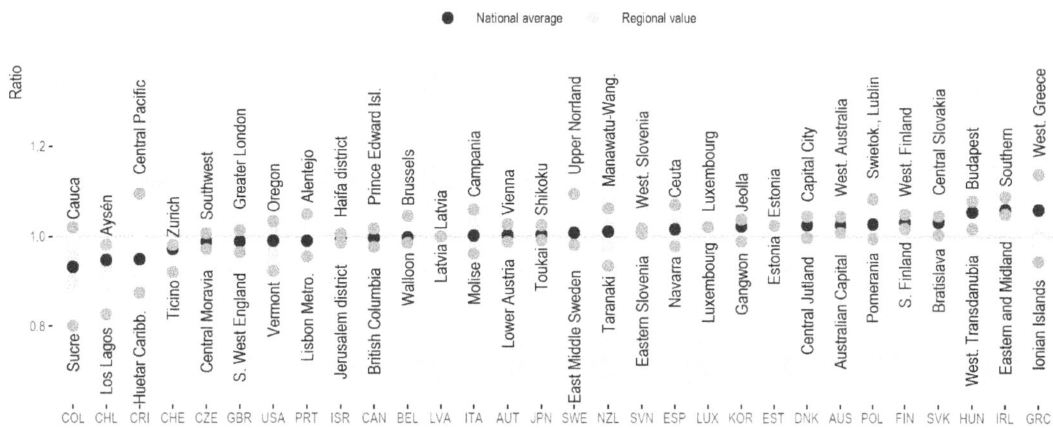

StatLink https://stat.link/uv5ghl

1.3. Difference between male and female employment rates in large regions (TL2), 2022 Q2

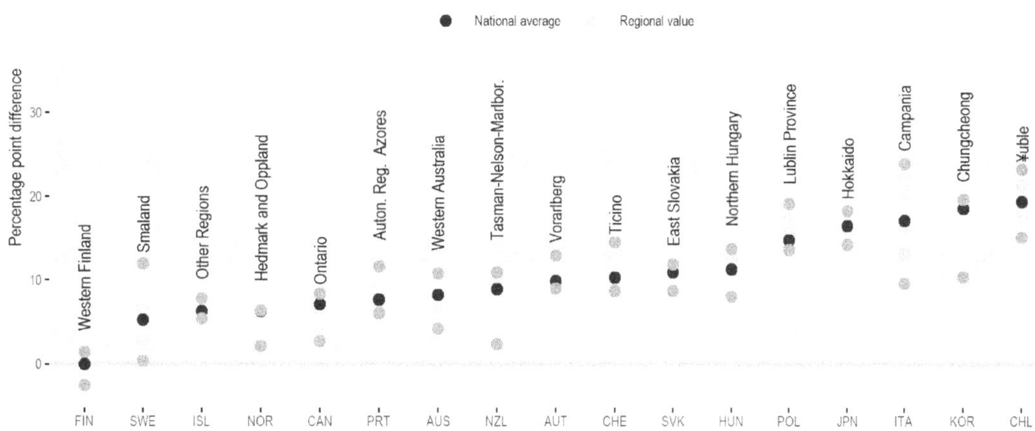

StatLink https://stat.link/3kiguw

1.4. Unemployment rates in 2022 Q2: North and South Americas

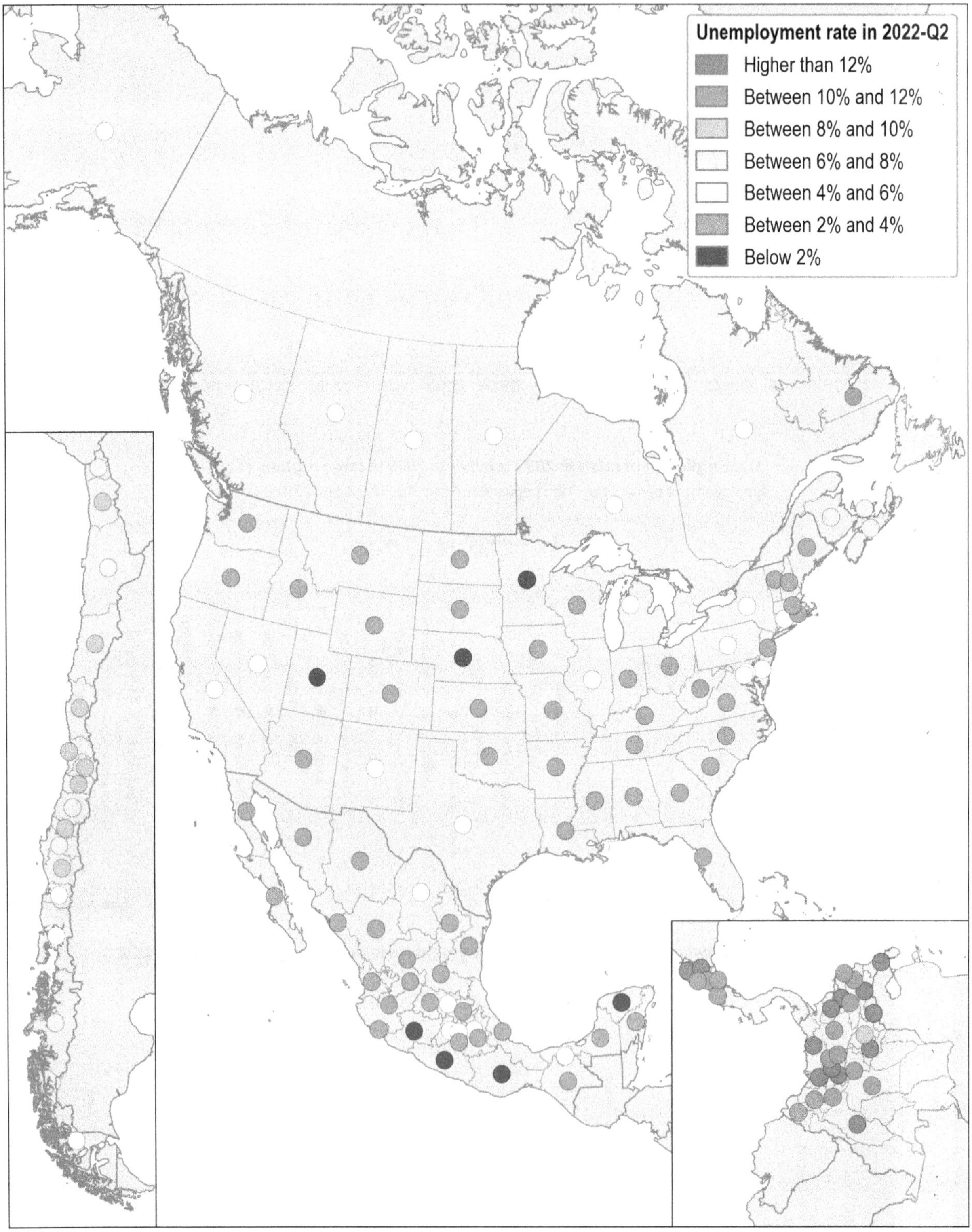

StatLink https://stat.link/ktujqe

1.5. Unemployment rates in 2022 Q2: Europe and Asia-Pacific

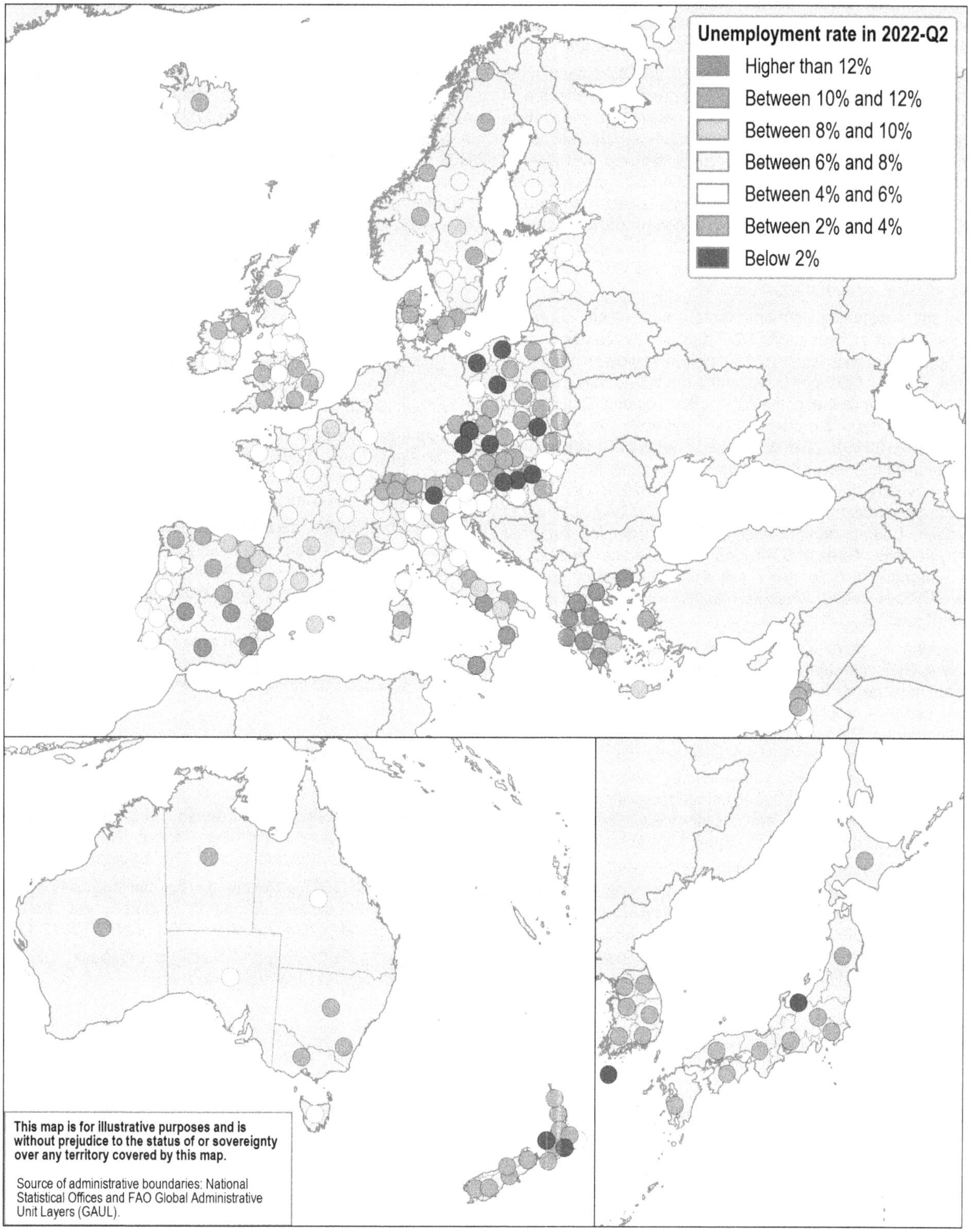

StatLink https://stat.link/iktcx9

Economic growth and polarisation across regions

Due to COVID-19, GDP in 2020 declined by more than 9% in the worst-hit regions. Over the last decade, non-metropolitan regions – especially those far from cities – continued to lag behind metropolitan regions in terms of GDP per capita.

GDP per capita fell across the vast majority of OECD regions in the first year of the COVID-19 pandemic. The large declines affected all types of regions across the rural-urban continuum: many with higher pre-pandemic levels of GDP and many others with lower pre-pandemic levels of GDP. Lower global demand, widespread travel bans and other measures to avoid COVID-19 contagion led to GDP declines even in countries and regions that managed to keep COVID-19 cases low. Although the pandemic did not increase regional disparities, the average gap in GDP per capita between metropolitan and non-metropolitan regions across OECD countries has also not receded over the last decade.

There is still substantial economic polarisation within countries (defined as the ratio of per capita GDP between its top and bottom 20% of regions) but polarisation did not generally worsen during the pandemic. In 2020, GDP per capita in the top 20% of large regions was, on average, twice that of the 20% bottom regions. Overall, half of OECD countries experienced a decrease in economic polarisation from 2010 to 2020 across large regions. The decreases in polarisation have been particularly large in Canada, Mexico, Peru and Türkiye, where there were large declines in 2020. Only 10 out of 33 countries became more polarised in 2020 and, in most of these cases, bottom regions declined more than top regions– especially in Chile, Korea and Sweden. Nevertheless, Mexico and Türkiye – along with Colombia – still show the starkest regional gaps in GDP per capita, whereas Canada and Korea show the smallest (Figure 1.6).

When looking at disparities over the last 20 years, regional inequality in GDP per capita is persistent, especially within OECD countries. These trends are measured by the Theil index of regional GDP per capita – a composite index of inequality within and between countries. Measures of within-country inequality appear to be slightly higher than two decades ago, although their rise was concentrated in 2005-12 and within-country inequality for large (TL2) and small (TL3) regions has remained roughly constant since then. On the other hand, between-country inequality has steadily declined over the last two decades (Figure 1.7, Panels A and B).

Some of the largest within-country differences in regional GDP per capita are between metropolitan and non-metropolitan regions. Metropolitan regions had both higher initial levels of GDP per capita and faster growth than other types of regions, especially those far from metropolitan areas. The lack of convergence in growth implies large and persistent differences between rural and urban areas. Non-metropolitan regions near metropolitan ones kept pace with metropolitan regions from 2010-18 but grew at a slower pace afterwards (Figure 1.8) whereas regions far from metropolitan areas fell further behind metropolitan regions, especially from 2012-16.

In 2020, GDP per capita declined by 5% in the median region, 2% in the top 20% of regions and 9% in the hardest-hit regions. There were only a handful of regions with positive changes (Figures 1.9 and 1.10). Within countries, the median range across large (TL2) regions was 7 pp. Canada, Colombia and Türkiye had the largest ranges of outcomes in 2020 (all 3 countries had more than 30 pp differences in GDP growth rates between their top and bottom regions). At present, 2020 GDP data for small (TL3) regions are only available for 17 OECD countries. Based on this data, the distribution of 2019-20 percentage changes appear similar across metropolitan and non-metropolitan regions, although the variance is higher for non-metropolitan regions as some of them experienced more extreme positive and negative changes in 2020 compared to metropolitan regions in OECD countries.

Annual changes in 2020 mask substantial quarterly fluctuations because the pandemic generally had larger negative impacts on 2020 Q2 than other quarters. While annual GDP data show rebounds for most countries in 2021, regional data are not yet available. Moreover, some countries that managed to keep COVID-19 transmission low in 2020 (e.g. Australia, Japan) had more infections in 2021-22. Beyond 2021, substantial uncertainty remains about the future trajectory of GDP across OECD regions due to the longer-term impacts of the COVID-19 pandemic and the rise in energy prices following Russia's invasion of Ukraine.

Definitions

GDP per capita is measured as a region's purchasing power parity (PPP)-deflated output per capita (base year 2015). Annual deflators are measured at national levels.

Top and bottom 20% regions in a given year are those with the highest/lowest GDP per capita until the equivalent of 20% of the national population is reached (including a fraction of the regions that contain the 20% threshold).

The Theil index measures inequality in GDP per capita between OECD regions. It breaks down the overall inequality into inequality due to differences within countries and inequality due to differences across countries (see Annex C for more details).

Regions near metropolitan areas are TL3 regions in which half or more of the population can reach a metropolitan region with over 250 000 inhabitants in less than a one-hour drive.

Source

Fadic, M. et al. (2019), "Classifying small (TL3) regions based on metropolitan population, low density and remoteness", *OECD Regional Development Working Papers*, No. 2019/06, OECD Publishing, Paris, *https://doi.org/10.1787/b902cc00-en*.

Gluschenko, K. (2017), "Measuring regional inequality: to weight or not to weight?", *Spatial Economic Analysis*, Vol. 13/1, *https://www.tandfonline.com/doi/abs/10.1080/17421772.2017.1343491*.

OECD (2022), *OECD Regional Statistics (database)*, OECD, Paris, *http://dx.doi.org/10.1787/region-data-en*.

Figure notes

1.6: Regional polarisation is defined as the ratio of a country's top and bottom 20% of regions in terms of GDP per capita. Changes over time are measured as percentage changes in the top/bottom ratio by country.

1.7: Theil index two-year moving averages. 31 countries are considered for TL2 and 27 countries for TL3; indices are unweighted. Unweighted indices are used to reflect disparities in growth across administrative or statistical regions of OECD countries (Gluschenko, 2017).

1.8: GDP per capita growth is based on population-weighted averages for small regions (TL3) grouped by metropolitan/non-metropolitan typology. 1 586 regions across 28 OECD countries are considered.

1.6. Regional polarisation in GDP per capita, levels vs. 2019-20 percentage change

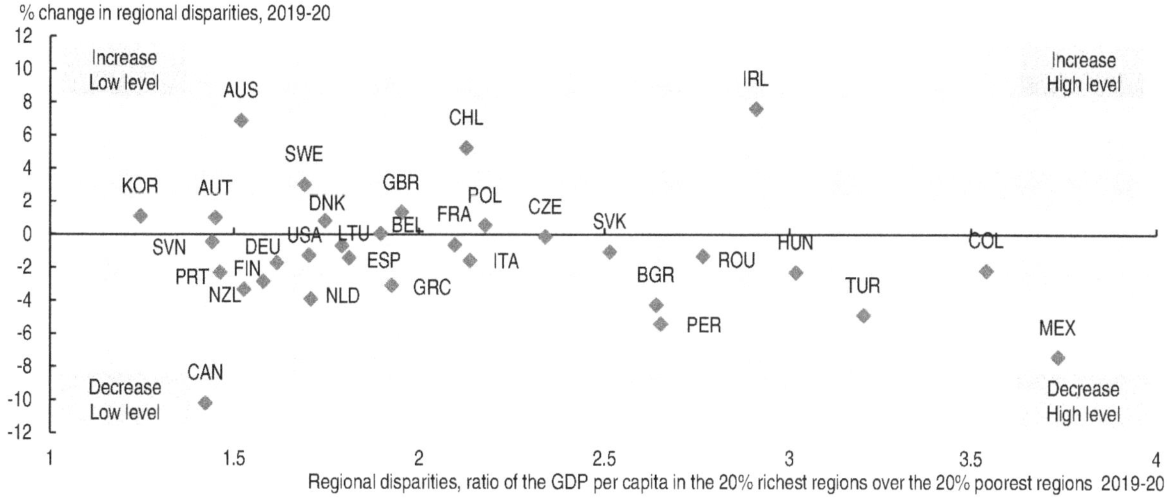

StatLink https://stat.link/q9k6g8

1.7. Theil inequality index of GDP per capita, 2000–20

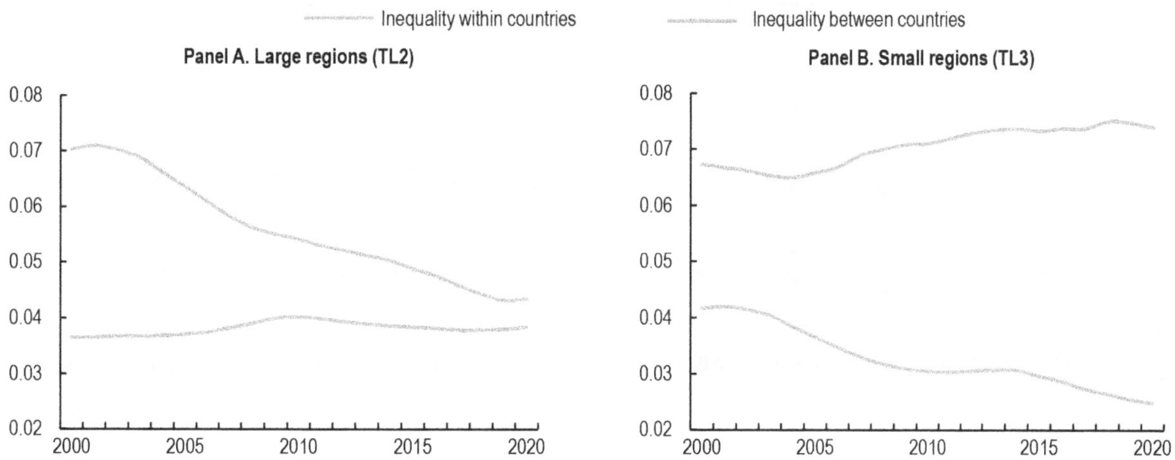

StatLink https://stat.link/t5xjzy

1.8. GDP per capita growth index by type of region relative to metropolitan regions, 2010–20

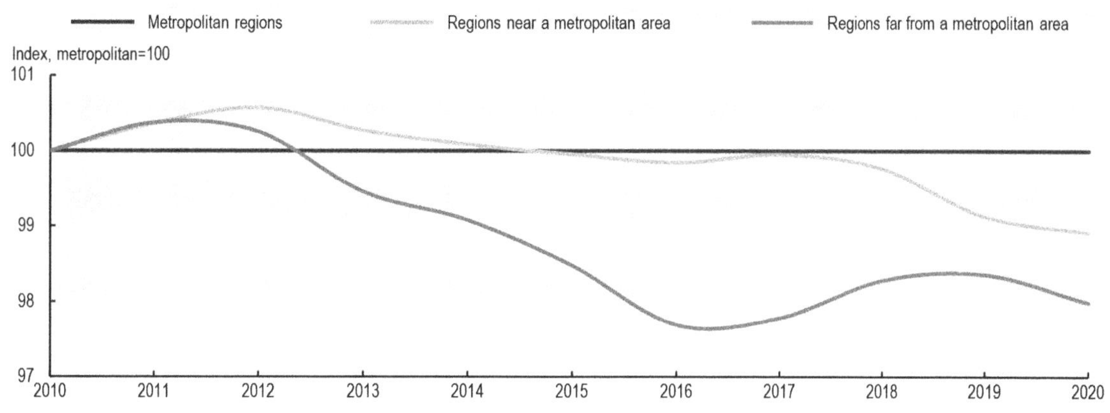

StatLink https://stat.link/2fa0m6

1.9. Change in GDP per capita between 2019 and 2020: North and South Americas

Large regions (TL2)

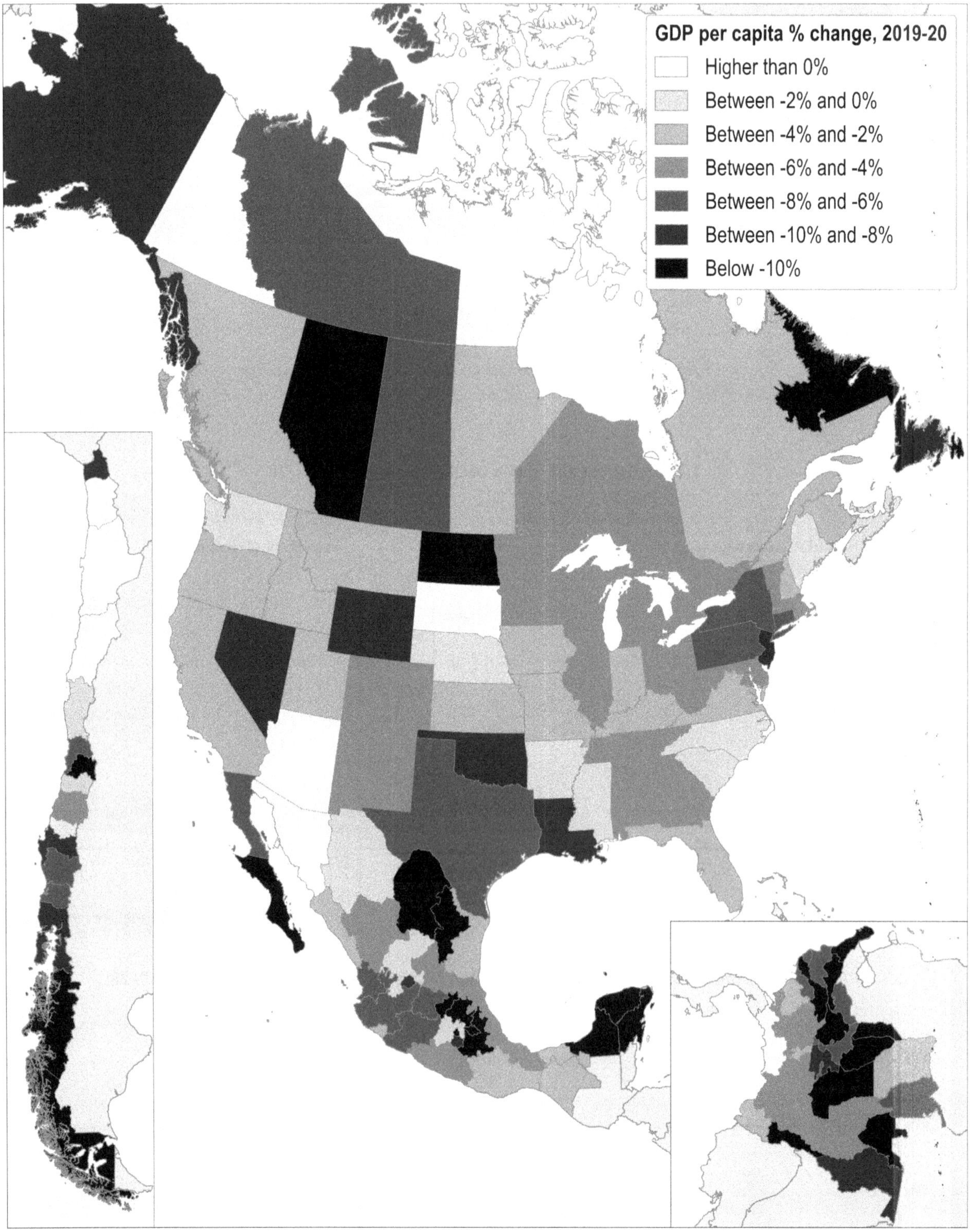

StatLink https://stat.link/hb564k

1.10. Change in GDP per capita between 2019 and 2020: Europe and Asia-Pacific

Large regions (TL2)

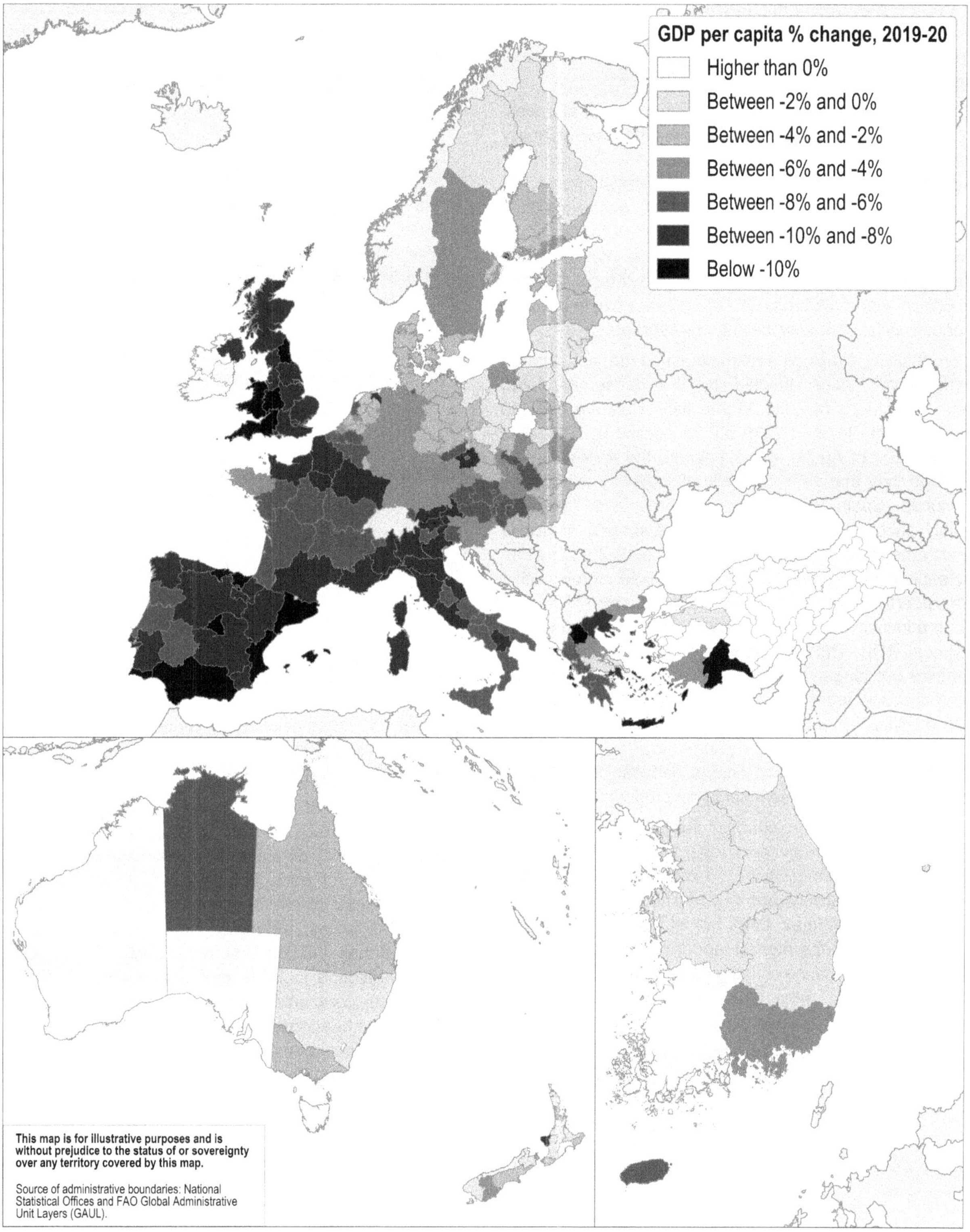

StatLink https://stat.link/xwzbk4

Productivity trends in regions

Labour productivity differences remain stark across regions. On average, productivity in the top region is nearly double that of the least-productive region. Despite positive growth in the majority of regions, half of OECD countries had at least one region with negative productivity growth over the 2005-20 period.

Productivity is a key contributor to economic growth and well-being. Labour productivity in OECD regions differs substantially both between and within countries (Figure 1.11). On average, within countries, labour productivity in the most productive region is nearly double the productivity of the least productive region. Differences are especially stark in Chile and Mexico: in these countries, the most productive region is more than five times as productive as the least productive region. Overall, around 60% of workers across OECD countries live in a region with productivity levels below the national average.

While productivity rankings within countries do not change frequently, some were affected by the pandemic-related economic disruptions in 2020. Within Italy, Calabria had the lowest productivity level in 2019 but its decline in 2020 was smaller than that of Apulia, which became the lowest-ranked region within Italy that year. Similarly, the Canary Islands fell below Murcia, Spain, due to the pandemic and Tasmania (previously second from the bottom in Australia) swapped places with the state of South Australia for 2019-20. Only one country experienced a change in its top-ranked region: within Canada, Alberta moved down from the top position to third in terms of productivity levels in 2020 due to its disproportionately large drop in GDP. These short-term productivity fluctuations may reverse but longer-term changes are likely. On the one hand, the dramatic rise of remote working has the potential to increase productivity substantially, while on the other hand, labour market disruptions from the pandemic and multiple years of reduced mobility within and across national borders may have enduring negative consequences for productivity.

Concerning productivity growth over the last 15 years, more than half of OECD countries had at least 1 region with negative productivity growth from 2005-20 (15 out of 26 countries with regional data), while Greece and Italy had negative productivity growth in all regions (Figure 1.12). In half of OECD countries, the capital region had the highest labour productivity in 2020. Despite the outperformance of many capital regions in terms of productivity levels, in most countries, the highest rate of productivity growth was in a non-capital region.

On average, the productivity of regions far from cities continues to lag behind that of metropolitan regions, except in Korea. In the remaining 25 OECD countries, Belgium, Estonia and the Slovak Republic have the largest disparities between metropolitan regions and those regions far from cities, while Norway, Slovenia and Spain have the smallest disparities (Figure 1.13).

Definitions

Regional labour productivity Gross value added (GVA) per worker, based on place of work. Labour productivity is measured in 2015 constant prices, using OECD deflators and converted into constant USD PPPs. Annual deflators are measured at national levels.

Regions near metropolitan areas are TL3 regions in which half or more of the population can reach a metropolitan region with over 250 000 inhabitants in less than a 1-hour drive.

Source

Central Statistics Office of Ireland (n.d.), *Redomiciled PLCs*, *https://www.cso.ie/en/interactivezone/statisticsexplained/nationalaccountsexplained/redomiciledplcs/*.

OECD (2022), *OECD Regional Statistics (database)*, OECD, Paris, *http://dx.doi.org/10.1787/region-data-en*.

Figure notes

1.11 and 1.12: 2020 or latest available year: 2019 data for CHE, COL, GBR, NOR, NZL; 2017 data for JPN. TL3 regions for Estonia, Latvia and Lithuania.

1.13: 2020 or latest available year: 2019 data for AUT, CHE, DEU, ESP, FIN, GRC, ITA, LTU, LVA, NLD, NOT, POL, PRT, SWE, USA; 2016 data for JPN. Productivity measures use equal weights for each TL3 region. Countries are sorted in ascending order of average productivity for regions far from metropolitan areas. Ireland is not included in the analysis because it has the starkest productivity differences across regions, reflecting in large part the relatively high share of multinational companies with significant intellectual property assets with headquarters in (including those that have redomiciled to) Ireland, and Dublin in particular (Central Statistics Office of Ireland).

1.11. Labour productivity regional disparities, large regions (TL2), 2020

GVA per person employed, thousands of (PPP-adjusted) 2015 USD

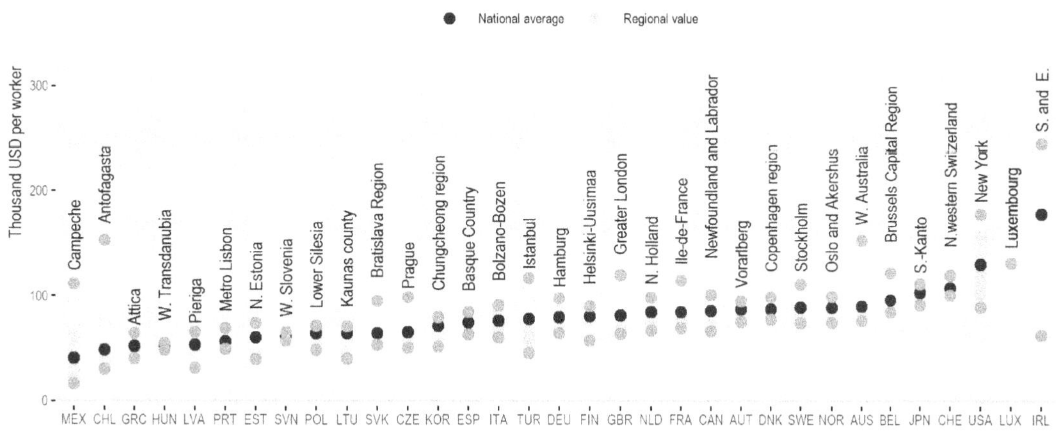

StatLink https://stat.link/5r6sv4

1.12. Labour productivity growth across large regions (TL2), 15-year average rates (2005-20)

Annualised growth in GVA per person employed, thousands of (PPP-adjusted) 2015 USD

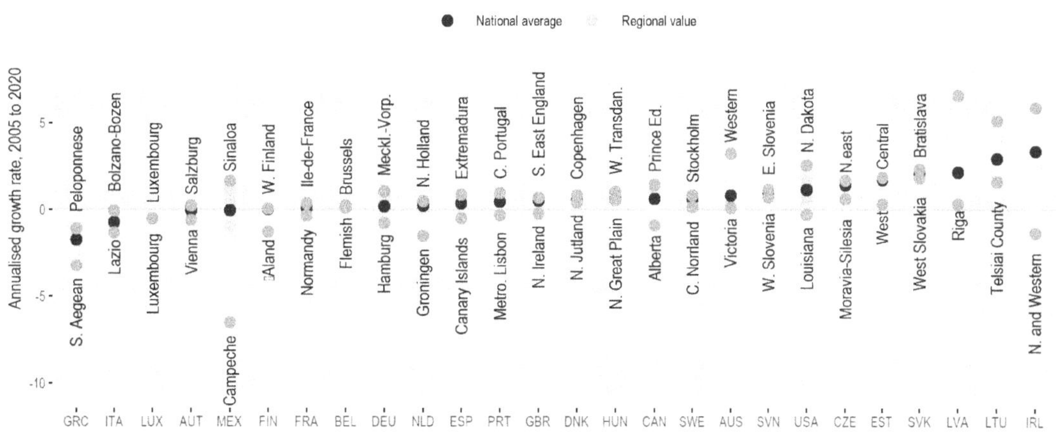

StatLink https://stat.link/8l9p6e

1.13. Labour productivity by type of region (TL3), 2020 or latest year

GVA per person employed, thousands of (PPP-adjusted) 2015 USD

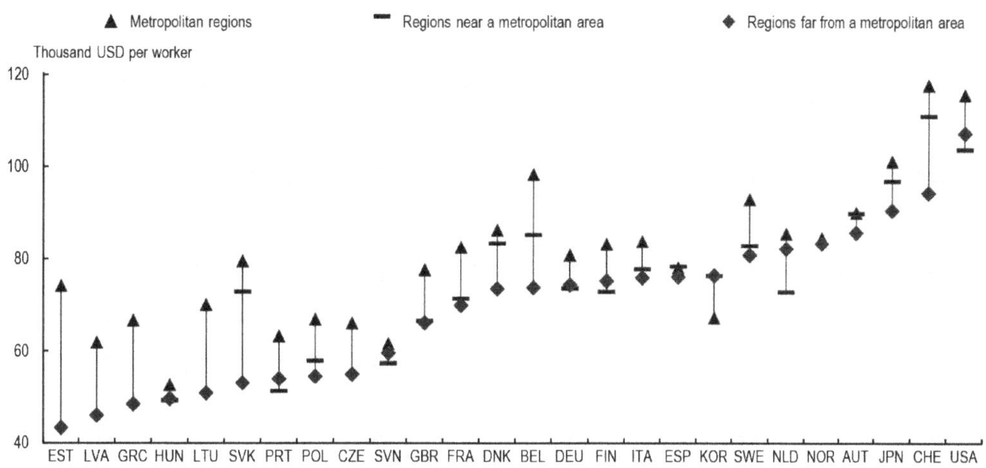

StatLink https://stat.link/mwu7e1

Regional attractiveness and integration: Tourism, trade and foreign direct investment (FDI)

COVID-19 triggered large declines in tourist stays, flights and tourism-related investment. The pandemic also prompted declines in international trade in many OECD regions. Across all sectors, FDI in OECD regions recovered quickly, yet longer-run trends of geographic concentration in FDI are persistent.

The emergence of COVID-19 around the globe led to travel bans and restrictions starting in March 2020 due to concerns over travellers contracting and transmitting the virus. While the tourism sector directly accounted for nearly 5% of GDP before 2020, it was severely curtailed by the pandemic (OECD, 2021). The fall in tourist activity had particularly adverse impacts on regions with large tourism sectors.

Across 25 OECD countries, all countries had at least 1 region in which tourist stays (number of nights spent in tourist accommodations) fell by half or more from 2019 to 2020, which includes the first 10 months of the COVID-19 pandemic (Figure 1.14). Island regions (e.g. Corsica in France, Greece's Ionian Islands and Spain's Balearic Islands), in addition to the Algarve region of Portugal, have the most tourist-centric economies in the OECD (OECD, 2020). These regions and many others in Greece and Spain had declines of more than 70% in tourist stays (Figure 1.16). Although larger cities have more diversified economies than tourist destinations, business travel and city stays also declined markedly during the pandemic. At least 5 metropolitan regions had 1-year declines of more than 70% in tourist stays: Brussels, Madrid, Prague, Santiago and Tel Aviv. The mean decline in air passengers was 70% and regions such as Drenthe (Netherlands), Moravia-Silesia (Czech Republic), Upper Austria and Wales experienced even larger declines (Figure 1.15).

A region's integration in global markets is related to trade openness, the ratio of its international trade (imports plus exports) to regional GDP. Trade openness has generally been expanding over the last decade (OECD, 2020). Some countries like Belgium, Slovenia and Switzerland have 1 or more regions in which trade openness exceeds 100%, leading to large within-country differences (Figure 1.16). However, the pandemic caused trade openness to fall in more than half of TL2 regions (of the 17 OECD countries with regional data for 2020). Regional data in 2021 is only available for a few countries but global trade data shows a sizeable recovery in 2021, despite continued supply-chain and transport disruptions along with climate and geopolitical concerns.

The pandemic also led to large falls in tourism-related FDI into OECD regions. FDI in accommodation and travel arrangement services fell by more than half, whereas overall FDI into OECD regions was only slightly weaker in 2020-21 compared to previous years. Similar to the pre-pandemic period, overall FDI inflows were highly concentrated geographically: around 15% of FDI in 2021 went to just 5 OECD regions: Chūgoku and Kyushu (Japan), North East and South East United Kingdom (UK), and Texas, United States (US). In a typical year, a handful of destination regions account for 15% or more of incoming investment into the OECD, partly because FDI flows often include some large transactions in which a single company makes a multi-billion-dollar investment (e.g. semiconductor project) in one place. Although the set of OECD destination regions receiving FDI changes over time, most regions that receive large inflows are those with already-high (top 30%) levels of GDP. Australia, Canada, the UK and the US are popular destinations, with some of their regions receiving very large FDI inflows in multiple years (especially Queensland, Australia; Ontario, Canada; Scotland and South East England, UK; California, New York and Texas, US).

Source

fDi Markets (2022), *Homepage*, Financial Times Limited, *https://www.fdimarkets.com/*.

OECD (2022), *OECD Regional Statistics (database)*, OECD, Paris, *http://dx.doi.org/10.1787/region-data-en*.

OECD (2021), *OECD Regional Outlook 2021: Addressing COVID-19 and Moving to Net Zero Greenhouse Gas Emissions*, OECD Publishing, Paris, *https://doi.org/10.1787/17017efe-en*.

OECD (2020), "From pandemic to recovery: Local employment and economic development", *OECD Policy Responses to Coronavirus (COVID-19)*, OECD, Paris, *https://read.oecd-ilibrary.org/view/?ref=130_130810-m60ml0s4wf&title=From-pandemic-to-recovery-Local-employment-and-economic-development*.

Figure notes

1.14: TL2 regions, except: Hungary TL2 with touristic regions; Poland Warsaw capital region and Mazowiecki region are merged. Countries are ranked in ascending order of country averages. Data include domestic and foreign tourist stays.

1.15: Data include domestic and foreign flight passengers.

1.16: TL2 regions, sorted in ascending order of the highest region. Trade openness is the sum of a region's international imports plus exports divided by its GDP.

1.17: TL2 regions, except Hungary TL2 with touristic regions; Poland Warsaw capital region and Mazowiecki region are merged. Data include domestic and foreign tourist stays.

1.14. Tourist stays by region: Percentage change in nights spent in accommodation, 2019-20

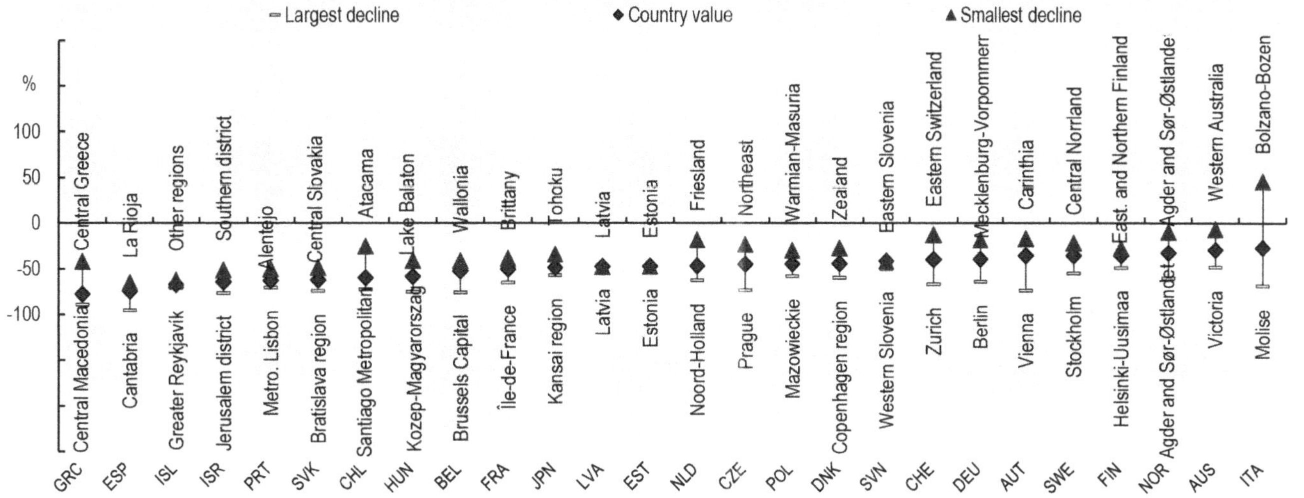

StatLink https://stat.link/0p574b

1.15. Flight passengers: Largest one-year percentage loss, Large (TL2) regions, 2019-20

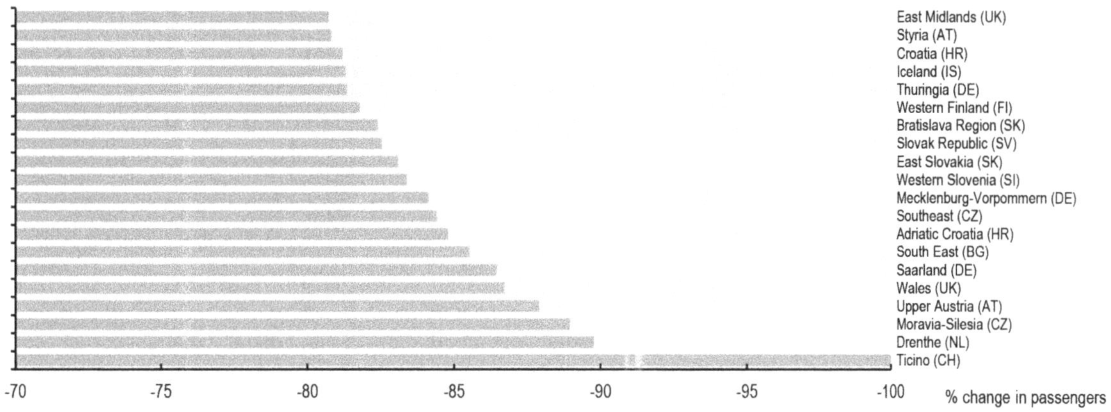

StatLink https://stat.link/czh03e

1.16. Trade openness in large (TL2) regions, 2019

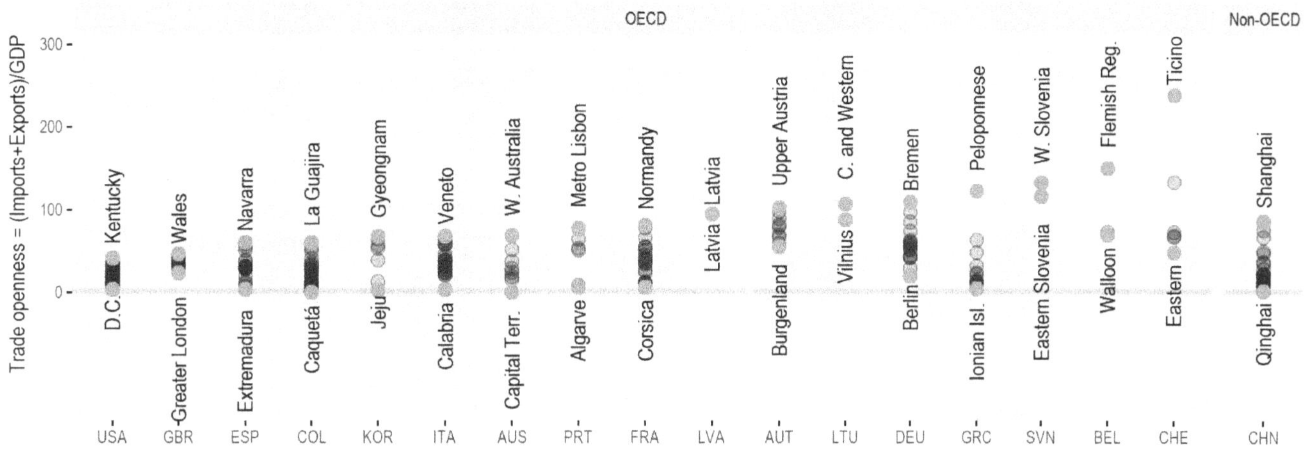

StatLink https://stat.link/4r8hxp

1.17. Tourist stays by region: Change in nights spent in accommodation, 2019–20

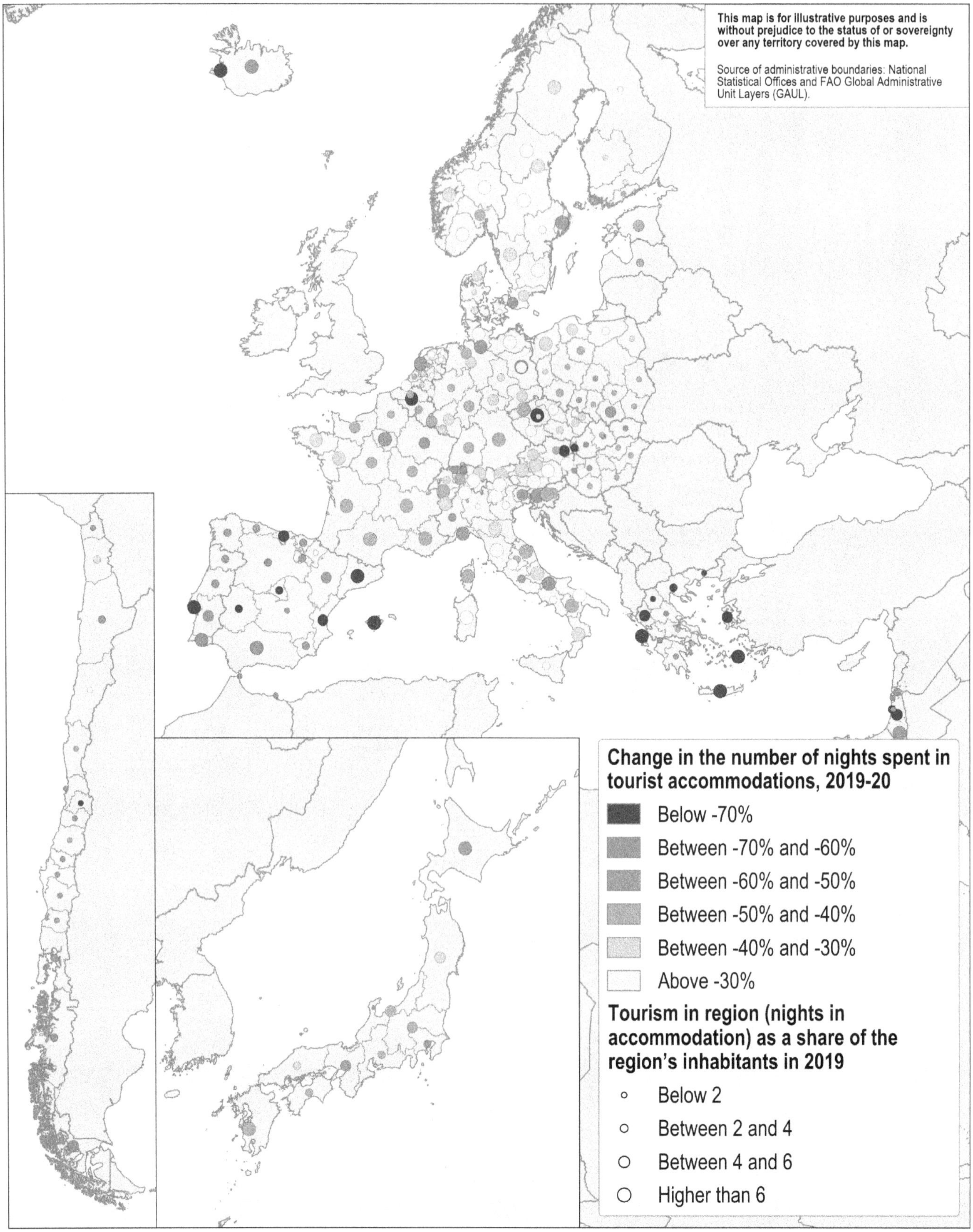

StatLink https://stat.link/4cb8kl

Cultural and creative sectors

Cultural and creative sectors (CCS) tend to concentrate in cities and capital regions, with shares of creative jobs in some capital regions double the country average.

CCS make cities and regions attractive places to work, live and visit. Moreover, CCS support economic growth because they have positive spill-overs on local economies as inputs to tourism and other economic activities. CCS also contribute to regional development by encouraging innovation, supporting health and well-being and contributing to the vibrancy of places (OECD, 2022).

CCS businesses and labour markets are clustered in cities and capital regions. Places with established cultural scenes (often large cities) help the sector's small firms and its workers share resources and knowledge. In most countries, capital regions have the highest shares of cultural employment (Figure 1.18). For example, in Germany, cultural employment makes up 10% of total employment in Berlin (6 pp higher than the national average) but only 3% in the Saxony-Anhalt region of Germany. In the Czech Republic and Hungary, the share of cultural employment in their capital regions (Prague and Budapest) is more than double their national average.

Over the 5 years preceding the COVID-19 crisis, employment in the cultural sector grew in 115 out of 170 large regions. However, this growth is relative, as the employment growth in culture exceeded total regional employment growth in only ten regions, including Liguria (Italy) or Upper Norrland (Sweden). There are large regional disparities in the evolution of the CCS employment share over the 2014-19 period, especially in Greece and Italy where the regional range between the highest region gaining in CCS share with the one losing the most exceeds two percentage points (Figure 1.19).

More than half of OECD regions saw declines in cultural employment between 2019 and 2020 (average employment decline of 1.5% during the first year of the pandemic). Nonetheless, in three-quarters of OECD regions, employment in CCS declined less than in other sectors. CCS employment may have been less affected during the pandemic because, while the pandemic containment measures had large negative impacts on sub-sectors of CCS such as museums and performing arts, other sub-sectors such as television and video games saw increases in activity (OECD, 2022). Furthermore, many CCS workers hold multiple jobs, thus job losses in other sectors of the economy might lead those who had previously worked in CCS as a second job to report it as their main employment (EENCA, 2020).

Regional governments remain a key source of financial support to CCS. Across all OECD countries for which there is available data, subnational governments spend a higher proportion of their budget on funding cultural services than national governments. Indeed, in 2019, around 60% of total government spending on culture came from regional governments across OECD countries. There was, however, significant variation across national contexts. For example, around 90% of cultural spending came from regional governments in Belgium, whereas this figure was only around 30% in Israel (Figure 1.20). Moreover, within countries, subnational spending on culture varies across regions. In Canada, the slightly broader category of government spending on culture (which includes recreational activities and religion) ranges from 1.3% in Prince Edward Island to 4% in British Columbia. Subnational financing for CCS may become even more important as national budgets are tighter now than before the COVID-19 crisis.

Definitions

Cultural and creative sectors (CCS). Industry sectors that produce or distribute goods or services with a high cultural value or creative input.

Cultural employment. Total employment in CCS businesses (including publishing, writing, design, photography, cinema, museums, libraries, news, and arts and entertainment, see Annex C) plus employment in cultural occupations (including teachers and artisans) in other sectors of the economy (Annex C).

Cultural employment statistics refer only to a person's main job. Since there is no official international definition of CCS or cultural occupations, the data presented here may differ significantly from national and regional reporting due to differences in categorisation.

Source

EENCA (2020), *The Status and Working Conditions of Artists and Cultural and Creative Professionals*, European Expert Network on Culture and Audiovisual.

OECD (2022), *The Culture Fix: Creative People, Places and Industries*, Local Economic and Employment Development (LEED), OECD Publishing, Paris, *https://doi.org/10.1787/991bb520-en*.

Figure notes

1.18: Data for Canada, Mexico, the UK and the US are from 2019. Data for Australia is from 2016. The minimum and maximum regional employment shares are only reported for countries with sufficient data for at least two regions.

1.19: Data from Eurostat.

1.20: Government expenditure by function (OECD COFOG).

1.18. Cultural employment as a share of total employment in large (TL2) regions, 2020 or latest year

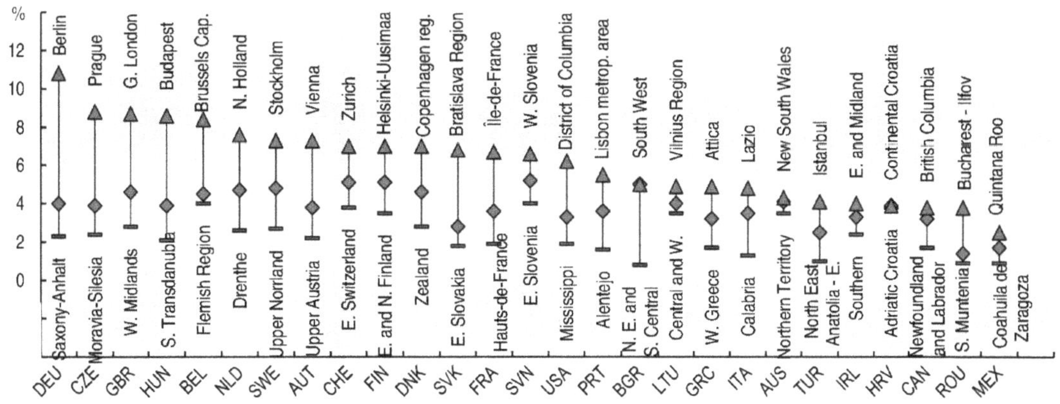

StatLink https://stat.link/ekpqrd

1.19. Change in shares of cultural employment in large (TL2) regions, 2014-19 (pre-pandemic)

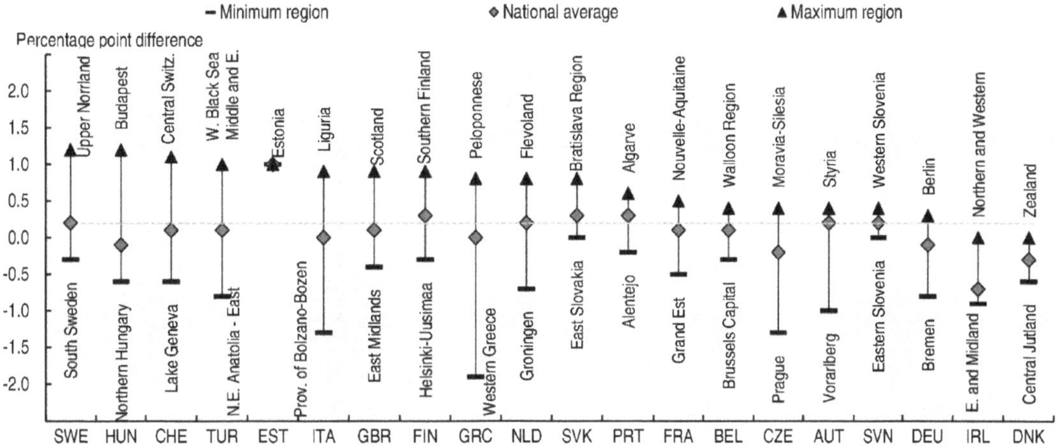

StatLink https://stat.link/d8nica

1.20. Subnational government spending on cultural services as a share of total government spending on cultural services, 2019

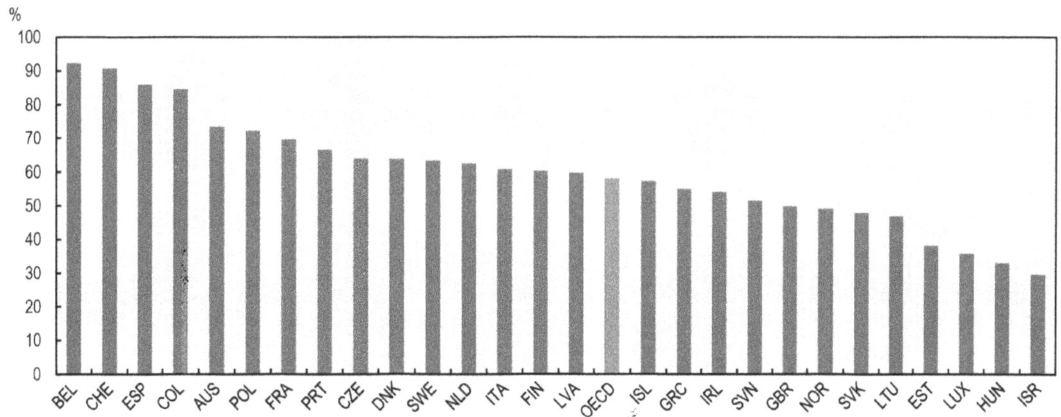

StatLink https://stat.link/f9d1hy

2. REGIONS AND CITIES IN ENVIRONMENTAL TRANSITION

Towards climate neutrality by 2050

Towards sustainable and resilient energy systems

Households in the energy and climate crises

Towards resilient and sustainable industries in regions

Sustainable transport in regions

Land use in cities

Sustainable agriculture and resilient forests in regions

Human settlements adapting to climate change

While most OECD countries aim for climate neutrality by 2050, progress is uneven between and within countries, with some regions still heavily relying on carbon-intensive energy sources.

This chapter examines progress on the environmental transition of regions through a wide range of indicators, including energy use, emissions by sector and exposure to extreme climate events.

Towards climate neutrality by 2050

Most OECD regions are far from meeting climate neutrality targets by 2050 and will have to undergo deep structural transformations.

Production-based greenhouse gas (GHG) emissions in OECD countries accounted for 30% of total emissions worldwide in 2018. Although the COVID-19 pandemic led to an unprecedented reduction of 5.8% in global CO_2 emissions due to lockdowns and restrictions, emissions rebounded by 5% in 2021 approaching the 2018-19 peak (IEA, 2022). To meet the 2015 Paris Agreement ambition of keeping global temperatures at no more than 1.5°C above pre-industrial levels, global average emissions per capita per year need to drop to under 2.1 tonnes of carbon dioxide equivalent (t CO_2-eq) by 2030 (UNEP-CCC, 2020). Many OECD countries have endorsed ambitious domestic GHG reduction targets by 2030 and plan to reach climate neutrality by 2050. The European Union (EU) endorsed a binding target of a reduction of at least 55% by 2030 compared to 1990. Similarly, the United States (US) plan a reduction of 50-52% by 2030 compared to 2005 and Australia by 43% over the same period.

However, recent trends in GHG emissions differ significantly across and within OECD countries. Indeed, in some regions, emissions have increased significantly despite the ambitious goals set at the national level. From 1990 to 2018, production-based emissions in Chile, Israel, Korea and Türkiye more than doubled for example, while in the United Kingdom (UK) and the Baltic states they declined by more than 40%.

Overall while emissions declined (by on average 23%) in 175 out of 432 OECD large regions between 1990 and 2018, they increased by more than 50% in 104 regions, with stark disparities often appearing in the same country. For example, in the US, emissions in North Dakota more than doubled, while they decreased by 30% in West Virginia (Figure 2.3).

Metropolitan regions register lower emissions per capita than other types of regions in almost all OECD countries. On average, emissions per capita in metropolitan regions are half those of regions far from a metropolitan area. Across OECD regions, emissions increased mostly in remote regions – by 14% – while remaining stable in other types of regions, although these trends vary significantly across countries. Metropolitan regions in European OECD countries are leading the transition to climate neutrality, as emissions per capita per year reached 7 t CO_2-eq in 2018, 27% lower than in 1990, the largest decline across all types of small regions (TL3). Metropolitan regions in South American OECD countries accounted for the lowest emissions per capita in 2018 with 2.9 t CO_2-eq. However, these regions have experienced the largest relative increase in emissions across the OECD (80%) since 1990. In Oceania and North America, although emissions increased across all types of regions, emissions per capita decreased, especially in metropolitan regions, which recorded a decline of 20% in emissions per capita since 1990 (Figures 2.1 and 2.2).

Most OECD regions are very far from reaching net zero by 2050. On average, regions will have to cut their emissions by a factor of 6 by 2030 to meet the United Nations (UN) target of 2.1 t CO_2-eq per capita. In 2018, only 5 large regions in OECD countries – located in Colombia, Costa Rica and Israel – had production-based emissions per capita estimates lower than this target, while 40% of regions had emissions per capita higher than 10 t CO_2-eq per capita. The US has the largest regional disparities, where the gap between the District of Columbia (3.6 t CO_2-eq per capita) and North Dakota (180.7 t CO_2-eq per capita) can be explained by the latter's shale oil industry. Large regional disparities also exist in Canada, Greece, the Netherlands and New Zealand.

Definition

Production-based or territorial emissions correspond to GHG emitted within a region and enable to set reduction targets. Emissions were estimated using the Emissions Database for Global Atmospheric Research (EDGAR), version 6 (Crippa et al., 2021), and expressed in CO_2-equivalents by considering the 3 main GHGs, namely CO_2, CH_4, and N_2O, and a 100-year global warming potential (GWP).

Some care is needed in looking only at production-based emissions as reductions can occur through outsourcing/off-shoring of carbon-intensive activities to other regions or countries, and subsequently importing the goods and/or services provided. Often these shifts are made to countries/ regions with more carbon-intensive production processes and less stringent regulations on carbon abatement. Currently, most OECD countries are net importers of GHG emissions (i.e. their consumption, including through imports, accounts for larger emissions than the emissions generated through their production of goods and services, including those for export markets).

Sources

Crippa, M. et al. (2021), "EDGAR v6.0 Greenhouse Gas Emissions", European Commission, Joint Research Centre (JRC), *http://data.europa.eu/89h/97a67d67-c62e-4826-b873-9d972c4f670b*.

IEA (2022), *Global Energy Review: CO_2 Emissions in 2021*, International Energy Agency, *https://www.iea.org/reports/global-energy-review-co2-emissions-in-2021-2*.

UNEP-CCC (2020), *Emissions Gap Report 2020*, United Nations Environment Programme, *https://www.unep.org/emissions-gap-report-2020*.

Figure notes

2.1: Regions near a metropolitan region in OECD Oceania register 182 t CO_2-eq/capita.

2.1-2.4: GHG estimates based on EDGAR.

2.1. Metropolitan regions register lower emissions per capita than other regions

GHG emissions per capita estimates (t CO_2-eq/capita) by type of small regions (TL3), 2018

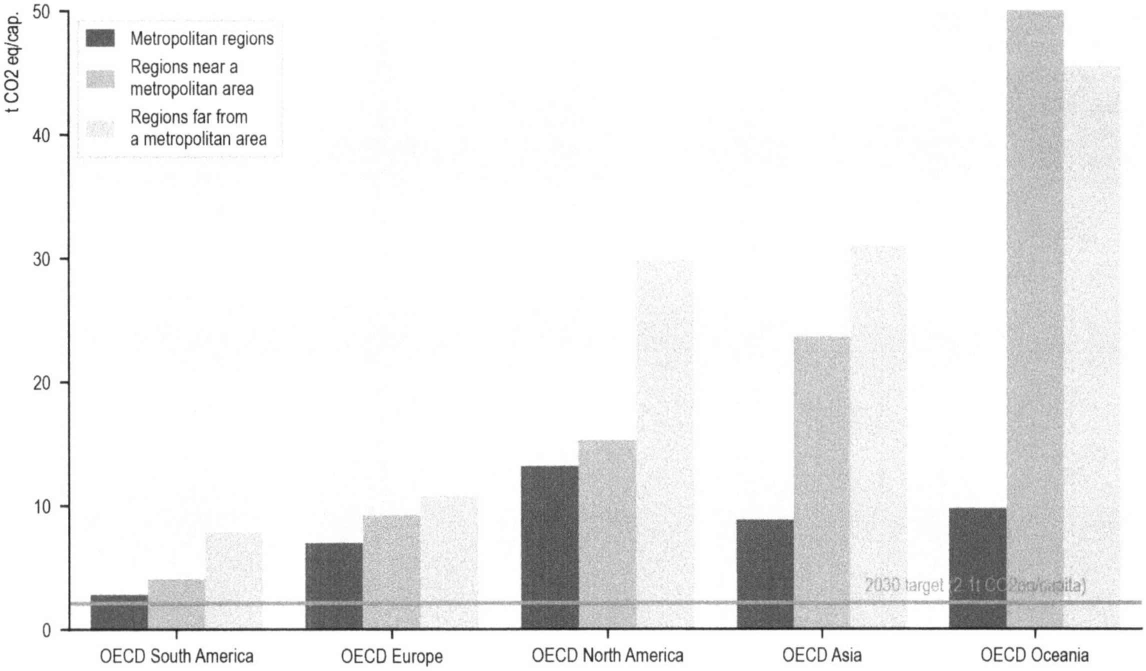

StatLink https://stat.link/biz26u

2.2. Emissions per capita decreased by more than 20% in metropolitan regions in OECD Europe, North America and Oceania

Percentage change in GHG emissions and emissions per capita by type of small regions (TL3), 1990-2018

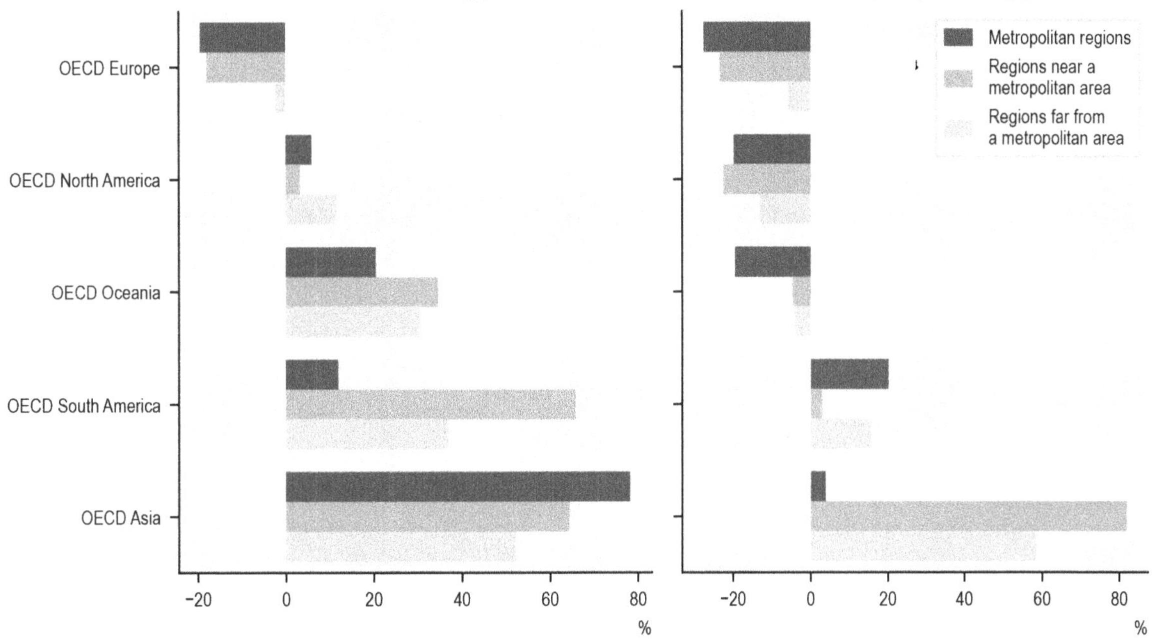

StatLink https://stat.link/4s8y79

2.3. OECD regions are still far from reaching climate neutrality goals by 2030, Americas

Total production-based GHG emissions per capita estimates (t CO_2-eq/capita), 2018; emission growth estimates (%) 1990-2018, OECD large regions (TL2)

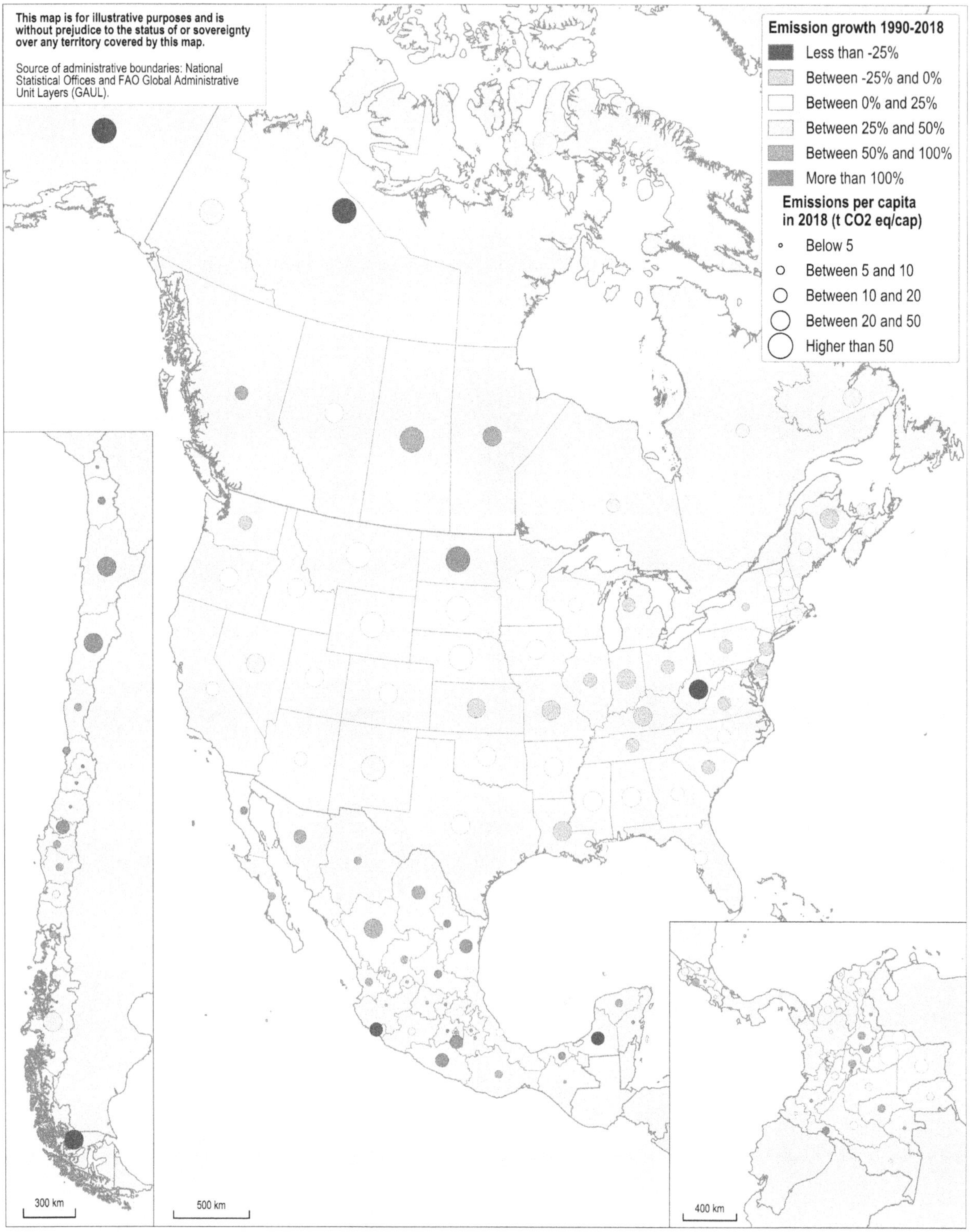

StatLink https://stat.link/e1pzdj

2.4. OECD regions are still far from reaching climate neutrality goals by 2030, Europe and Asia-Pacific

Total production-based GHG emissions per capita estimates (t CO_2-eq/capita), 2018; emission growth estimates (%) 1990-2018, OECD large regions (TL2)

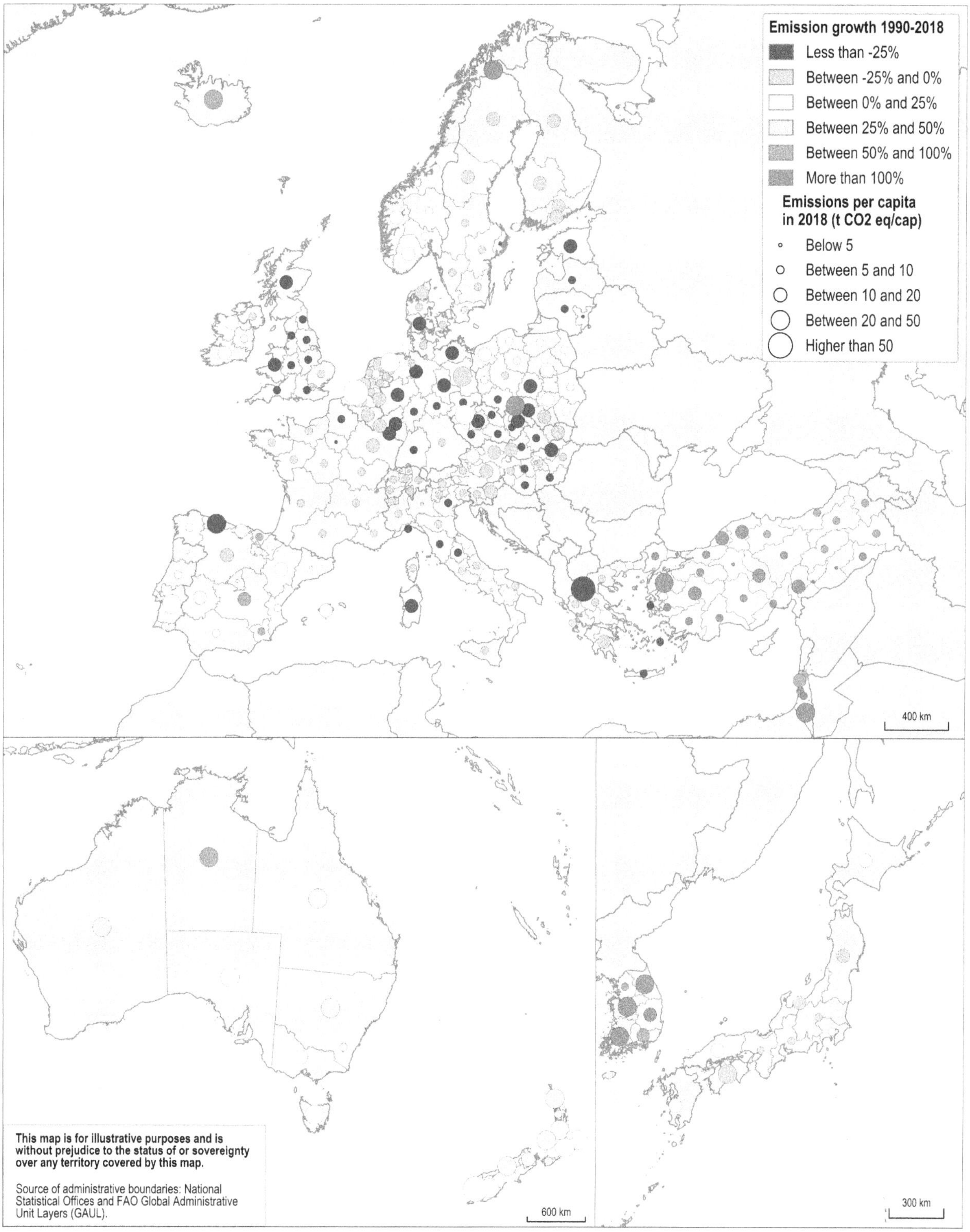

StatLink https://stat.link/eiklrc

Towards sustainable and resilient energy systems

Many OECD regions are still lagging in clean electricity generation.

Energy-related GHG emissions (from energy extraction, transformation and production) account for the largest share of production-based emissions across OECD countries (38% in 2018). The power industry accounts for the largest percentage (76%) of emissions in these activities, followed by oil refineries and transformation industry (14%) and fuel exploitation (11%). Since 1990, energy emissions have increased in almost two-thirds of OECD large regions.

Within OECD countries, metropolitan regions accounted for 58% of all energy-related emissions in 2018, 59% of emissions from power production and 71% of emissions from energy transformation, while accounting for 70% of the population. Remote regions on the other hand (hosting only 10% of the population) accounted for 42% of emissions from fuel exploitation (Figure 2.5).

Remote regions on average generate cleaner power, with more than half of their electricity produced from renewable sources. Metropolitan regions, on the other hand, tend to produce more carbon-intensive electricity (from coal and other fossil fuels), which in large part reflects the large land requirements of renewable installations compared to thermal power plants. (Figure 2.6). Whilst it is important to understand these spatial differences in energy systems, not least to identify which regions (and workers) are most likely to be affected by the green transition, it is important to note that the consumption of electricity follows very different spatial patterns.

While over one-third of regions generate most of their electricity from low-carbon sources, more than 50 regions spread across 19 OECD countries still rely on coal for most of the electricity they generate. Quebec (Canada), Auvergne-Rhône-Alpes (France) and Scotland (UK) rely on more than 90% of their electricity from nuclear or renewable sources and emit less than 100 g of CO2 eq. per kWh of electricity generated – almost 4 times below the OECD average (350 g CO2-eq/kWh). The carbon intensity of electricity production varies considerably within most OECD countries. For example, in Mexico, 12 of the top 14 producing states rely on fossil fuel for at least 70% of their electricity but Chiapas and Oaxaca produce more than 90% of electricity from renewable sources (Figures 2.7, 2.8 and 2.9).

More than 50 OECD European regions rely on natural gas – in large part imported – for more than half of their electricity generation. In Germany for example, which imports more than 90% of its natural gas – of which half was from Russia before Russia's war of aggression against Ukraine (IEA, 2021b) – several regions such as North Rhine-Westphalia are heavily dependent on gas for electricity generation. While gas consumption in OECD European countries has remained stable over the past 2 decades, natural gas production has been decreasing since 2004, accounting for only 65% of total gas consumption in 2019 (IEA, 2021a). In Europe, about 20 regions – including Budapest (Hungary), Groningen (Netherlands) and Lazio (Italy) – use gas for more than 60% of their electricity production (Figure 2.9).

Recent price shocks to natural gas have created steep increases in the cost of electricity production from gas, which may create, at least in the short term, challenges for the green transition, as gas is significantly less carbon-intensive per unit of energy than other fossil fuels such as coal. For example, in the region of Lublin, Poland, with high use of gas, electricity production is three times less carbon-intensive than in the Greater Poland region, which relies heavily on coal.

Definition

Emissions from the energy industry in regions were estimated using EDGAR, version 6 (Crippa et al., 2021) and expressed in CO_2-eq. Energy industry emissions include those from the power industry, oil refineries and transformation industry, and fuel exploitation. Fuel exploitation refers to fugitive emissions occurring when extracting oil, natural gas or coal.

Indicators on the production of electricity and carbon intensity of electricity production are based on the Global Power Plant Database (GPPD) (Byers et al., 2021) and the harmonised global dataset on wind and solar installations (Dunnett et al., 2020). Renewable energy sources include hydropower, wind, waste, biomass, wave and tidal, geothermal and solar. Fossil fuels include coal, oil, petroleum coke and natural gas.

For more details, see methodology in Annex C.

Sources

Byers, L. et al. (2021), *A Global Database of Powerplants*, World Resources Institute, *https://www.wri.org/publication/global-power-plant-database*.

Crippa, M. et al. (2021), *EDGAR v6.0 Greenhouse Gas Emissions (dataset)*, Joint Research Centre (JRC), European Commission, *http://data.europa.eu/89h/97a67d67-c62e-4826-b873-9d972c4f670b*.

Dunnett, S. et al. (2020), "Harmonised global datasets of wind and solar farm locations and power", *Scientific Data*, Vol. 7/1, p. 190, *https://doi.org/10.1038/s41597-020-0469-8*.

IEA (2021a), *Key World Energy Statistics 2021*, International Energy Agency, *https://www.iea.org/reports/key-world-energy-statistics-2021*.

IEA (2021b), "World – Natural Gas imports by origin (Edition 2020)", *IEA Natural Gas Information Statistics (database)*, International Energy Agency, *https://doi.org/10.1787/45b645ba-en*.

2.5. Fuel extraction emissions are concentrated in remote regions

Emissions from the energy sector by type of small region (TL3), 2018

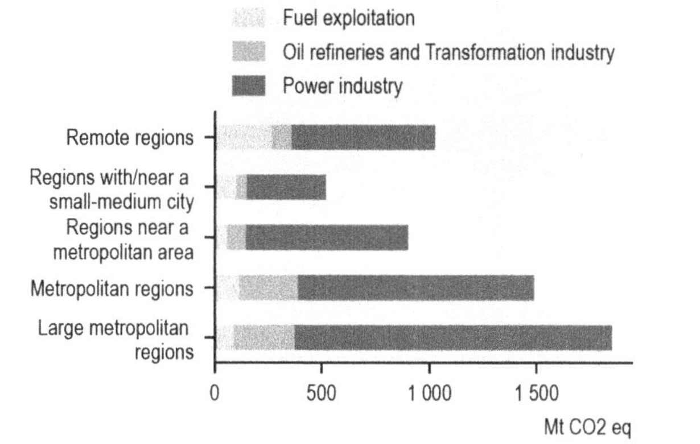

StatLink https://stat.link/k50bsw

2.6. Remote regions tend to generate cleaner electricity than other regions

Share of electricity by source and by type of small regions (TL3), 2019

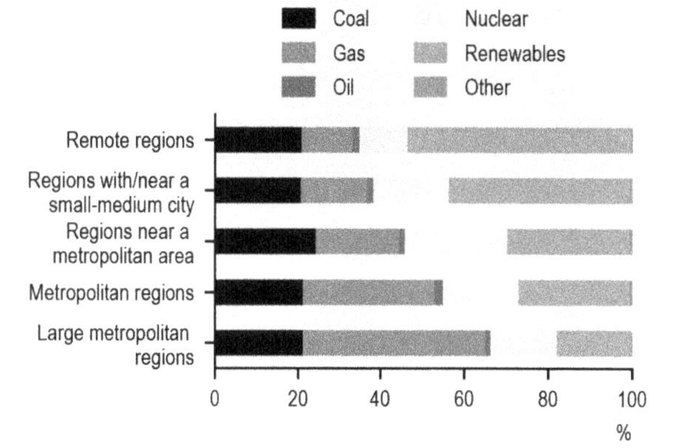

StatLink https://stat.link/2wse7a

2.7. More than 50 European regions rely mainly on natural gas for electricity generation

Share of natural gas in electricity generation (%), 2019, European OECD large regions (TL2)

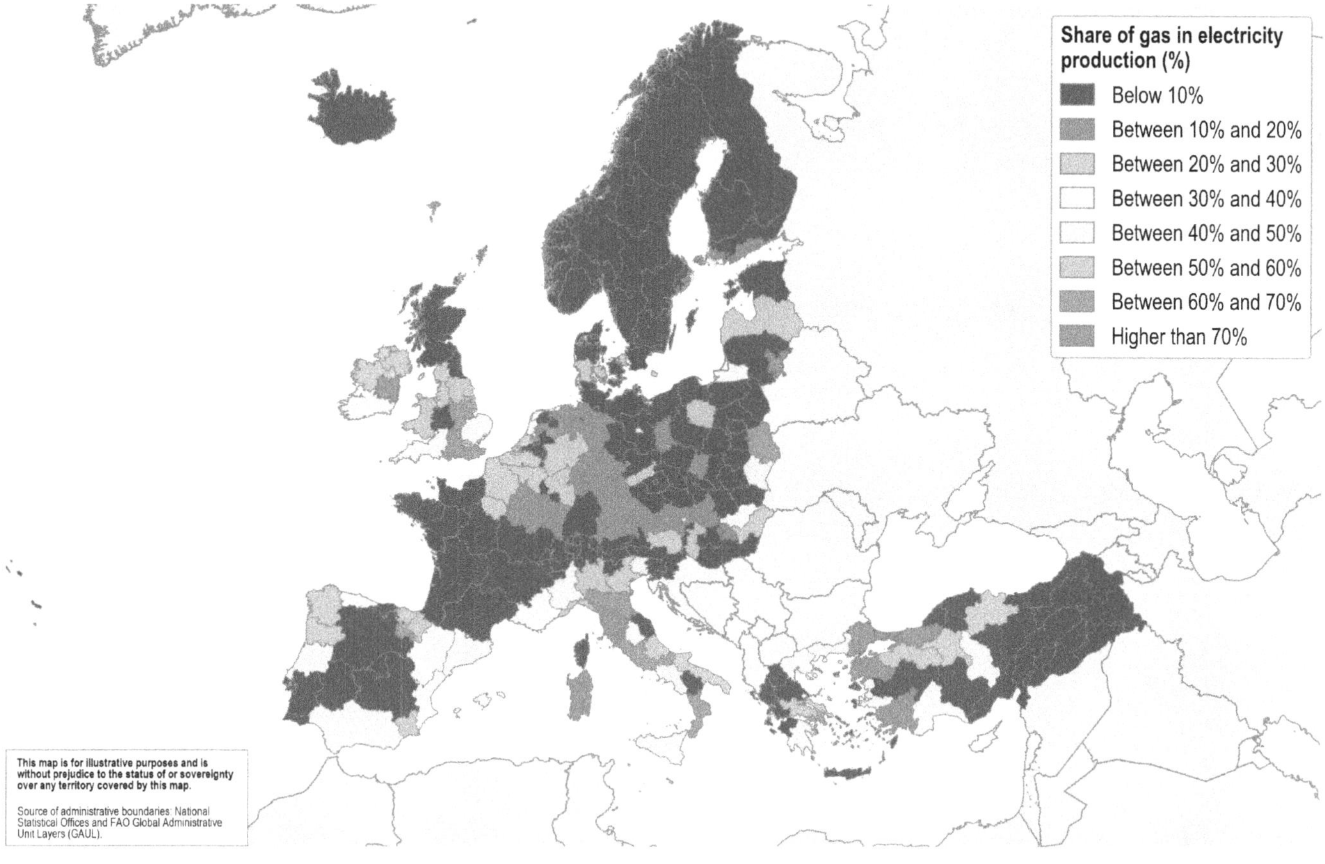

StatLink https://stat.link/b16hrx

2.8. Many regions still lag behind in low-carbon electricity production, Americas

Carbon intensity of electricity generation (g CO_2 eq/kWh) and gross electricity production (GWh), 2019, large regions (TL2)

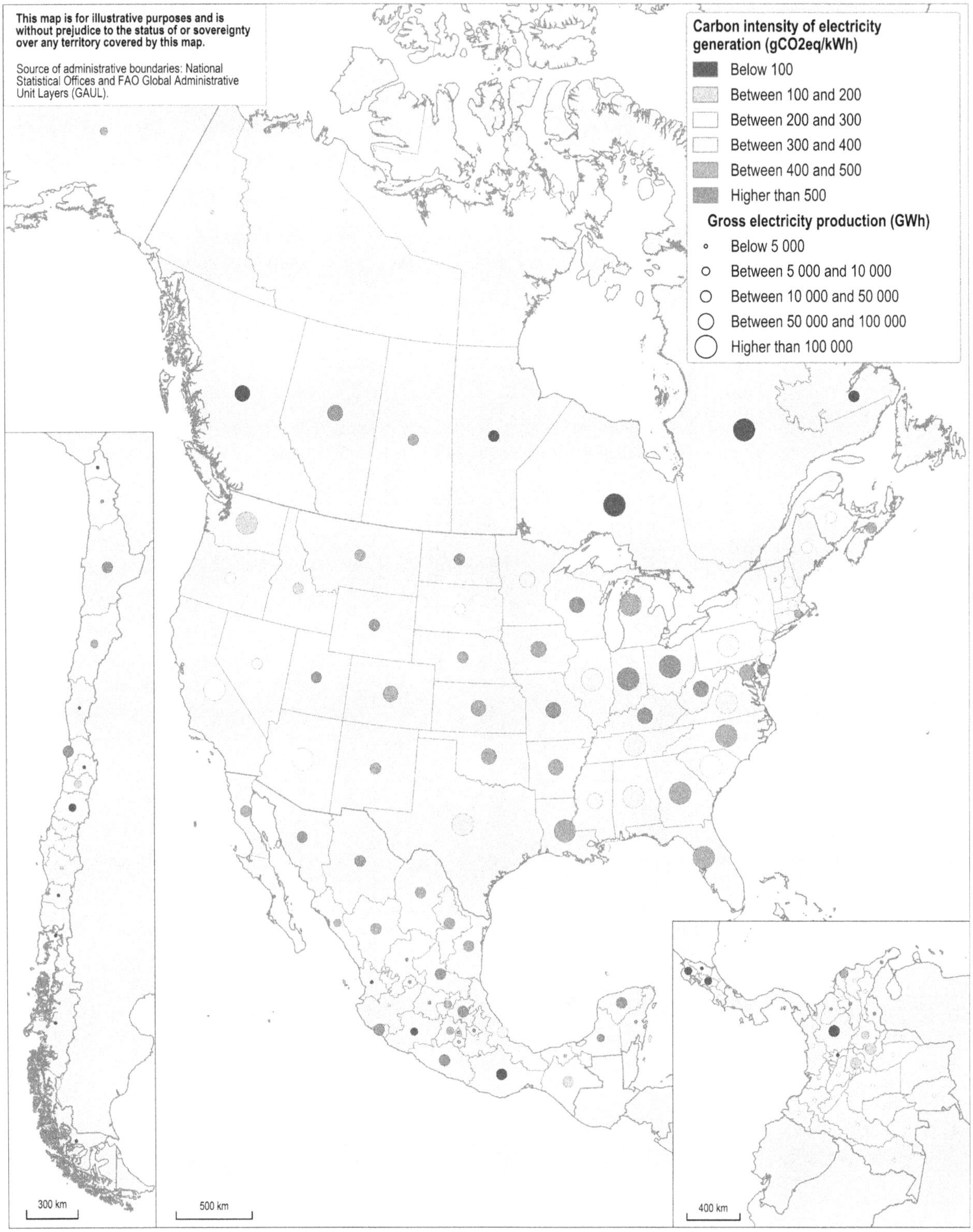

StatLink https://stat.link/1li7m6

2.9. Many regions still lag begind in low-carbon electricity production, Europe and Asia-Pacific

Carbon intensity of electricity generation (g CO_2 eq/kWh) and gross electricity production (GWh), 2019, large regions (TL2)

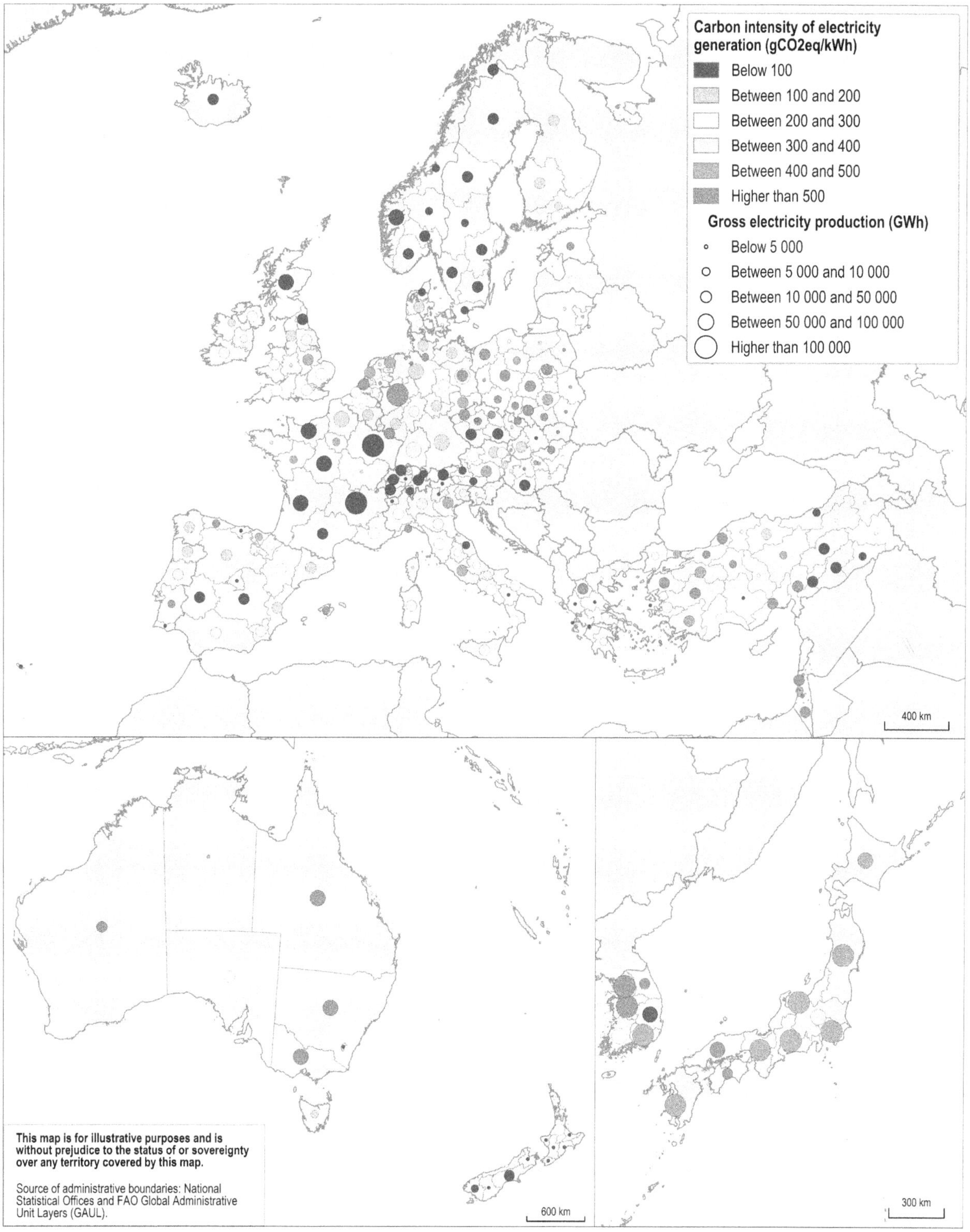

StatLink https://stat.link/1b4za8

Households in the energy and climate crises

In OECD regions, households have an important role to play to meet climate neutrality goals.

In OECD countries, direct building emissions (excluding purchased electricity and construction) accounted for 11% of GHG emissions in 2018 (Crippa et al., 2021). Direct building emissions have declined since 2000 (-11%) due to efficiency gains and despite the continuing growth in housing area per capita. However, buildings are still off track to achieve carbon neutrality by 2050 (IEA, 2022) and will have an important role to mitigate dependency on imported natural gas. Within countries, building emissions show differences that can only be partly explained by climate factors. For example, in Germany, building emissions per capita in Brandenburg are three times higher than in Bremen (Figure 2.10). Since 2000, building emissions per capita decreased in three-quarters of OECD large regions, with Swedish regions experiencing a decrease of more than 75%. However, not all OECD regions have seen declines, indeed many regions in the Baltic states, Colombia and Türkiye saw increases.

Space heating accounts for the largest share (64%) of energy consumption for European households (Eurostat, 2019) and natural gas is the leading energy source for space heating. By retrofitting their dwellings, households can play an important role in reducing both their energy consumption and dependencies on natural gas.

Heating degree days (HDD) provide a measure of weather-induced heating needs, albeit without accounting for building efficiency. In the US, heating needs in Florida are around 15 times lower than in Minnesota. Large disparities are also observed in smaller countries such as Italy, where the Aosta Valley region and the province of Bolzano-Bozen have at least four times more heating needs than Apulia, Sardinia and Sicily. Both Italy and the US are in the top 10 OECD countries in terms of natural gas consumption per capita in the residential sector. Rises in energy prices disproportionately impact low-income households. Indeed, in the UK – the country with the third-highest gas consumption per capita in the residential sector in Europe (IEA, 2022) – regions north of London tend to have both lower income and slightly higher heating needs (Figure 2.11).

In addition to energy consumption, households play an important role in lowering materials consumption, by reducing waste and increasing recycling. In 2018, waste accounted for 4% of domestic GHG emissions in OECD countries (Crippa et al., 2021). Large disparities in municipal waste generation per inhabitant exist across and within OECD countries. Israel and Luxembourg record on average almost three times the municipal waste per inhabitant observed in Colombia and regional disparities are particularly stark in Canada, Sweden and Latin American countries. In Mexico, for example, the average resident of Mexico City generates three times more waste than in Oaxaca (Figure 2.12). Over the past decade, most East European countries, as well as Colombia, Korea and Mexico have increased per capita waste. Recycling is still very limited in Türkiye and Latin America but very developed in many European countries, notably in Austria, Belgium, the Netherlands, Norway and Sweden, where close to 100% of municipal waste is recycled in most large regions. Capital regions often record the highest recycling rates within their respective countries, such as Australia, Belgium or France. Many European capital regions also show the largest decline in per capita waste in their respective countries (Figure 2.13).

Definition

Emissions from buildings and waste in regions were estimated using EDGAR, version 6 (Crippa et al., 2021), and expressed in CO_2-eq. Building emissions only refer to direct emissions. The carbon intensity of purchased electricity and construction materials is not included.

Heating degree days (HDD) measure the heating needs of buildings. It is the sum of the differences between the mean outdoor air temperature and a standard temperature (15°C) (Mistry, 2019).

Recycled municipal waste includes waste that undergoes material recycling or other forms of recovery (including energy recovery, composting). Landfilling is excluded.

Sources

Crippa, M. et al. (2021), *EDGAR v6.0 Greenhouse Gas Emissions*, Joint Research Centre (JRC), European Commission, *http://data.europa.eu/89h/97a67d67-c62e-4826-b873-9d972c4f670b*.

Eurostat (2019), *Share of Fuels in the Final Energy Consumption in the Residential Sector by Type of End-use, https://appsso.eurostat.ec.europa.eu/nui/show.do?dataset=nrg_d_hhq&lang=en*.

IEA (2022), "OECD - Natural gas supply and consumption", *IEA Natural Gas Information Statistics (database), https://doi.org/10.1787/data-00481-en*.

IEA (2022), *Buildings*, International Energy Agency, *https://www.iea.org/reports/buildings*.

Mistry, M. (2019), "A high-resolution (0.25 degree) historical global gridded dataset of monthly and annual cooling and heating degree days (1970-2018) based on GLDAS data", PANGAEA, *https://doi.org/10.1594/PANGAEA.903123*.

Figure notes

2.12: 2013 for EST, LUX; 2014 for TUR; 2016 for CAN; 2017 for CHL; 2018 for JPN; 2019 for AUT, COL, ESP, FRA, HUN, ISR, ITA.

2.13: 2013 for CZE, EST, LUX; 2014 for TUR; 2015 for DEU; 2017 for AUS, CHL; 2018 for FRA, JPN; 2019 for AUT, HUN, ISR, ITA.

2.10. Building emissions

Building emissions per capita (t CO_2-eq/capita) estimates, OECD large regions (TL2), 2018

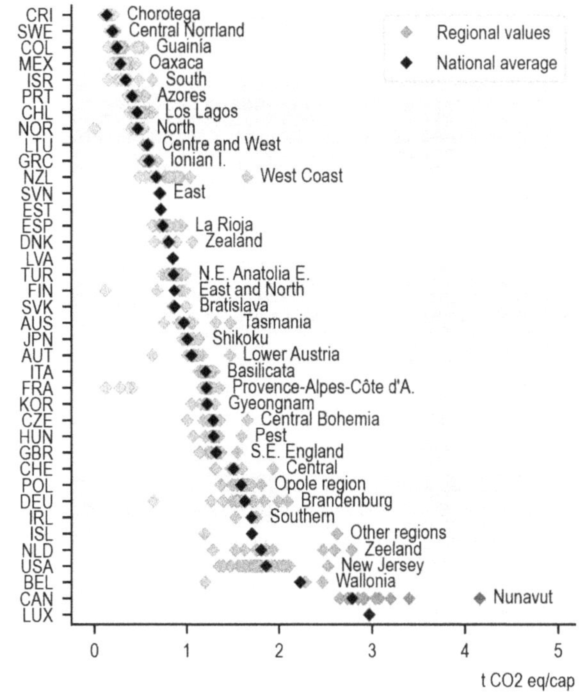

StatLink https://stat.link/q1yat5

2.11. Heating needs

HDD (with reference temperature 15°C), OECD large regions (TL2), 2010-18

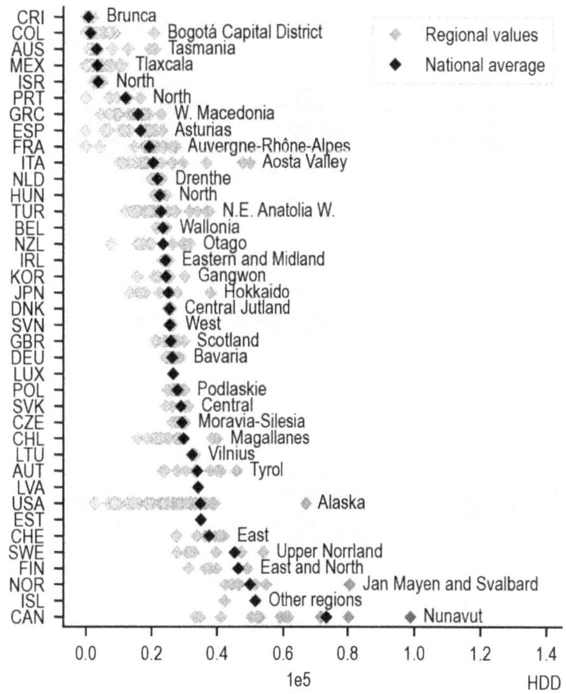

StatLink https://stat.link/aepdct

2.12. Municipal waste per capita

Municipal waste volume per capita, OECD large regions (TL2), 2020

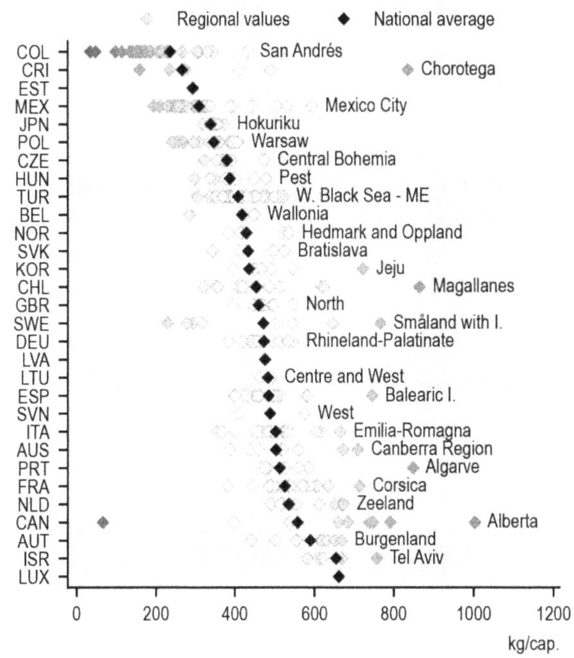

StatLink https://stat.link/ftw52r

2.13. Non-recycled municipal waste per capita

Non-recycled waste per capita, OECD large regions (TL2), 2020

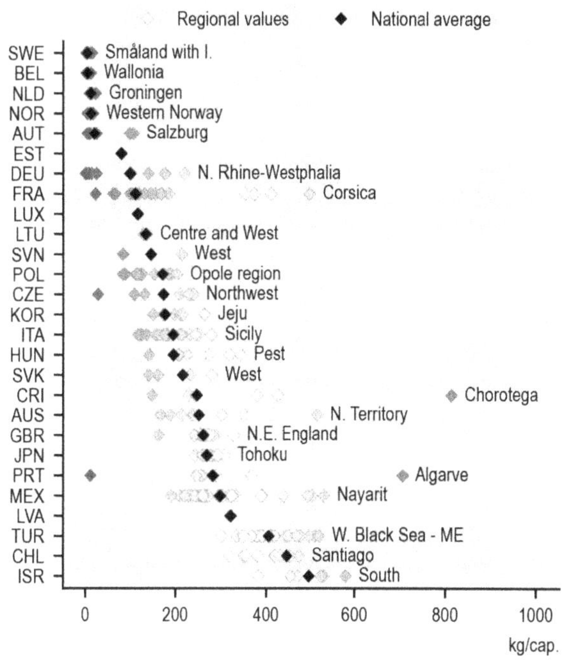

StatLink https://stat.link/k4ln7j

Industrial regions will have to undergo deep transformations to meet climate neutrality goals.

In OECD countries, the manufacturing sector (including oil refineries and the transformation industry) is the third-largest contributor to territorial emissions after the energy and transport sectors, accounting for 20% of total emissions (Crippa et al., 2021), while accounting for 12% of total employment. With a 27% reduction in GHG emissions since 1970, manufacturing is the sector with the largest decline in emissions. This can be explained by a drop in employment driven in part by globalisation, as in many OECD countries manufacturing industries have been relocated offshore. Metropolitan regions experienced the largest decline in manufacturing emissions (-31%) but, in remote regions, they increased by 7%. Within the manufacturing industry, emissions are particularly concentrated in four specific sectors: the manufacture of coke and petroleum products; of chemicals and chemical products; of non-metallic mineral products (i.e. cement); and of basic metals (i.e. steel). In EU27 countries, these 4 sectors account for 80% of total manufacturing GHG emissions. These sectors can drive the differences in manufacturing emissions observed within OECD countries. For example, in the Netherlands, the manufacturing emissions per unit of gross value added (GVA) in the region of Zeeland are almost seven times higher than in Limburg. Although the manufacturing industry accounts for more than 20% of total GVA in both regions, emissions in Zeeland are particularly high due to the manufacture of chemicals and chemical products (Figure 2.14).

The transition to climate neutrality will affect more strongly regional economies with high employment shares in emission-intensive manufacturing sectors. In European OECD countries, the regions with the highest share of employment in the four most-emitting manufacturing sectors are Northwest (Czech Republic), Rhineland-Palatinate, Saxony-Anhalt (Germany) and North Middle Sweden, where such sectors account for around 7% of total regional employment (Eurostat, 2021). Emissions are particularly high in specific regions. For example, emissions in the four most-emitting manufacturing sectors are concentrated in Lower Saxony, North Rhine-Westphalia and Rhineland-Palatinate for Germany (OECD, 2022) (Figure 2.16).

The manufacturing sector also tends to be more energy-intensive compared to other sectors. In 2019, for OECD countries, manufacturing accounted for 18% of the total final energy consumption, 30% of natural gas consumption and 25% of electricity consumption (IEA, 2022b). Manufacturing industries heavily relying on energy are unevenly distributed within countries, making some regions' economies more vulnerable to increases in energy prices. Within OECD countries, the most energy-intensive region consumes on average 16 times more energy per unit of GVA than the least energy-intensive region. This occurs as the most energy-intensive manufacturing sectors can be very concentrated in a few places. For example, in Greece, the Netherlands and Norway, most of the national employment in the manufacturing of coke and refined petroleum products is concentrated in one single region (Peloponnese, South Holland and Western Norway) (Figure 2.15).

Definition

Manufacturing industry emissions in OECD regions were estimated using EDGAR, version 6 (Crippa et al., 2021) and expressed in CO_2-eq. Manufacturing industry emissions include combustion for manufacturing, oil refineries and transformation industry, chemical processes, non-metallic minerals production, iron and steel production, non-ferrous metals production and non-energy use of fuels and solvents and products use.

Emissions in **key manufacturing sectors** in European regions were estimated using EU-ETS matched with the ORBIS database (OECD, 2022). Emissions are expressed in CO_2-eq and include CO_2, N_2O, CH_4 and F-gases. Key manufacturing sectors refer to the manufacture of coke and refined petroleum products (NACE 19), chemicals and chemical products (NACE 20), non-metallic mineral products (NACE 23) and basic metals (NACE 24).

See Annex C for more details.

Sources

Crippa, M. et al. (2021), *EDGAR v6.0 Greenhouse Gas Emissions*, Joint Research Centre (JRC), European Commission, *http://data.europa.eu/89h/97a67d67-c62e-4826-b873-9d972c4f670b*.

Eurostat (2021), "Structural Business Statistics data by NUTS 2 regions and NACE Rev. 2 (from 2008 onwards)", *https://appsso.eurostat.ec.europa.eu/nui/show.do?dataset=sbs_r_nuts06_r2&lang=en*.

IEA (2022a), "OECD - Natural gas supply and consumption", *IEA Natural Gas Information Statistics (database)*, *https://doi.org/10.1787/data-00481-en*.

IEA (2022b), "World energy balances", *IEA World Energy Statistics and Balances (dataset)*, *https://doi.org/10.1787/data-00512-en*.

OECD (2022), "Regional industrial transitions to climate neutrality: Identifying vulnerable regions", OECD, Paris.

Figure notes

2.14: 2017 for JPN. Only regions where the GVA in manufacturing is higher than USD 10 billion (constant prices, constant purchasing power parity [PPP], base year 2015) are represented.

2.16: The top four high-emission manufacturing sectors are the manufacture of coke and refined petroleum products (NACE 19), of chemicals and chemical products (NACE 20), of non-metallic mineral products (NACE 23) and of basic metals (NACE 24).

2.14. Regional disparities in manufacturing emissions intensity

Emissions per unit of GVA in manufacturing, 2018, OECD large regions (TL2)

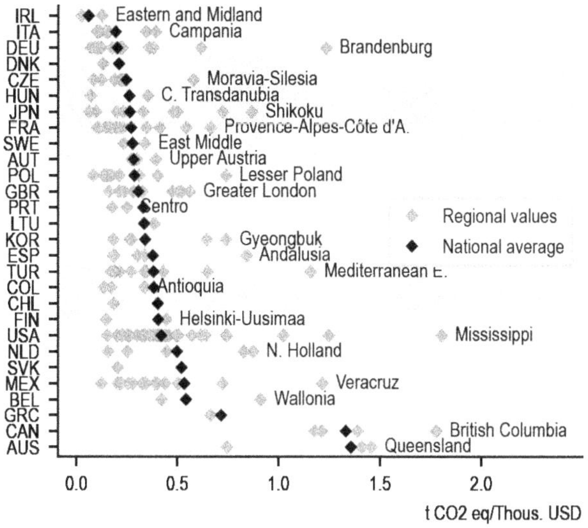

StatLink https://stat.link/3jlc2t

2.15. Manufacturing energy intensity is concentrated in a few regions

Manufacturing energy consumption per unit of GVA, 2018, European large regions (TL2)

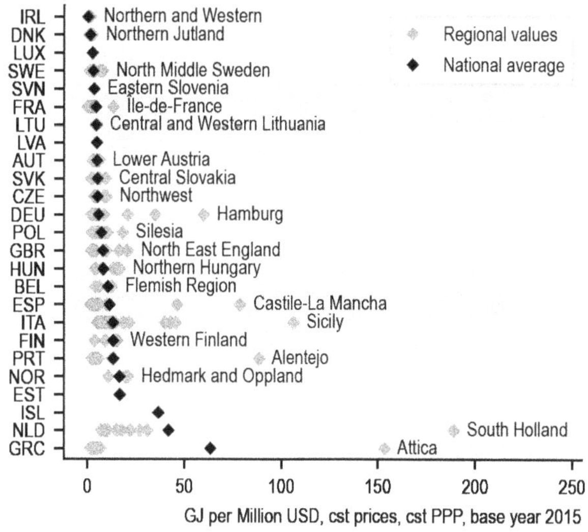

StatLink https://stat.link/j5n61e

2.16. Manufacturing emissions are concentrated in a few regions

Emissions (kt CO2 eq) and employment share (%) in the top four high-emission manufacturing sectors, OECD European large regions (TL2), 2019

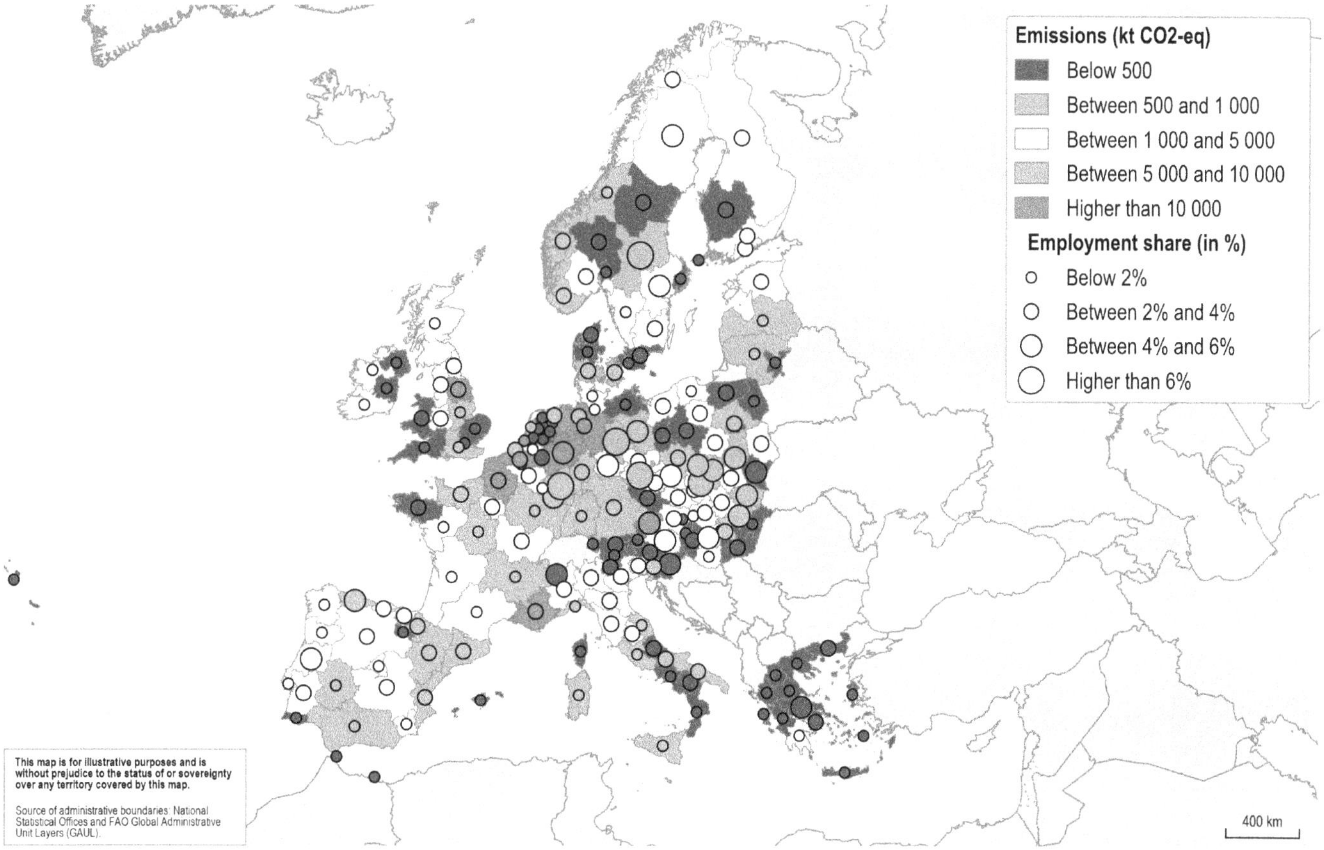

StatLink https://stat.link/d7epr5

Sustainable transport in regions

With higher access to public transport, more developed electric mobility and lower private vehicle ownership per capita, capital regions are leading the way to more sustainable transport.

The transport sector is the second-largest contributor to GHG emissions (24% in 2018) in OECD countries after the energy sector. Transport witnessed the largest increase in emissions, doubling from 1970 to 2018. Road transport accounted for 88% of emissions within this sector in 2018 (excluding international shipping and international aviation) (Crippa et al., 2021). Despite an improvement in vehicle energy efficiency, the distances travelled and the vehicle numbers, size and mass increased, leading to higher fuel consumption and related emissions. Differences in road emissions per capita within countries are particularly high, especially in Oceania and North America. On average, remote regions have over three times higher road transport emissions per capita than large metropolitan regions. Such disparities can originate from differences in population densities, the number of private vehicles per capita and access to public transport and services (Figures 2.20 and 2.21).

The transport sector accounted for over one-third of the total final energy consumption and two-thirds of oil products consumption in 2019 in OECD countries. Reaching climate neutrality and cutting oil use requires further development of public transport, reducing private car use in large cities and accelerating the adoption of electric and more efficient vehicles (IEA, 2022). Private vehicle ownership is concentrated in specific types of regions in OECD countries. In Asian and most European countries, non-metropolitan regions record more vehicles per inhabitant than metropolitan regions. However, in Australia, Mexico, Türkiye and East European countries, metropolitan regions record higher vehicles per capita than other regions, maybe driven by higher living standards in metropolitan regions. Within-country differences are largest in North America and Southern Europe. For example, in Italy, Aosta Valley recorded almost 1 800 vehicles per 1 000 inhabitants, the highest number of private vehicles per capita across OECD regions and more than 3 times the vehicles per capita observed in Liguria (Figure 2.17).

During the last two decades, the number of private vehicles per capita decreased in most European regions, especially capital regions. Greater London, UK, has seen a 12% decline in per capita private vehicle ownership since 2000. On the other hand, in many regions of Chile, Mexico and the US, private vehicle ownership has increased significantly. In the regions of Morelos and Tlaxcala (Mexico) for example, the number of private vehicles per capita in 2020 was four times higher than in 2001. Regarding the adoption of electric mobility, Norway ranks first, with 22% of its private vehicle fleet being electric or hybrid. In most OECD countries, capital regions are leading the adoption of electric or hybrid vehicles. This may be explained by shorter average travel distances and higher accessibility of charging stations. In the region of Oslo and Viken (Norway), almost 30% of private vehicles are either electric or hybrid as of 2020, an increase of 20 percentage points (pp) in only 4 years. Brussels Capital Region (Belgium), Budapest (Hungary), Greater London (UK) and Stockholm (Sweden) recorded a share of around 7% in the same year (Figure 2.18).

Ensuring good accessibility to public transport in cities is essential not only to reduce GHG emissions but also to reduce congestion and air pollution, and to improve quality of life. On average, across the OECD's largest cities, 83% of the population can access a bus stop and 31% can access a metro or tram stop within a 10-minute walk. Buses provide better coverage across a city transport network but their frequency tends to be more variable and their speed is lower than metros. Northern and Western European cities, as well as Auckland (New Zealand), tend to have the best access to public transport. In terms of metro or tram stops, Southern European cities show relatively lower accessibility (e.g. Lisbon 21% or Athens 22%) than Central and Northern European cities (Figure 2.19).

Definition

Road transport emissions in regions were estimated using EDGAR, version 6, and expressed in CO_2-eq.

Motor vehicles include road vehicles, other than motorcycles, intended for the carriage of passengers and designed to seat no more than nine persons including the driver.

Public transport stop locations were extracted from Open Street Map (Haklay and Weber, 2008) for the largest city of each OECD country. Walking times were calculated using Mapbox API.

Sources

Crippa, M. et al. (2021), *EDGAR v6.0 Greenhouse Gas Emissions*, Joint Research Centre (JRC), European Commission, *http://data.europa.eu/89h/97a67d67-c62e-4826-b873-9d972c4f670b*.

Haklay, M. and P. Weber (2008), "OpenStreetMap: User-generated street maps", *IEEE Pervasive Computing*, Vol. 7, pp. 12-18.

IEA (2022), *A 10-Point Plan to Cut Oil Use*, International Energy Agency, *https://www.iea.org/reports/a-10-point-plan-to-cut-oil-use*.

Figure notes

2.17: 2009 for CAN; 2010 for ESP; 2011 for EST; 2012 for LUX; 2013 for JPN; 2014 for ISL and TUR; 2019 for ISR and DEU; 2020 for AUS, CHE, CHL, CZE, FIN, GBR, GRC, IRL, ITA, KOR, LTU, MEX, NLD, NOR, POL, SVK, SVN and USA.

2.18: 2020 for CHE, GBR, IRL, KOR, MEX, NOR, POL, SVN, SWE; 2021 for AUT, BEL, FRA, HUN, LVA, SVK.

2.17. Private vehicle ownership in regions

Private motor vehicles per 1 000 inhabitants in large regions (TL2), 2021

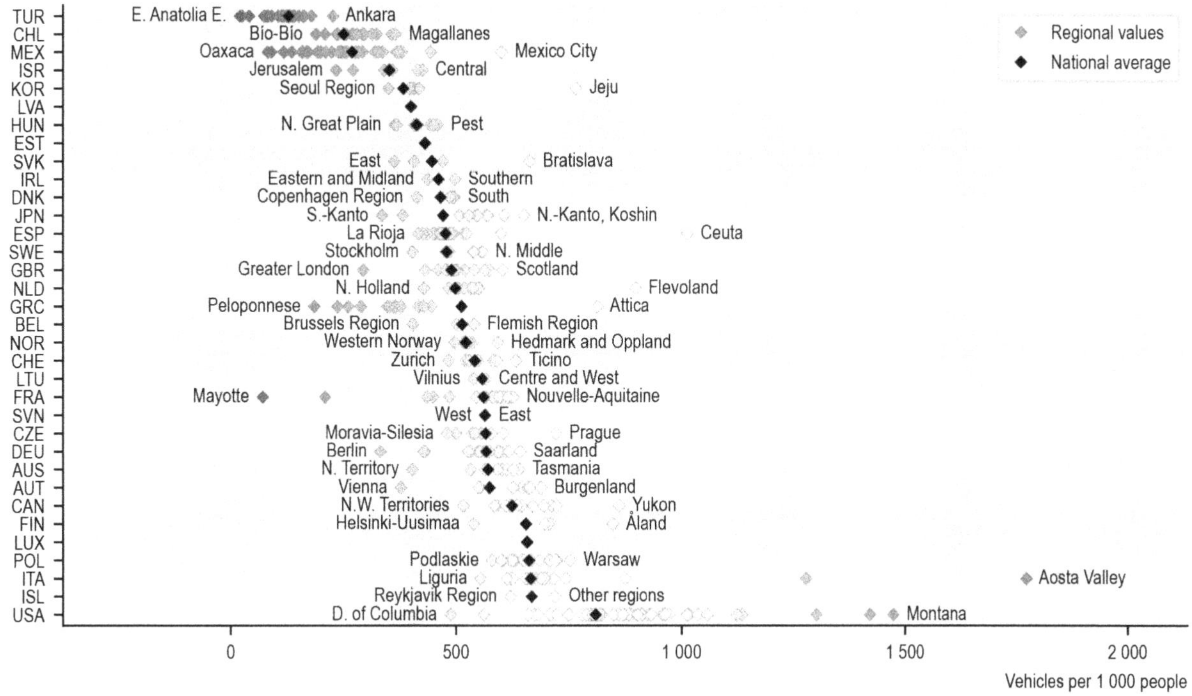

StatLink https://stat.link/xmvwg5

2.18. Norway leads electric and hybrid mobility

Share of private electric or hybrid vehicles (%) in large regions (TL2), 2020-21

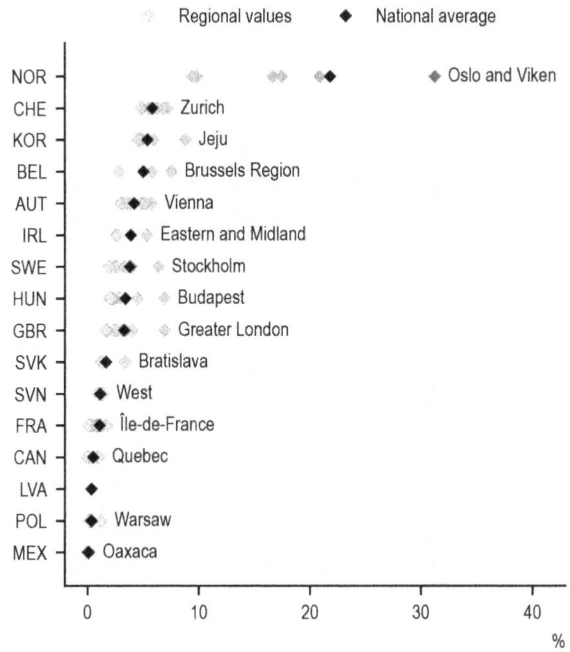

StatLink https://stat.link/bi2dac

2.19. The largest cities in OECD countries provide good access to public transport

Share of population with access to public transport (within 10-min walk), largest functional urban area (FUA) per country

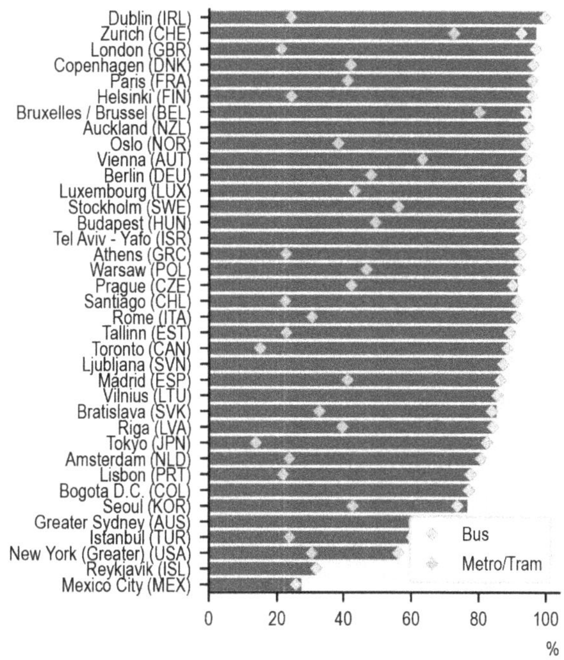

StatLink https://stat.link/w9bj58

2.20. Regional disparities in road transport emissions, Americas

Road transport emissions per capita (t CO_2-eq/capita) estimates in 2018 and emissions per capita growth 2000-18, OECD large regions (TL2)

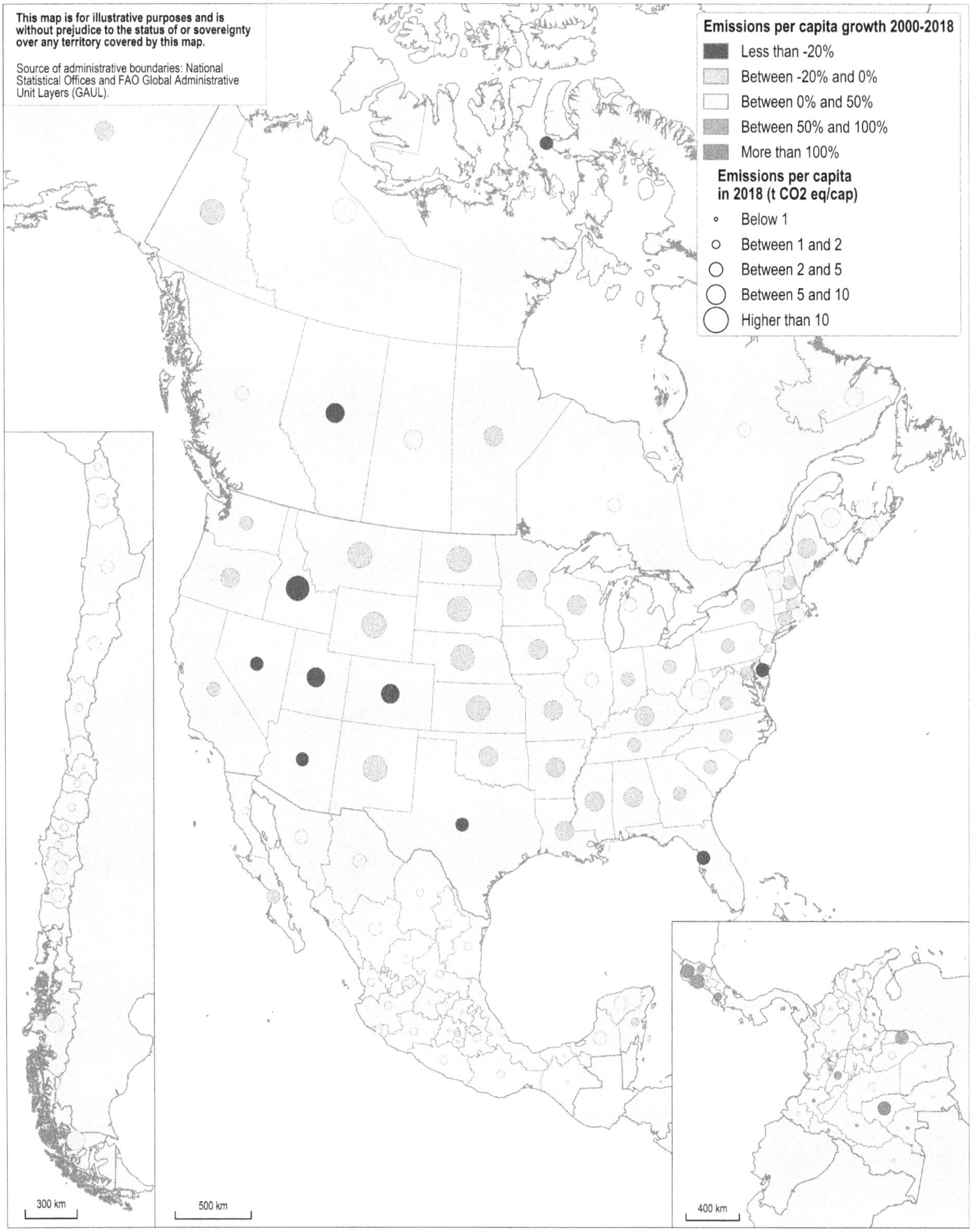

StatLink https://stat.link/tzroi9

2.21. Regional disparities in road transport emissions, Europe and Asia-Pacific

Road transport emissions per capita (t CO_2-eq/capita) estimates in 2018 and emissions per capita growth 2000-18, OECD large regions (TL2)

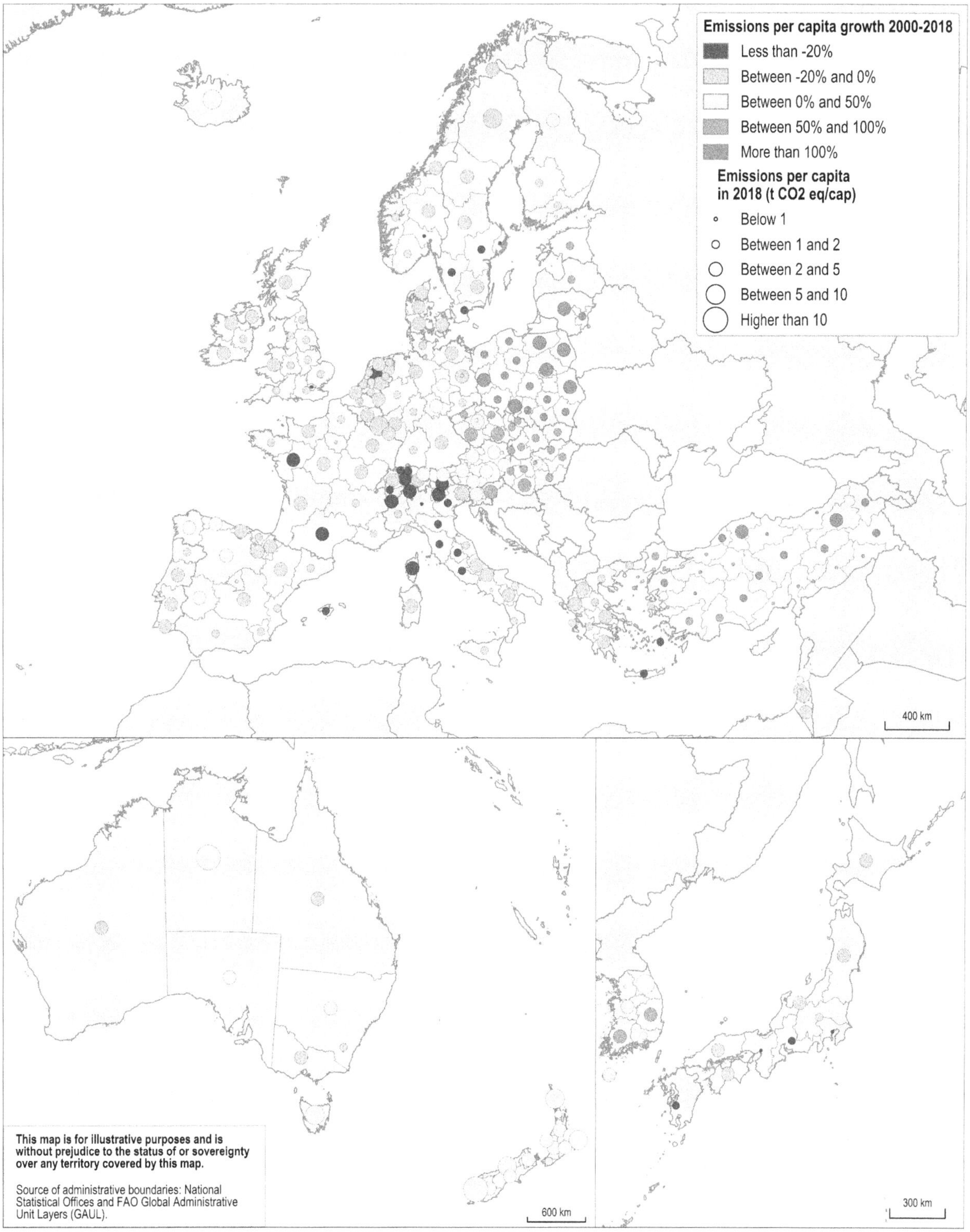

StatLink https://stat.link/l9ac4y

Land use in cities

The average amount of residential built-up area per inhabitant varies substantially across OECD countries, from 40 m^2 per capita in Korea to 460 m^2 in Finland.

Cities are continuing to concentrate on increasing shares of the global population. Over the last few decades, cities' population has been characterised by both physical expansion and increasing densities (OECD/EC, 2020). Both processes affect the shape of their built environment, which in turn can have implications in terms of environmental footprint and capacity to provide services. For example, cities with fragmented and sprawling structures can make it more difficult to provide public transport and increase energy consumption and related CO_2 emissions (UN-Habitat, 2018).

The amount of residential space per capita in cities differs remarkably across countries and tends to be higher in countries with high gross domestic product (GDP) per capita. Cities' residential built-up area can range from about 40-60 m^2 per inhabitant in Colombia, Korea and Türkiye to about 450 m^2 per inhabitant in Finland, New Zealand and the US. Notwithstanding the large variation in residential built-up areas per capita, there is no common pattern across countries. Within several countries, such as Australia, Chile, New Zealand and the US, the residential built-up area per capita varies relatively widely between FUAs (Banquet et al., 2022) (Figure 2.22).

Commuting zones drive up the total built-up area per capita of OECD metropolitan areas. As land prices are lower and developing land tends to be easier outside of the dense urban centres, land in commuting zones tends to be used more extensively. In several countries, such as Ireland and Latvia, cities with relatively low built-up area per capita coexist with others showing very high levels. In those countries, the relatively large FUA-wide built-up areas are primarily driven by spread-out land use in commuting zones (rather than in cities) (Figure 2.23).

A second dimension to characterise the shape of urban settlements is the height of buildings. The recent estimates of building heights released by the European Commission (EC) Joint Research Centre (JRC) at the global level allowed for assessing differences in average building heights between OECD metropolitan areas. FUAs in Korea and Japan record the highest average building height across OECD countries (more than 8 m). As expected, due to the higher demand for central locations, building height in the city is higher than in its commuting zone, with a difference of 3.4 metres, on average. The average building height tends to increase with city size. Cities with more than 1.5 million inhabitants record an average building height of 9.3 m, while those with less than 250 000 people have an average building height of 7.7 m. Comparing average building height with built-up area per capita enables to find consistent patterns within different macro-regions. Metropolitan areas located in OECD North America tend to have low average building height and higher built-up area per capita, reflecting a higher horizontal spread compared to the OECD average. Cities in OECD Asia and Oceania are on the other hand much more "compact" as they register both relatively low levels of built-up area per capita and higher average building heights. Cities in OECD Europe and South America show both low levels of built-up area per capita and medium levels of building height (Figure 2.24).

Definition

Built-up is here defined in terms of land use. Not only are building footprints included but also surrounding areas such as gardens. Residential areas refer to urban fabrics and isolated structures. Industrial and commercial areas include industrial, commercial, public, military and private units, mineral extraction and dump sites, construction sites and land without current use. These estimates are based on satellite imagery data (Sentinel-1 and -2) using deep learning models.

Sources

Banquet, A. et al. (2022), "Monitoring land use in cities using satellite imagery and deep learning", *OECD Regional Development Papers*, No. 28, OECD Publishing, Paris, *https://doi.org/10.1787/dc8e85d5-en*.

JRC (2022), *GHSL Data Package 2022: Public Release GHS P2022*, European Commission, *https://data.europa.eu/doi/10.2760/19817*.

OECD/European Commission (2020), *Cities in the World: A New Perspective on Urbanisation*, OECD Urban Studies, OECD Publishing, Paris, *https://doi.org/10.1787/d0efcbda-en*.

UN-Habitat (2018), *SDG 11 Synthesis Report 2018: Tracking Progress Towards Inclusive, Safe, Resilient and Sustainable Cities and Human Settlements*, United Nations Human Settlements Programme, Nairobi.

Figure notes

2.22 and 2.24: Built-up surface estimated for 2021 using the OECD land use model (Banquet et al., 2022). Population counts estimated for 2020 based on GHS-POP 2022 release (JRC, 2022).

2.22. Residential and commercial/industrial built-up area per capita in FUAs, 2021

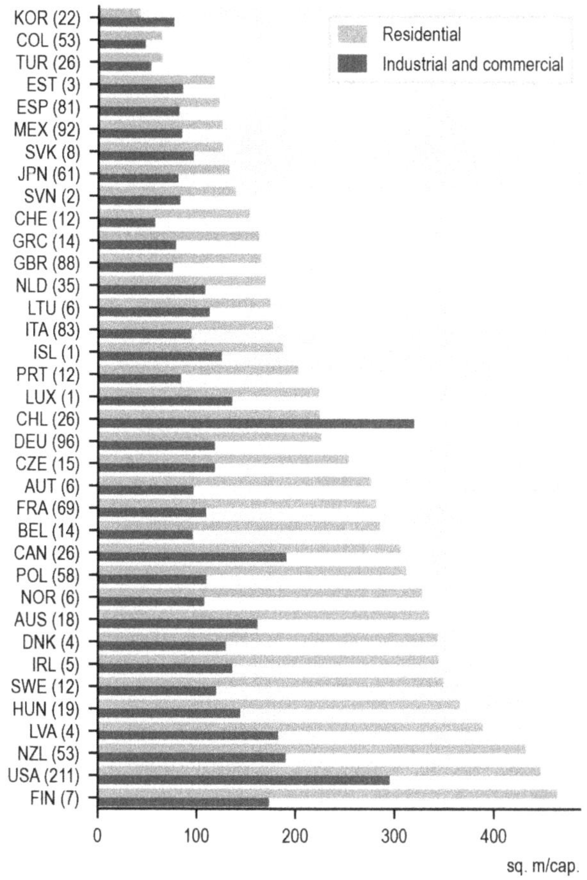

StatLink https://stat.link/z9qvjm

2.23. Residential built-up area in cities and their commuting zones, 2021

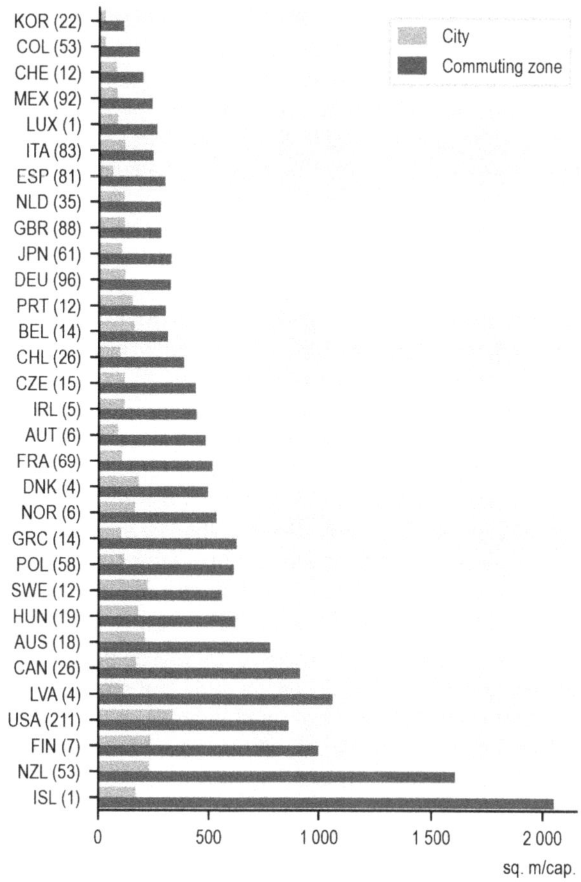

StatLink https://stat.link/mufknq

2.24. Built-up area and building height in cities

Average built-up area per capita (m²/person) and building height (m) in FUAs of more than 500 000 inhabitants, 2021

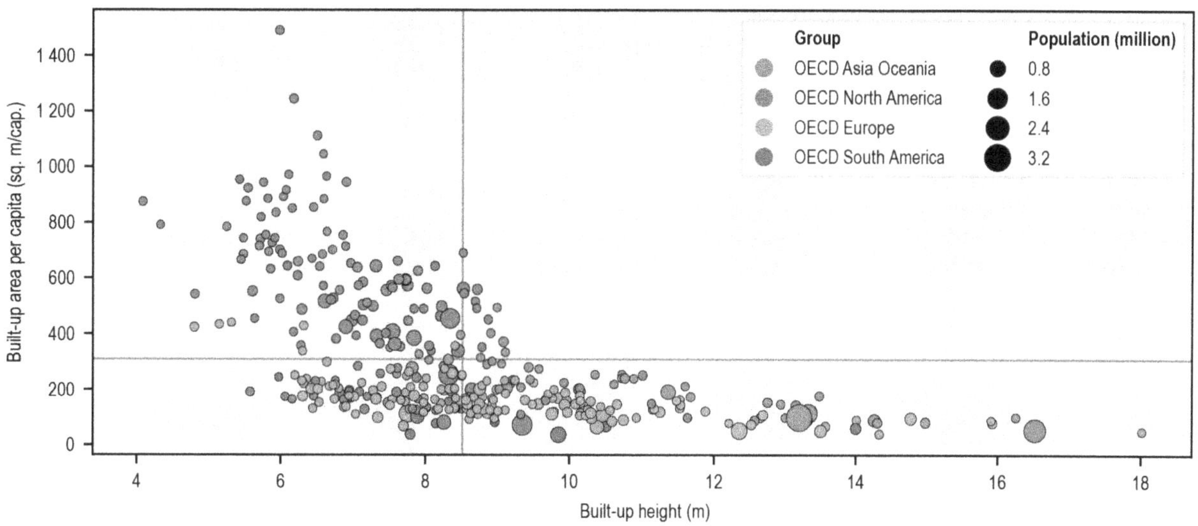

StatLink https://stat.link/ngjhbp

Changes in temperatures and precipitations have led to a notable decrease in soil moisture in many OECD regions.

Agriculture accounted for 9% of total production-based emissions in 2018 in OECD countries. While total GHG emissions declined by 6% during the last 2 decades, agriculture emissions increased by 4% over the same period in OECD countries (Crippa et al., 2021). Emissions in this sector mainly reflect methane (CH_4, 65%) emitted by animals and rice cultivation and nitrous oxide (N_2O, 33%) released from pastures and crops using nitrogen fertilisers. Modelled pathways that limit global warming to 1.5°C above pre-industrial levels involve deep reductions in emissions of methane by 35% or more by 2050 relative to 2010 (IPCC, 2018). One-quarter of OECD regions produce 70% of the emissions from the agriculture sector. New South Wales (Australia) and Iowa and Texas (US) had the highest emissions in agriculture in 2018. These 3 regions treble the emissions of more than 95% of OECD regions. In terms of emissions per unit of GVA, the most emission-intensive regions are Southern Ireland, the region of Canterbury in New Zealand, Wales in the UK and Montana in the US. This corresponds to territorial emissions and does not reflect the carbon footprint of agricultural products and their export to distant locations (Figure 2.25).

Rising prices of energy and fertilisers, as well as the increasing frequency and intensity of climate hazards, put pressure on the agricultural sector and food security. Increased temperatures and changes in precipitation distribution can lead to droughts, which directly affect agricultural yields. Drought is here measured in terms of percentage change in soil moisture compared to 1981-2010 (reference period). In one-third of OECD regions, croplands' soil moisture decreased by more than 3% over the past 5 years compared to 1981-2010. Across and within OECD countries, the impact of droughts on agriculture differs widely. Among the most affected regions, Tolima in Colombia and Chihuahua in Mexico experienced a soil moisture decline of about 10% over the past 5 years compared to the reference period. In these 2 regions, GVA in agriculture, forestry and fishing account for a significant share of total GVA (respectively 17% and 7%), which makes the economy of these regions particularly vulnerable (Figure 2.27).

Wildfires have also been affecting agricultural lands and forests. In terms of relative surface, the most impacted regions are the Canberra region (Australia) where 52% of the forest area burned in the past 5 years, followed by Attica in Greece and Central Portugal. In terms of cropland exposure, more than 3% of the croplands were burned in the past 5 years in Australia, Costa Rica, Mexico and Türkiye. In the region of South-eastern Anatolia – Middle (Türkiye), around 20% of the cropland area burned over the past 5 years, corresponding to a total area of 5 500 km^2 (Figure 2.26).

Definition

Agricultural emissions in regions were estimated using EDGAR, version 6 and expressed in CO_2-eq.

Droughts can be defined in three ways: agricultural, hydrological or meteorological. Meteorological droughts mainly focus on low precipitations at a certain time and usually precede the other types of droughts. Here droughts are defined in terms of cropland soil moisture anomaly, i.e. the percentage change in soil moisture compared to the reference period 1981-2010.

Sources

Artes Vivancos, T. et al. (2019), “A global wildfire dataset for the analysis of fire regimes and fire behaviour”, *Scientific Data*, Vol. 6, p. 296.

Crippa, M. et al. (2021), *EDGAR v6.0 Greenhouse Gas Emissions*, Joint Research Centre (JRC), European Commission, *http://data.europa.eu/89h/97a67d67-c62e-4826-b873-9d972c4f670b*.

ECMWF (2022), “ERA5-Land monthly averaged data from 1950 to present”, European Centre for Medium-Range Weather Forecasts, *https://cds.climate.copernicus.eu/cdsapp#!/dataset/reanalysis-era5-land-monthly-means?tab=overview*.

ESA CCI (2019), “Land cover classification gridded maps from 1992 to present derived from satellite observations”, European Space Agency Climate Change Initiative.

IPCC (2018), *Global Warming of 1.5°C*, Intergovernmental Panel on Climate Change, *https://doi.org/10.1017/9781009157940.001*.

Figure notes

2.26: Only large regions with at least 5% of their territory covered by forests are represented.

2.25. Regional agricultural emissions

Emissions from agriculture in Mt CO_2-eq in large regions (TL2), 2018

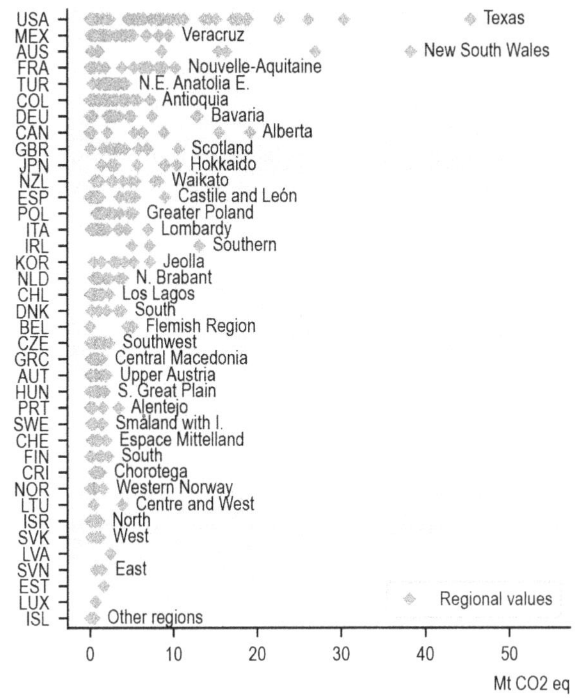

StatLink https://stat.link/hbaxkr

2.26. Regional exposure to forest fires

Forest area burned as a % of total forest area in large regions (TL2), 2017-21

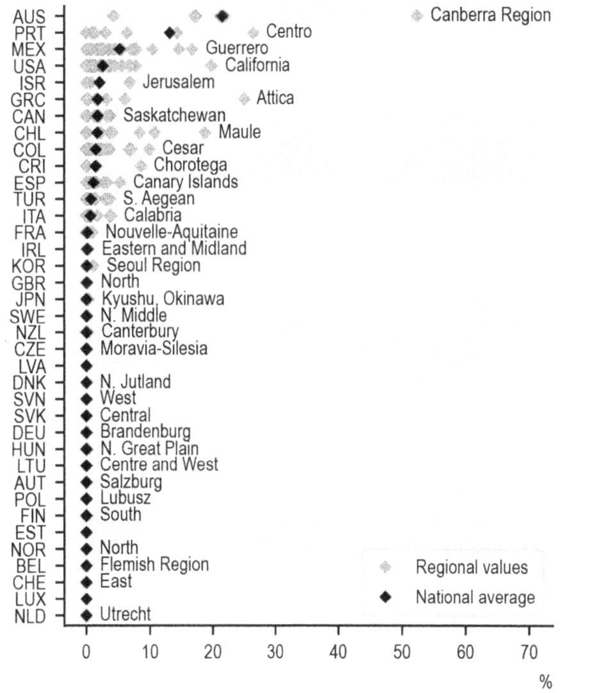

StatLink https://stat.link/wuz8t3

2.27. Regional exposure to agricultural droughts

Percentage change in croplands' soil moisture in large regions (TL2), 2017-2021 compared to 1981-2010

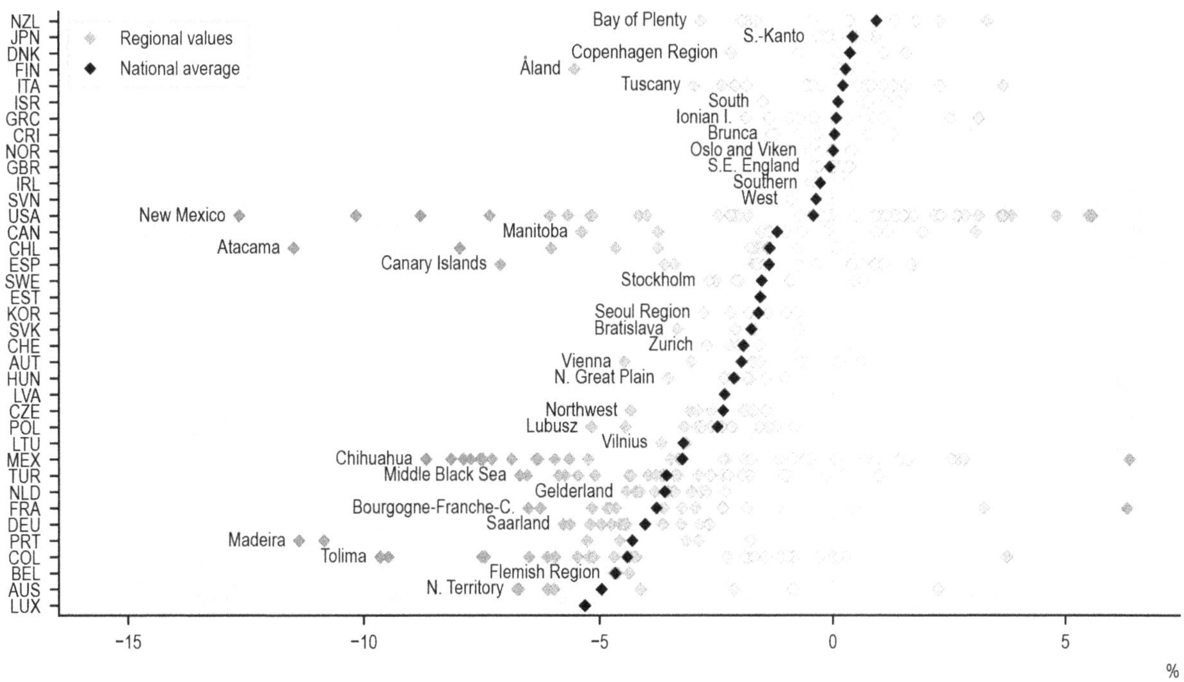

StatLink https://stat.link/8elz0s

Human settlements adapting to climate change

Many OECD regions and cities are becoming increasingly exposed to various climate-related hazards, such as heat waves, wildfires and flooding.

Climate change has caused substantial damage to people, settlements and infrastructures, due to the increase in frequency and intensity of extreme weather events, such as heat waves, wildfires, droughts and flooding. Nearly all (95%) regions in OECD countries have been more exposed to heat stress over the past 5 years than in 1981-2010 (reference period). Heat stress has been particularly high and increased fastest in Central America and the Mediterranean Basin. Costa Rica and Israel have been hit particularly hard, as their populations experienced on average more than 140 days per year of strong heat stress, over 25 days more than during 1981-2010. The region of Córdoba (Colombia) experienced an average of 267 days per year of very strong heat stress, a 70-day longer period than during 1981-2010 (Figure 2.28).

Cities are particularly impacted by heat waves, as the temperature tends to be higher than in the surrounding areas due to the urban heat island effect. This phenomenon results from high building density, heat from human activities, building materials and limited vegetation. Extreme heat in cities has a significant impact on health and affects disproportionately low-income neighbourhoods due to fewer green areas and higher building density. In the past 5 years, almost half of OECD cities witnessed a summer daytime heat island effect of more than 3°C. The urban heat island intensity varies across OECD cities, depending on the population size and the climate zone. Built-up lands in cities with more than 250 000 inhabitants are on average 3°C warmer than their surrounding area, this difference being almost twice as high as in cities with less than 100 000 inhabitants. Cities located in Japan, Korea and the Eastern US are more affected by this phenomenon than other OECD cities. These disparities can be explained by differences in climate, urban planning cultures and vegetation (Figures 2.32 and 2.33). Adaptation policies are consequently particularly needed in cities to mitigate the impact of heat waves. This implies working on building materials and promoting green areas. In this respect, shares of green areas can be very different in OECD cities. In Ireland, Norway, Switzerland and the UK, cities include three times more green areas relative to the total area than those in Chile, Japan or Mexico. In per capita terms, cities located in the US record the highest green area per capita with 300 m^2/person, compared to 26 m^2/person in Chile or Türkiye (Figure 2.31).

Increasing heat stress has also been combined with more frequent and intense wildfires in OECD regions. Over the past 5 years, population exposure to wildfires has been particularly high in Chile, Israel, Italy, Mexico, Portugal and Türkiye. In 29 regions located in Latin America, Australia and the Mediterranean Basin, more than 50% of the population has been exposed to wildfires over the past 5 years. In some regions such as in Ñuble (Chile), the share of people exposed to wildfires was higher than 90% (Figure 2.29).

Climate change is also impacting the water cycle, leading to more frequent river flooding. Without higher protection standards, flood events are projected to happen more often on all continents, especially in Asia, America and Europe (Alfieri et al., 2017). Here, river flooding is assessed by looking at past events occurring on average every 100 years, referred to as 100-year floods. Latvia, the Netherlands and the Slovak Republic are the most exposed countries with more than 30% of the population exposed to floods. In 61 OECD regions, more than 30% of the population is exposed to river floods. Bremen, Gelderland, Hamburg and South Holland, are the most exposed European OECD large regions, with more than 50% of their population at risk (Figure 2.30).

Definition

Green areas refer to trees, shrublands and grasslands.

Exposure to wildfires refers to the population located within a 5 km buffer around fires.

Population exposure to strong heat stress is defined using the Universal Thermal Climate Index (UTCI) which measures the impact of atmospheric conditions on the human body:

- 32°C < UTCI < 38°C: strong heat stress.
- 38°C < UTCI < 46°C: very strong heat stress.
- UTCI > 46°C: extreme heat stress.

The **urban heat island intensity** is here defined for a FUA as the difference in land surface temperature between the built-up area and its surroundings.

See methodology in Annex C.

Sources

Alfieri, L. et al. (2017), "Global projections of river flood risk in a warmer world", *Earth's Future*, Vol. 5/2, pp. 171-182, *https://doi.org/10.1002/2016ef000485*.

Artes Vivancos, T. et al. (2019), "A global wildfire dataset for the analysis of fire regimes and fire behaviour", *Scientific Data*, Vol. 6, p. 296.

CDS (2022), "Thermal comfort indices derived from ERA5 reanalysis", Copernicus Climate Change Service Climate Data Store.

Dottori, F. et al. (2021), *River Flood Hazard Maps for Europe and the Mediterranean Basin Region*, Joint Research Centre (JRC), European Commission.

Wan, Z., S. Hook and G. Hulley (2021), *MODIS/Aqua Land Surface Temperature/Emissivity Daily L3 Global 1 km SIN Grid V061*.

Zanaga, D. et al. (2021), *ESA WorldCover 10 m 2020 v100*, *https://doi.org/10.5281/zenodo.5571936*.

2.28. Population exposure to heat stress

Additional days per year of strong heat stress or worse (UTCI > 32°C) over 2017-21, compared to 1981-2010, OECD large regions (TL2)

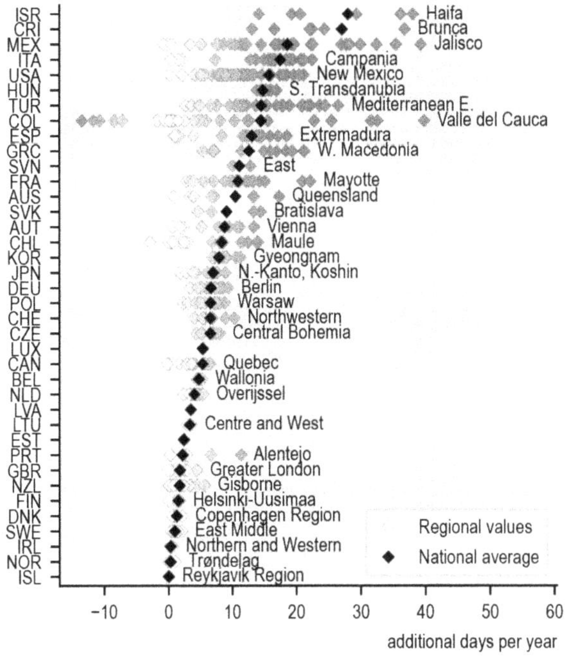

StatLink https://stat.link/fdnb4c

2.29. Population exposure to fires

Share of the population exposed to at least one fire over 2017-21 in OECD large regions (TL2)

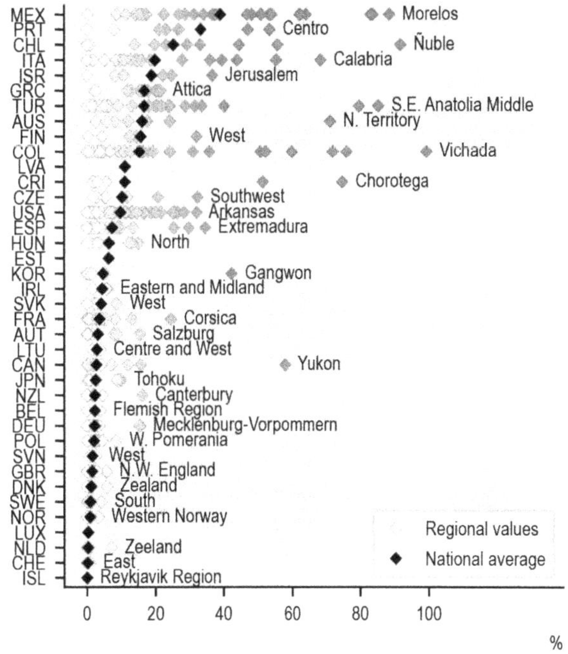

StatLink https://stat.link/ksefga

2.30. Population exposure to floods

Share of the population exposed to 100-year river floods in large regions (TL2), 2015

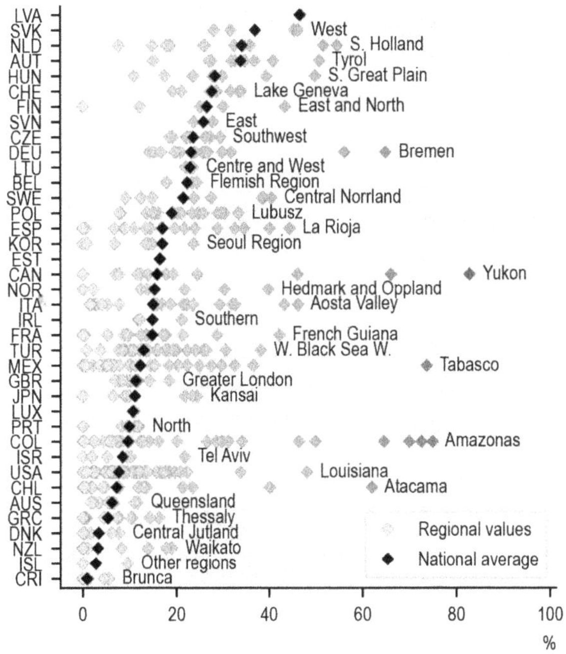

StatLink https://stat.link/s26qhd

2.31. Green areas in metropolitan areas

Green areas (trees, grasslands and shrublands) as % of the total area in FUA's urban centres, 2020

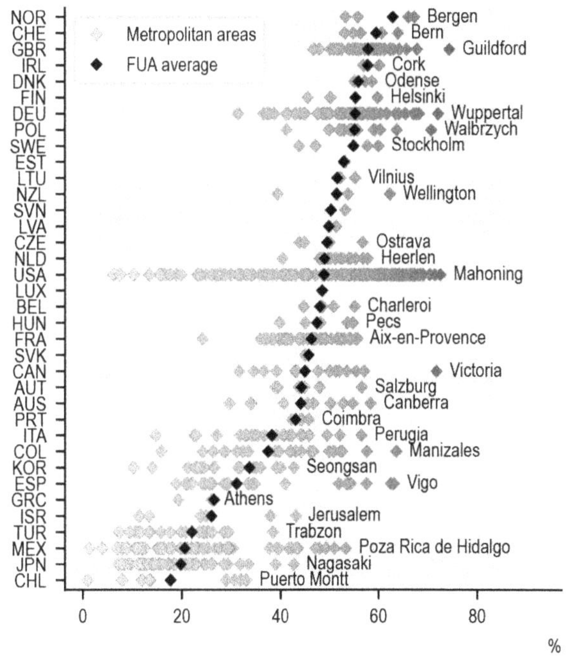

StatLink https://stat.link/skflq0

2.32. Large metropolitan areas are more impacted by the urban heat island effect, Americas

Average summer daytime urban heat island intensity (°C), FUA, 2017-21

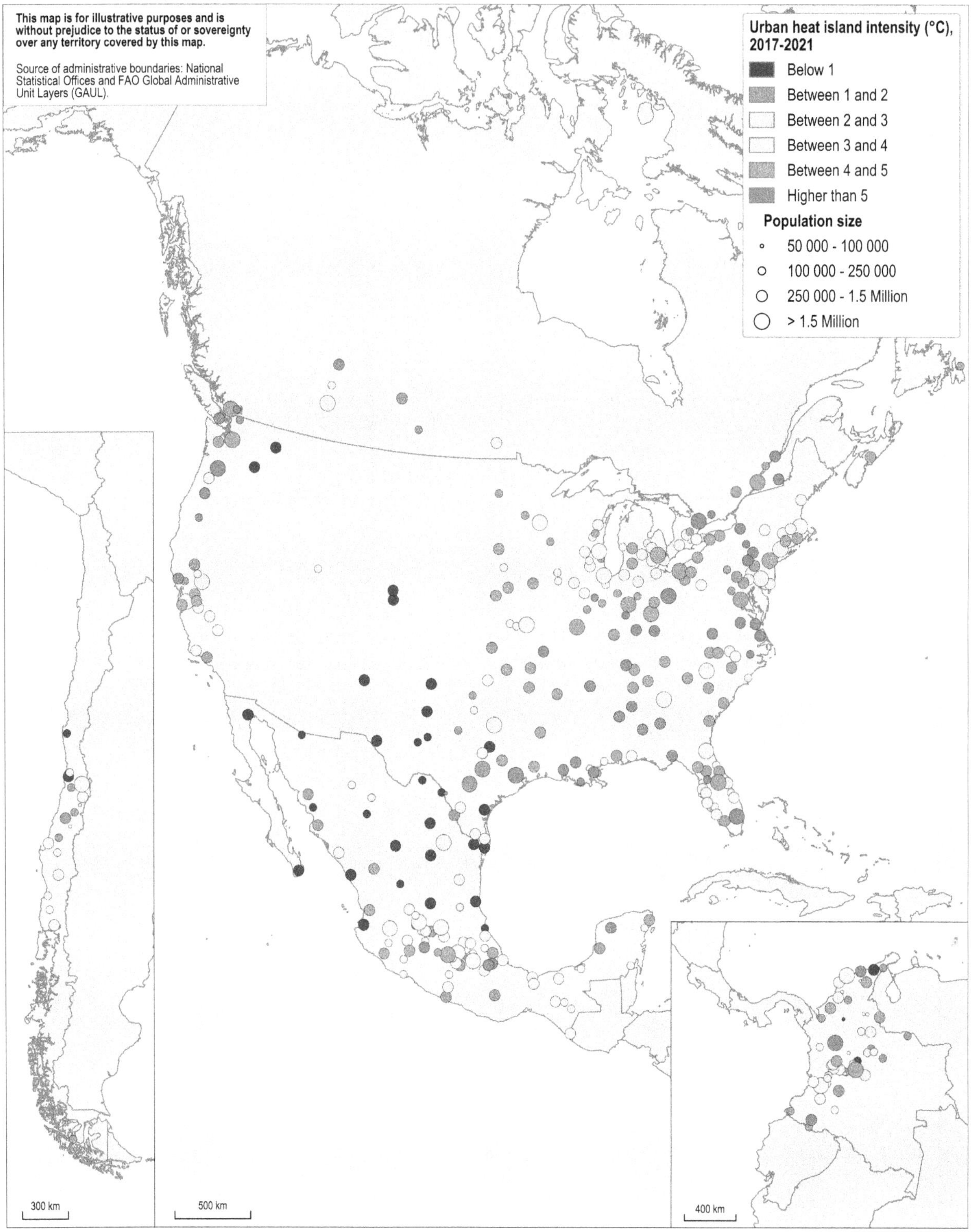

StatLink https://stat.link/txpc4z

2.33. Large metropolitan areas are more impacted by the urban heat island effect, Europe and Asia-Pacific

Average summer daytime urban heat island intensity (°C), FUA, 2017-21

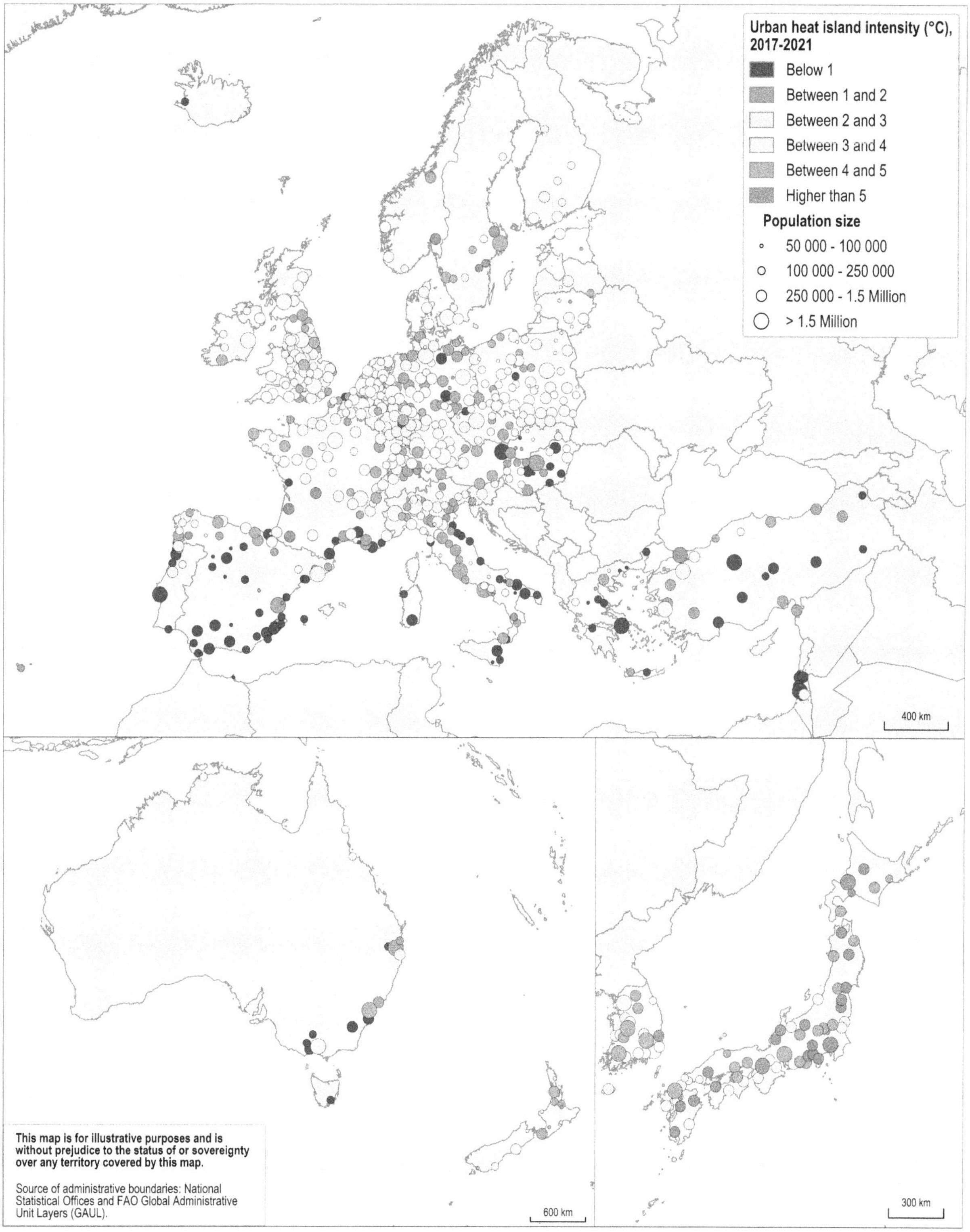

StatLink https://stat.link/6znxpc

3. REGIONS AND CITIES FACING DEMOGRAPHIC CHANGE

This chapter presents an overview of socio-demographic trends in regions and cities across OECD countries. It discusses how the projection of population trends, ageing and urbanisation are playing out in regions and cities. The chapter presents indicators of the elderly dependency rate, within-country residential mobility, population growth and decline. It also documents the presence and integration of migrants in regional labour markets.

Population growth across OECD cities and rural areas

Most OECD countries experienced an increase in the share of the population living in cities.

Over the last 50 years, the population in OECD countries has concentrated around large and densely populated regions. The concentration of the population within a country is shaped by many factors including the distribution of economic activities within the country and the presence of public services or amenities. In 2015, almost half of the population of OECD countries (49%) lived in cities, which represented only 6% of the total OECD surface area. Of the remaining population, 26% lived in towns and semi-dense areas and 24% in rural areas.

Across OECD countries, the distribution of population across different types of settlements is highly uneven. While more than 60% of the population lived in cities in Chile, Colombia, Japan and Korea, less than 20% of the population lived in such areas in the Slovak Republic and Slovenia (Figure 3.2). On average, rural areas accounted for around one-quarter of the population and 98.5% of the land area in OECD countries. In countries such as Ireland, the Slovak Republic and Slovenia, one out of two people lived in rural regions which is double the OECD average (Figure 3.1).

Since 2000, the share of the population living in cities has increased by around 3 percentage points (pp) across the OECD, mainly at the expense of rural areas (Figure 3.3). During this period, the share of the population in towns and semi-dense areas and rural areas has decreased on average by 1.3 and 1.5 pp respectively. The relative growth of cities was particularly strong in Iceland, New Zealand and Türkiye, where their population share rose by over 7 pp.

Sources

OECD (2022), *OECD Regional Statistics (database)*, OECD Pu blishing, Paris, *http://dx.doi.org/10.1787/region-data-en.*

Reference years and territorial level

2000-15, TL3 regions are classified according to metropolitan access classification (see below for further details).

Definitions

Degree of urbanisation: This typology reflects the urban-rural continuum and proposes three classes instead of the dichotomy of urban or rural. The three classes are: i) cities (or densely populated areas); ii) towns and semi-dense areas (or intermediate density areas); and iii) rural areas (or thinly populated areas).

Access to metropolitan areas typology: The proposed classification distinguishes TL3 regions based on the level of access to metropolitan areas (Fadic et al., 2019). At a first level, regions where at least half of the regional population live in a metropolitan area of at least 250 000 inhabitants are considered "metropolitan" regions, and as "non-metropolitan" otherwise. Metropolitan regions are further distinguished as "large metro" regions if they include or are part of a metropolitan area of at least 1.5 million inhabitants. "Non-metropolitan" regions are sub-classified in regions "with access to a metro" if half of its population can reach a metropolitan area within a 60-minute drive. When half of the regional population can reach only a smaller-sized city (between 50 000 and 250 000 inhabitants), the region is classified as "with access to a small/medium city". In all other cases, the region is classified as "remote". The classification relies on the concept of FUAs (Dijkstra et al., 2019; OECD, 2012) to delineate metropolitan areas of at least 250 000 inhabitants or smaller-sized cities.

Further information

Territorial grids and regional typology (Annex B).

Eurostat (2013), *Urban-Rural Typology*, *http://ec.europa.eu/eurostat/web/rural-development/methodology*.

Figure notes

3.1-3.3: The OECD average corresponds to the population-weighted average of 38 OECD countries.

3.1. Distribution of area by the degree of urbanisation
Area share of each type of settlement

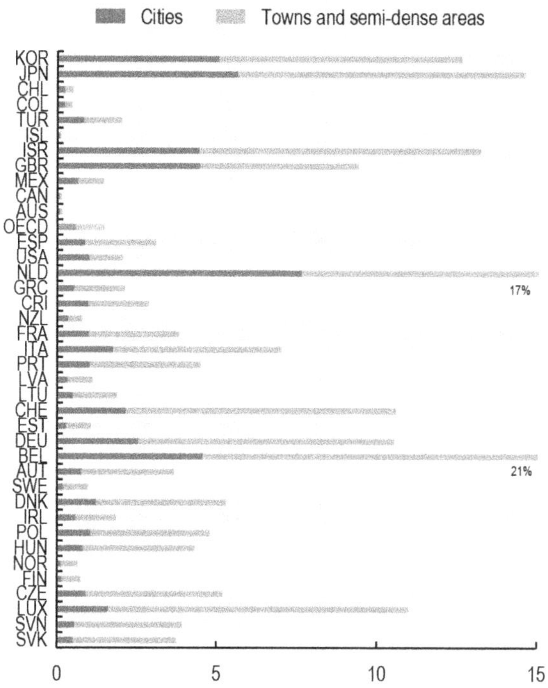

StatLink https://stat.link/5a4sv6

3.2. Distribution of population by the degree of urbanisation
Population share of each type of settlement

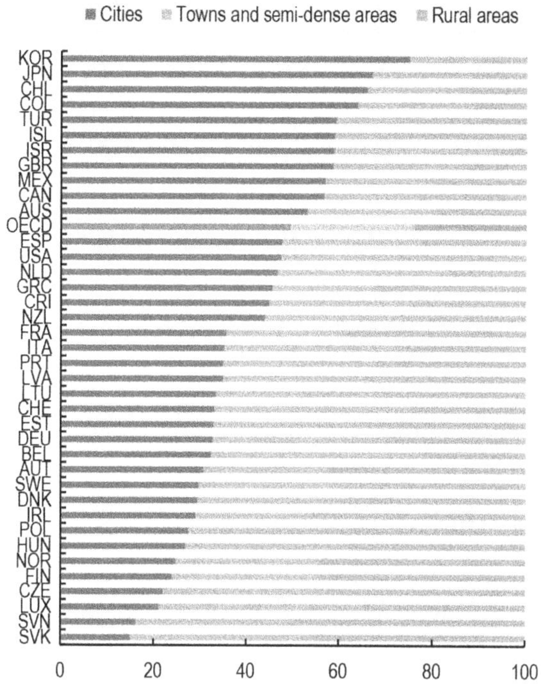

StatLink https://stat.link/s1zfoj

3.3. Change in the share of population by degree of urbanisation, 2000-15
Change in the share of population by type of area over the total population

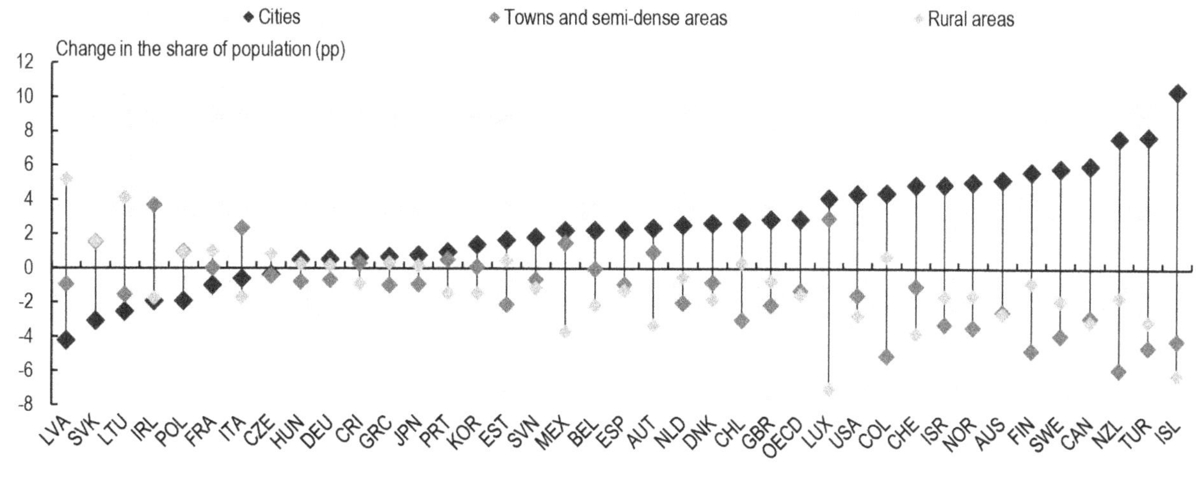

StatLink https://stat.link/lfxkrp

Global trends in city population growth

Populations will continue to concentrate in metropolitan areas.

In the past decades, the population in OECD countries has slowly gravitated towards large, densely populated regions and cities. This trend is consistent with the evidence that, as countries develop, they have larger shares of the urban population (OECD/European Commission, 2020). The existing literature points to different reasons for the increasing geographic concentration of people, from the economic advantages of agglomeration – including economic opportunities and amenities (Combes and Gobillon, 2015) – to geographical factors such as rivers or access to the sea (Nieves et al., 2017). Today, cities house almost half of the OECD population while this share is even larger when accounting for commuting areas surrounding cities.

The spatial concentration of the population in metropolitan regions is expected to continue in the next two decades. According to the available population projections for 27 OECD countries, the population living in metropolitan regions is expected to remain roughly unchanged, while the population in regions near a metropolitan area and those far from a metropolitan area are expected to shrink by 2.8% and 2.3% respectively (Figure 3.4). As a consequence, while the share of the population living in metropolitan regions is expected to slightly increase from 66% to 67% by 2040, the population shares of regions near a metropolitan area are expected to decline from 16% to 15% and from 18% to 17% for regions far from a metropolitan area (Figure 3.5).

An increasing share of the OECD population will move into large cities and their commuting zones (functional urban areas, FUAs). Based on population projections made by the European Union (EU) (Schiavina, Freire and MacManus, 2022), between 2020 and 2030, the OECD population living in FUAs will increase from 950 million to 1 billion inhabitants (Figure 3.6). The population is expected to increase in larger FUAs with more than 1 million inhabitants, while the population in smaller FUAs is expected to shrink. The population living in FUAs with a population of less than 250 000 inhabitants or between 250 000 and one million inhabitants are expected to shrink by 4% and 3% respectively. In contrast, the population living in FUAs with a population of between 1 and 5 million inhabitants is projected to grow by around 5% by 2030, relative to the population levels in 2020. FUAs with a population of above 5 million inhabitants will experience the fastest growth. The population living in these large FUAs is projected to grow by 20%.

Sources

OECD calculations are based on data from Eurostat and national statistical institutes.

Reference years and territorial level

2020-40, TL3 regions are classified according to metropolitan access classification (see below for further details).
3.6: Data corresponds to 37 OECD countries, excluding Costa Rica.

Definition

Access to metropolitan areas typology: The proposed classification distinguishes TL3 regions based on the level of access to metropolitan areas (Fadic et al., 2019). At a first level, regions where at least half of the regional population live in a metropolitan area of at least 250 000 inhabitants are considered "metropolitan" regions, and as "non-metropolitan" otherwise. Metropolitan regions are further distinguished as "large metro" regions if they include or are part of a metropolitan area of at least 1.5 million inhabitants. "Non-metropolitan" regions are sub-classified in regions "with access to a metro" if half of its population can reach a metropolitan area within a 60-minute drive. When half of the regional population can reach only a smaller-sized city (between 50 000 and 250 000 inhabitants), the region is classified as "with access to a small/medium city". In all other cases, the region is classified as "remote". The classification relies on the concept of FUAs (Dijkstra et al., 2019; OECD, 2012) to delineate metropolitan areas of at least 250 000 inhabitants or smaller-sized cities.

Further information

Combes, P.P. and L. Gobillon (2015), "The empirics of agglomeration economies", in *Handbook of Regional and Urban Economics*, Elsevier, Vol.5, pp.247-348, *https://doi.org/10.1016/B978-0-444-59517-1.00005-2*.

Dijkstra, L., H. Poelman and P. Veneri (2019), "The EU-OECD definition of a functional urban area", *OECD Regional Development Working Papers*, No. 2019/11, OECD P ublishing, Paris, *https://doi.org/10.1787/d58cb34d-en*.

Fadic, M. et al. (2019), "Classifying small (TL3) regions based on metropolitan population, low density and remoteness", *OECD Regional Development Working Papers*, No. 2019/06, OECD Publishing, Paris, *https://doi.org/10.1787/b902cc00-en*.

Nieves, J.J. et al. (2017), "Examining the correlates and drivers of human population distributions across low-and middle-income countries", *Journal of the Royal Society Interface*, Vol. 14/137, p. 20170401.

OECD/European Commission (2020), Cities in the World: A New Perspective on Urbanisation, OECD Urban Studies, OECD Publishing, Paris, https://doi.org/10.1787/d0efcbda-en.

OECD (2012), *Redefining "Urban": A New Way to Measure Metropolitan Areas*, OECD Publishing, Paris, *http://dx.doi.org/10.1787/9789264174108-en*.

Schiavina M., S. Freire and K. MacManus (2022), *GHS-POP R2022A - GHS Population Grid Multitemporal (1975-2030)*, Joint Research Centre (JRC), European Commission, *http://data.europa.eu/89h/d6d86a90-4351-4508-99c1-cb074b022c4a*.

Figure notes

3.4-3.5: Data corresponds to 25 OECD countries in Europe, Japan and Korea with available data.

3.4. Expected population by region typology, 2020-40

Total population relative to levels in 2020

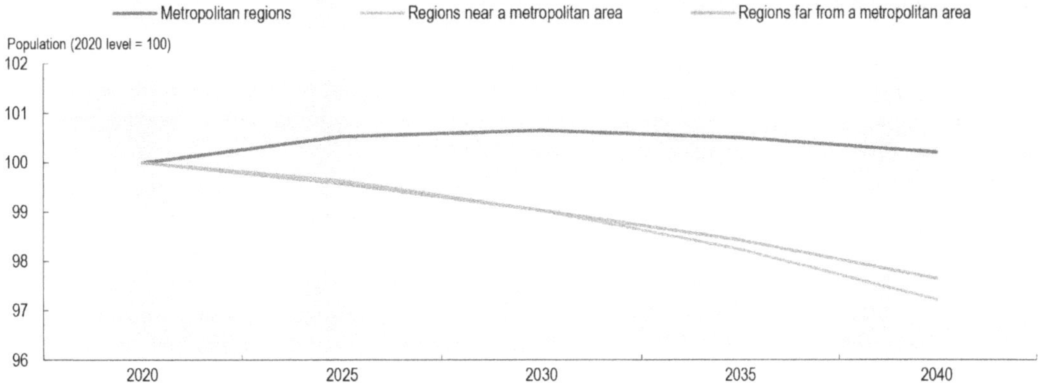

StatLink https://stat.link/l6guso

3.5. Distribution of population by type of region, 2020-40

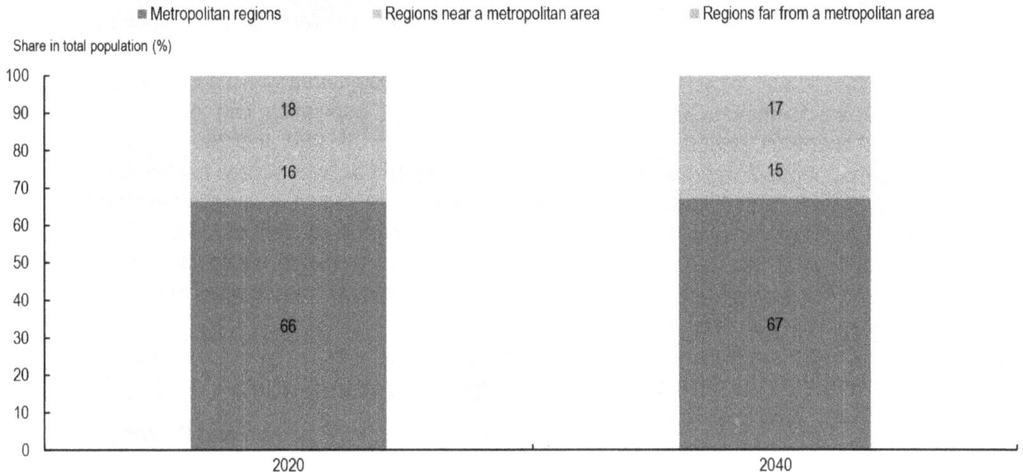

StatLink https://stat.link/1mlo8j

3.6. Changes in OECD population in FUAs, 2020-30

Population relative to levels in 2020

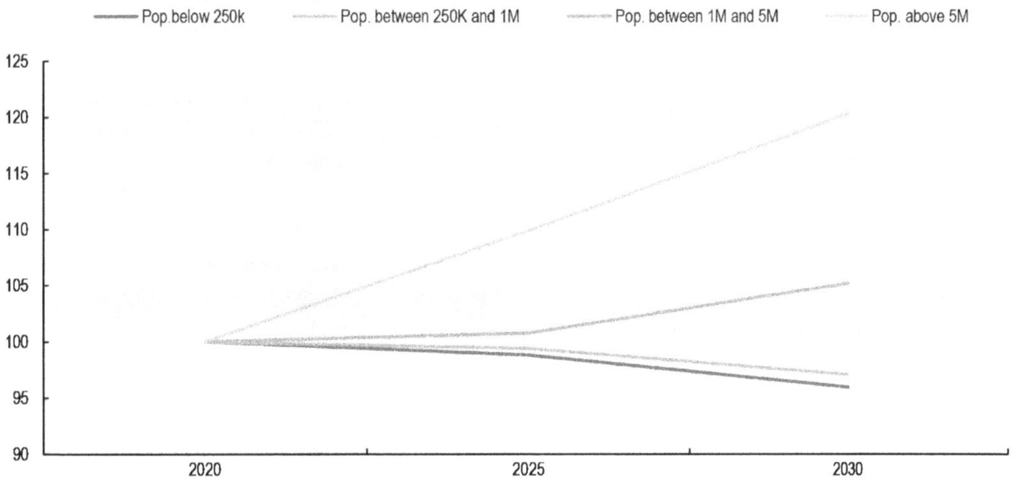

StatLink https://stat.link/7sty1h

Ageing population

Populations are expected to continue ageing, especially in non-metropolitan areas.

The population has been stagnating or declining in many OECD countries while ageing at the same time, which presents many challenges and opportunities. Older individuals typically receive public pensions and use public services such as healthcare more intensively than younger people, which can entail greater financial burdens on the working-age population and future generations. Although ageing will be present in all types of regions in the next two decades, some places will be more concerned than others.

Non-metropolitan regions will experience population ageing the most. Across the OECD, elderly dependency rates remain significantly lower in metropolitan regions compared to other regions (Figure 3.7). As the population ages, the elderly share of the population (i.e. those above 65 years old) will increase in all 3 types of regions but the increase will be largest in regions far from a metropolitan region (Figure 3.7). While the share of the elderly is expected to increase by 8 percentage points, reaching 29% in these areas, it is expected to increase by 6 pp to 25% in metropolitan regions, and by 7 pp to 27% in regions near a metropolitan region.

These expected ageing trends are common to almost all OECD countries (Figure 3.8). In most countries, dependency rates will remain significantly lower in metropolitan regions compared to other regions (Figure 3.8). This is particularly the case in countries where all non-metropolitan regions have relatively high elderly dependency rates, such as Japan, Korea and Lithuania. In these countries, all non-metropolitan regions have elderly dependency rates above 35% (reaching 42% in Korea). Elderly dependency rates in metropolitan regions remain below 31% in all OECD countries, with the exception of Japan and Korea where the rates are 35% and 33% respectively.

Sources

OECD calculations are based on data from Eurostat and national statistical institutes.

Reference years and territorial level

2020-40, TL3 regions are classified according to metropolitan access classification (see below for further details).

Definitions

The elderly population is the population aged 65 years and over.

The elderly dependency ratio is defined as the ratio between the elderly population and the working-age population (15-64 years).

The elderly share is defined as the ratio between the elderly population and the total population.

Access to metropolitan areas typology: The proposed classification distinguishes TL3 regions based on the level of access to metropolitan areas (Fadic et al., 2019). At a first level, regions where at least half of the regional population live in a metropolitan area of at least 250 000 inhabitants are considered "metropolitan" regions, and as "non-metropolitan" otherwise. Metropolitan regions are further distinguished as "large metro" regions if they include or they are part of a metropolitan area of at least 1.5 million inhabitants. "Non-metropolitan" regions are sub-classified as regions "with access to a metro" if half of its population can reach a metropolitan area within a 60-minute drive. When half of the regional population can reach only a smaller-sized city (between 50 000 and 250 000 inhabitants), the region is classified as "with access to a small/medium city". In all other cases, the region is classified as "remote". The classification relies on the concept of FUAs (Dijkstra et al., 2019; OECD, 2012) to delineate metropolitan areas of at least 250 000 inhabitants or smaller-sized cities.

Further information

Dijkstra, L., H. Poelman and P. Veneri (2019), "The EU-OECD definition of a functional urban area", *OECD Regional Development Working Papers*, No. 2019/11, OECD P ublishing, Paris, *https://doi.org/10.1787/d58cb34d-en*.

Fadic, M. et al. (2019), "Classifying small (TL3) regions based on metropolitan population, low density and remoteness", *OECD Regional Development Working Papers*, No. 2019/06, OECD Publishing, Paris, *https://doi.org/10.1787/b902cc00-en*.

OECD (2012), *Redefining "Urban": A New Way to Measure Metropolitan Areas*, OECD Publishing, Paris, *http://dx.doi.org/10.1787/9789264174108-en*.

Figure notes

3.7-3.8: Data corresponds to 27 OECD countries for which data is available. It includes 25 European countries, Japan and Korea.

3.7. The share of elderly in the population by area typology, 2020 and 2040

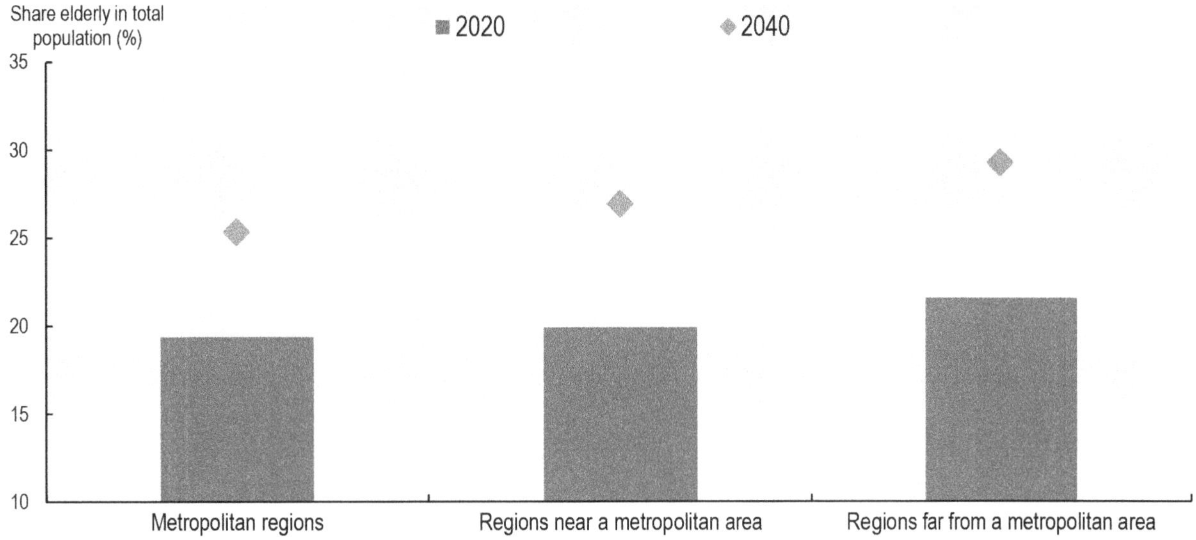

StatLink https://stat.link/7v1imr

3.8. The share of elderly population by country and region typology, 2040 projection

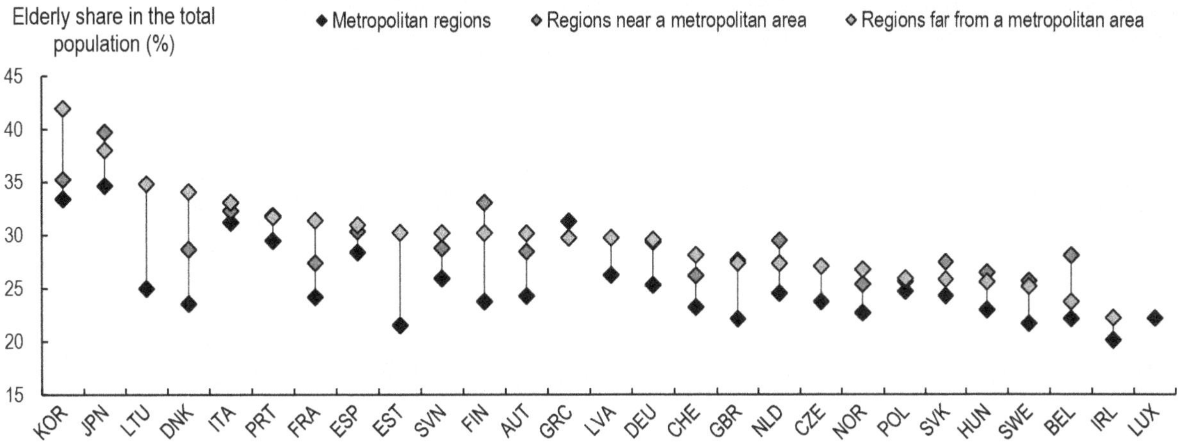

StatLink https://stat.link/ozhbn4

Mobility across regions

Most people who change regions within a country move to metropolitan regions.

People relocate across regions for numerous regions, including to access better jobs or education opportunities or to benefit from better amenities. While some of these flows are not necessarily permanent, they can affect the demographic structure of regions by changing the age composition.

In the 28 OECD countries, 29 million people changed their region of residence each year, on average, between 2016 and 2019. While regional data are not yet available for all countries in 2020, it appears that COVID-19 sparked some temporary moves across regions but reduced other types of inter-regional moves, leading to net declines in inter-regional migration in many OECD countries. In 2019, inter-regional movers corresponded to 2.7% of the total population in the OECD area, ranging from around 5% in Korea, the Netherlands and the United Kingdom (UK) to less than 0.7% in Italy, Poland and the Slovak Republic (Figure 3.9).

Inter-regional migration does not affect all regions of a country in the same way. While metropolitan regions and regions close to a city tend to experience positive net inflows, others are often facing net outflows. In the 28 OECD countries with available data from 2016 to 2019, metropolitan regions and regions near a metropolitan area experienced net in-migration flows, gaining an average of 10.5 and 7 persons per every 10 000 inhabitants respectively (Figure 3.11). In contrast, regions far from a metropolitan area faced net out-migration flows, losing an average of 10 persons for every 10 000 people. Looking at individual regions, Parinacota (Chile), Sejong (Korea) and Flagstaff (United States, US) were the regions with the highest positive annual net migration rate during the last 4 years considered, with gains of 9%, 4% and 3% of the regional population respectively (Figure 3.10). In contrast, during the same period, Suhl (Germany), Oost-Go (Netherlands) and Anchorage (US) experienced net out-migration that corresponded to losses of 7.8%, 4.2% and 3.7% of their populations.

Young people between 15 and 29 years old account for more than half of the total within-country flows. In almost all OECD countries for which data is available, young people move almost exclusively to metropolitan regions, with educational and professional opportunities likely driving such flows (Figure 3.12). Greece and Portugal are exceptions, as these two countries were the only ones where regions far from metropolitan regions received net inflows of young migrants since 2016.

Sources

OECD (2022), *OECD Regional Statistics (database)*, OECD Publishing, Paris, *http://dx.doi.org/10.1787/region-data-en*.

Reference years and territorial level

2016-19; TL3 or TL3 regions classified according to metropolitan access classification (see below for further details).

Definitions

Inter-regional movers: Data refer to yearly flows of the population from one TL3 region to another TL3 region in the same country (regional migration). Outflows are represented as the number of persons who left the region the previous year to reside in another region of the same country, while inflows are represented as the number of new residents in the region coming from another region of the same country.

The net migration flow is defined as the difference between inflows and outflows in a region. A negative net migration flow means that more people left the region than entered it.

Access to metropolitan areas typology: The proposed classification distinguishes TL3 regions based on the level of access to metropolitan areas (Fadic et al., 2019). At a first level, regions where at least half of the regional population live in a metropolitan area of at least 250 000 inhabitants are considered "metropolitan" regions, and as "non-metropolitan" otherwise. Metropolitan regions are further distinguished as "large metro" regions if they include or they are part of a metropolitan area of at least 1.5 million inhabitants. "Non-metropolitan" regions are sub-classified as regions "with access to a metro" if half of its population can reach a metropolitan area within a 60-minute drive. When half of the regional population can reach only a smaller-sized city (between 50 000 and 250 000 inhabitants), the region is classified as "with access to a small/medium city". In all other cases, the region is classified as "remote". The classification relies on the concept of FUAs (Dijkstra et al., 2019; OECD, 2012) to delineate metropolitan areas of at least 250 000 inhabitants or smaller-sized cities.

Further information

Territorial grids and regional typology (Annex B).

Dijkstra, L., H. Poelman and P. Veneri (2019), "The EU-OECD definition of a functional urban area", *OECD Regional Development Working Papers*, No. 2019/11, OECD Publishing, Paris, *https://doi.org/10.1787/d58cb34d-en*.

Fadic, M. et al. (2019), "Classifying small (TL3) regions based on metropolitan population, low density and remoteness", *OECD Regional Development Working Papers*, No. 2019/06, OECD Publishing, Paris, *https://doi.org/10.1787/b902cc00-en*.

OECD (2012), *Redefining "Urban": A New Way to Measure Metropolitan Areas*, OECD Publishing, Paris, *http://dx.doi.org/10.1787/9789264174108-en*.

Figure notes

3.9-3.12: Average values for 2016-19 (4-year period).

3.12: Regions with a large city includes those with large and very large cities.

3.9. Annual rate of inter-regional movers by country, 2016-19

Flows across TL3 regions within a country, % of the total population

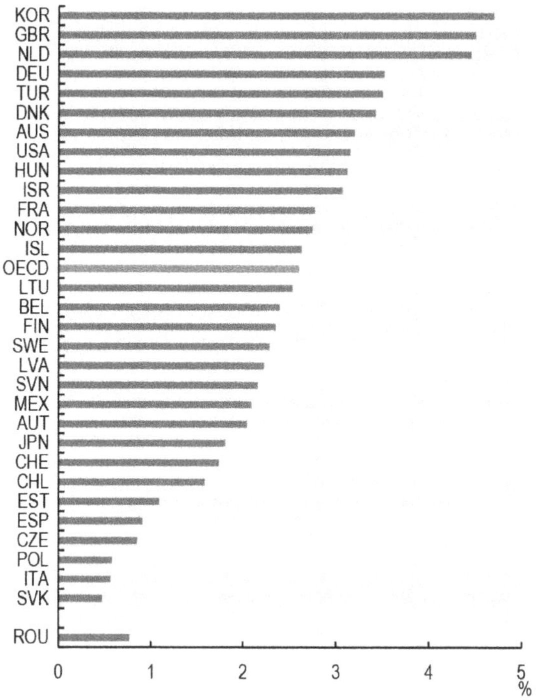

StatLink https://stat.link/rgjudv

3.10. Annual rate of inter-regional movers across small regions, 2016-19

Net flows across TL3 regions within a country, % of the total population

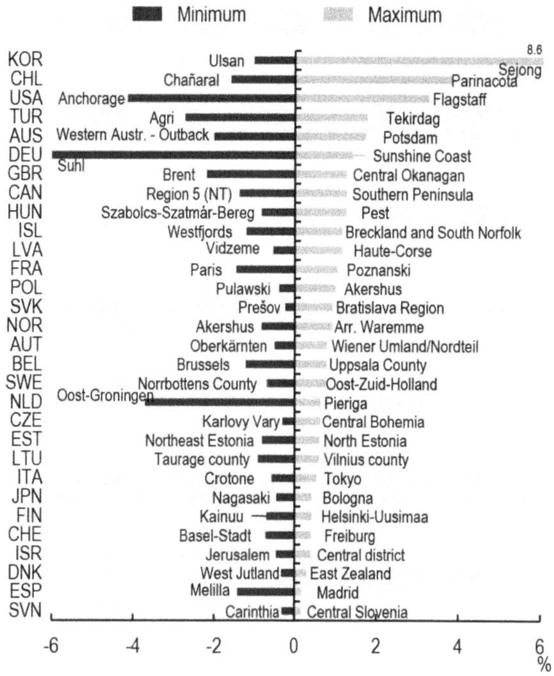

StatLink https://stat.link/qa2hz6

3.11. Annual regional population flows by type of region, 2016-19

Net flows across regions per 10 000 population

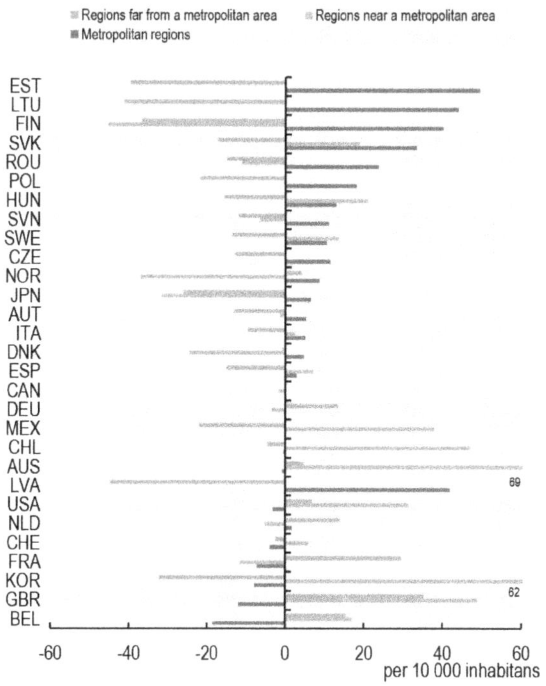

StatLink https://stat.link/4trl60

3.12. Share of young movers by type of region, 2016-19

Positive net population flows of youth (15 to 29 years old) across regions

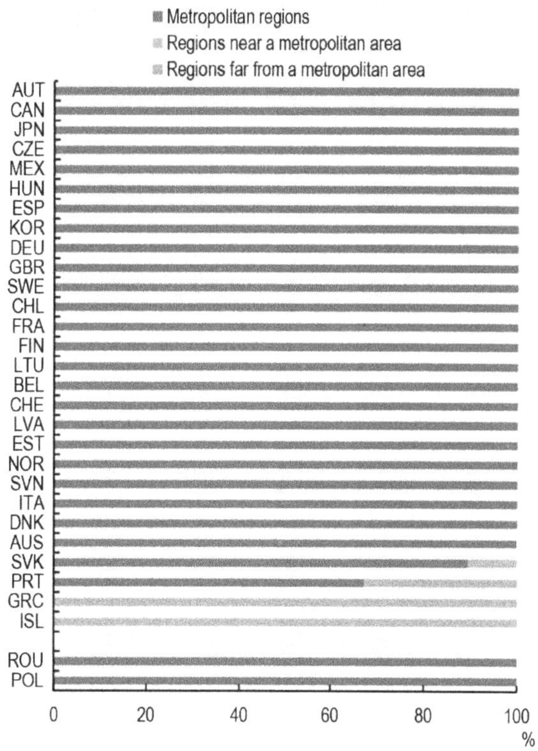

StatLink https://stat.link/60mr87

Presence of international migrants by type of region

Eight out of every ten migrants live in metropolitan regions in OECD countries, but only seven out of ten native-born.

In a context of widespread ageing and shrinking working-age population across OECD regions, international migration is one important source of potential inflows of people in regional economies. In 2019, 5.3 million new permanent migrants settled in OECD countries, an increase of around 25% since 2010. New migrants come with a variety of skills and socio-demographic characteristics and include for instance highly-qualified foreign doctors, nurses and scientists, as well as individuals working in low-skilled occupations. While regional data is not yet available for 2020, permanent migration inflows to OECD countries are estimated to have fallen by more than 30%, due in part to widespread restrictions on international travel and migration. This halted population growth in several OECD countries, including Australia and Germany (OECD, 2022a).

The share of migrants (foreign-born population) over the total population has a very diverse magnitude across OECD countries. For example, while 14% of the population in OECD were migrants in 2019, that share was 47% in Luxembourg and only 1% in Mexico (OECD, 2022b). The presence of migrants also differs within OECD countries. In some regions, migrants represent one-fourth of the population, while in others a negligible share. On average, the regional variation is stark, with a 15-percentage point difference between the region with the highest and lowest share of migrants within the same country (Figures 3.15 and 3.16). Belgium and the UK record the largest regional differences (above 35 percentage points) among OECD countries, while Denmark, Norway, Sweden and Switzerland display relatively small regional variations.

Compared to the native-born population, migrants are more likely to settle in large and dense regions, where they can benefit from agglomeration advantages including employment opportunities and social networks. Accordingly, more than half of the foreign-born population (53%) in the 22 OECD countries with available data live in large metropolitan regions, i.e. regions that contain a metropolitan area of more than 1.5 million inhabitants, 13 pp higher than for native-born population (Figure 3.13). In contrast, less than a fifth of migrants (19%) reside in non-metropolitan regions, compared to almost a third (30%) of the native-born population. The difference in the location of migrants and native-born populations is particularly striking in remote regions and regions near a metropolitan area. Remote regions account for 5% of the native-born population while only 3% of migrants. Similarly, regions near small/medium-sized cities account for 12% of the native-born population, but only 6% of migrants (Astruc-Le Souder et al., forthcoming).

In most OECD countries, migrants continue concentrating in cities. On average, cities host 68% of the migrant population, while towns and semi-dense areas, and rural areas host 22% and 9% of migrants over the total population respectively (Figure 3.14). Since 2015, the share of migrants has increased in all types of areas, but more strongly in cities. Between 2015 and 2019, the share of migrants living in cities increased from 11% to 14%. During the same period, the share of migrants in towns and semi-dense areas, and rural areas increased by two and one pp respectively.

Sources

OECD (2022), *OECD Migrant Municipal Database*, OECD, Paris (accessed June 2022).

Reference years and territorial level

2019 or latest available year, NUTS1 or NUTS2 (TL2) depending on data availability.

2015-20, municipalities

Definitions

International migrants: The terms "migrants and "foreign-born" are used interchangeably. Migrants are defined by place of birth. The migrant population is defined as the population born in a country different from the one of residence. Unlike citizenship, this criterion does not change over time, it is not subject to country differences in legislation and it is thus adequate for international comparisons.

Access to metropolitan areas typology: The proposed classification distinguishes TL3 regions based on the level of access to metropolitan areas (Fadic et al., 2019). At a first level, regions where at least half of the regional population live in a metropolitan area of at least 250,000 inhabitants are considered as 'metropolitan regions, and as 'non-metropolitan' otherwise. Metropolitan regions are further distinguished in 'large metro' regions if they include or they are part of a metropolitan area of at least 1.5 million inhabitants.' Non-metropolitan' regions are sub-classified in regions' with access to a metro' if half of its population can reach a metropolitan area within a 60-minute drive. When half of the regional population can reach only a smaller-sized city (between 50,000 and 250,000 inhabitants), the region is classified as 'with access to a small/medium city'. In all other cases, the region is classified as 'remote'. The classification relies on the concept of functional urban areas (FUAs) (Dijkstra et al., 2019; OECD, 2012) to delineate metropolitan areas of at least 250,000 inhabitants or smaller-sized cities.

Degree of urbanisation: This typology reflects the urban-rural continuum and proposes three classes instead of only the dichotomy urban or rural. The three classes are 1) cities (or densely populated areas); 2) towns and semi-dense areas (or intermediate density areas), and; 3) rural areas (or thinly populated areas).

Further Information

Territorial grids and regional typology (Annex B)

Astruc-Le Souder, M., J. Hesse, C. Hoffmann, L. Kleine-Rueschkamp, C. Mas, C. Özgüzel (forthcoming), "Going granular - A new database on migration in municipalities across the OECD". OECD Regional Development Working Papers

Dijkstra, L., H. Poelman and P. Veneri (2019), "The EU-OECD definition of a functional urban area", OECD Regional Development Working Papers, No. 2019/11, OECD Publishing, Paris, *https://doi.org/10.1787/d58cb34d-en.*

Fadic, M., J.E. Garcilazo, A. Moreno-Monroy and P.Veneri (2019), "Classifying small (TL3) regions based on metropolitan population, low density and remoteness", OECD Regional Development Working Papers, No. 2019/06, OECD Publishing, Paris, *https://doi.org/10.1787/b902cc00-en.*

OECD (2022a), International Migration Outlook 2022, OECD Publishing, Paris, *https://doi.org/10.1787/30fe16d2-en.*

OECD (2022b), The Contribution of Migration to Regional Development, OECD Regional Development Studies, OECD Publishing, Paris, https://doi.org/10.1787/57046df4-en.

OECD (2012), Redefining "Urban": A New Way to Measure Metropolitan Areas, OECD Publishing, Paris, *http://dx.doi.org/10.1787/9789264174108-en.*

Figure notes

3.13: The underlying sample covers the entire local resident population.

3.14: 2019 or latest available year. Data for the UK are limited to England and Wales. The underlying sample covers the entire local resident population.

3.15-3.17: The figures present the share of foreign-born among 15-64-year-olds.

3.13. Distribution of the foreign- and native-born population by type of TL3 region, 2019 or the latest available year

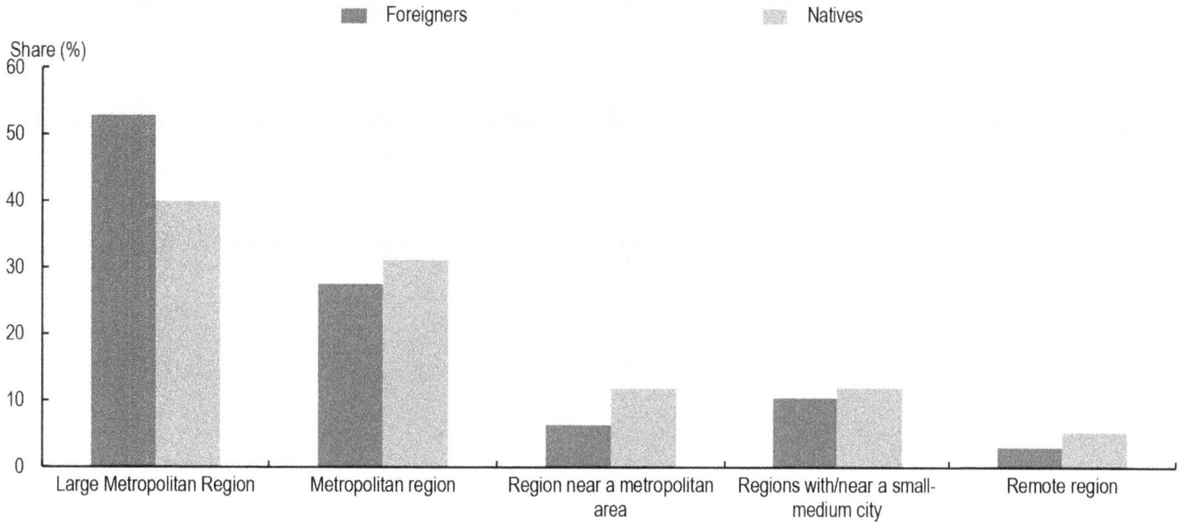

StatLink https://stat.link/vwpybs

3.14. Migrants live mainly in cities

The distribution of foreign-born population by the degree of urbanisation, 2020 or latest available year

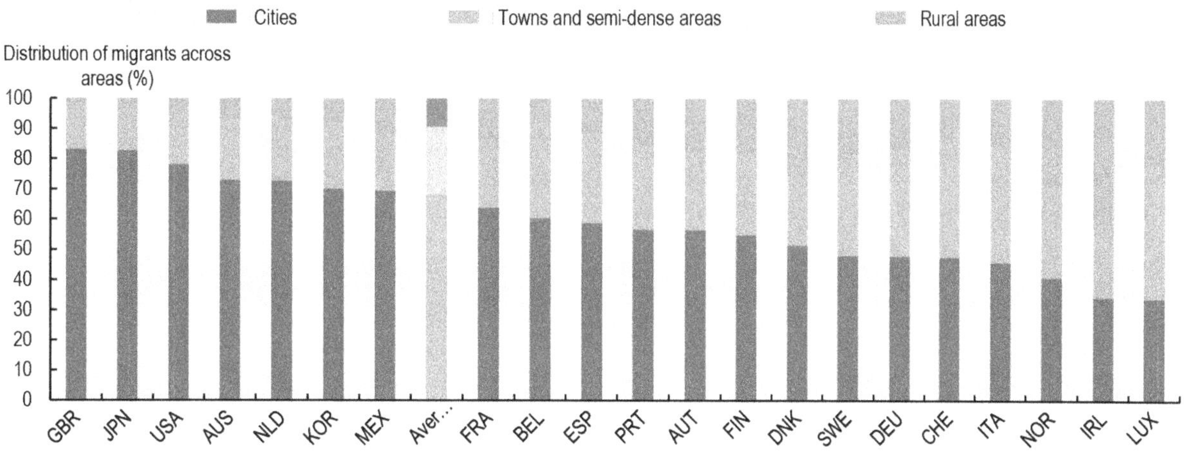

StatLink https://stat.link/j83flh

3.15. Migrant population across OECD regions, Europe, Asia and Oceania, 2019

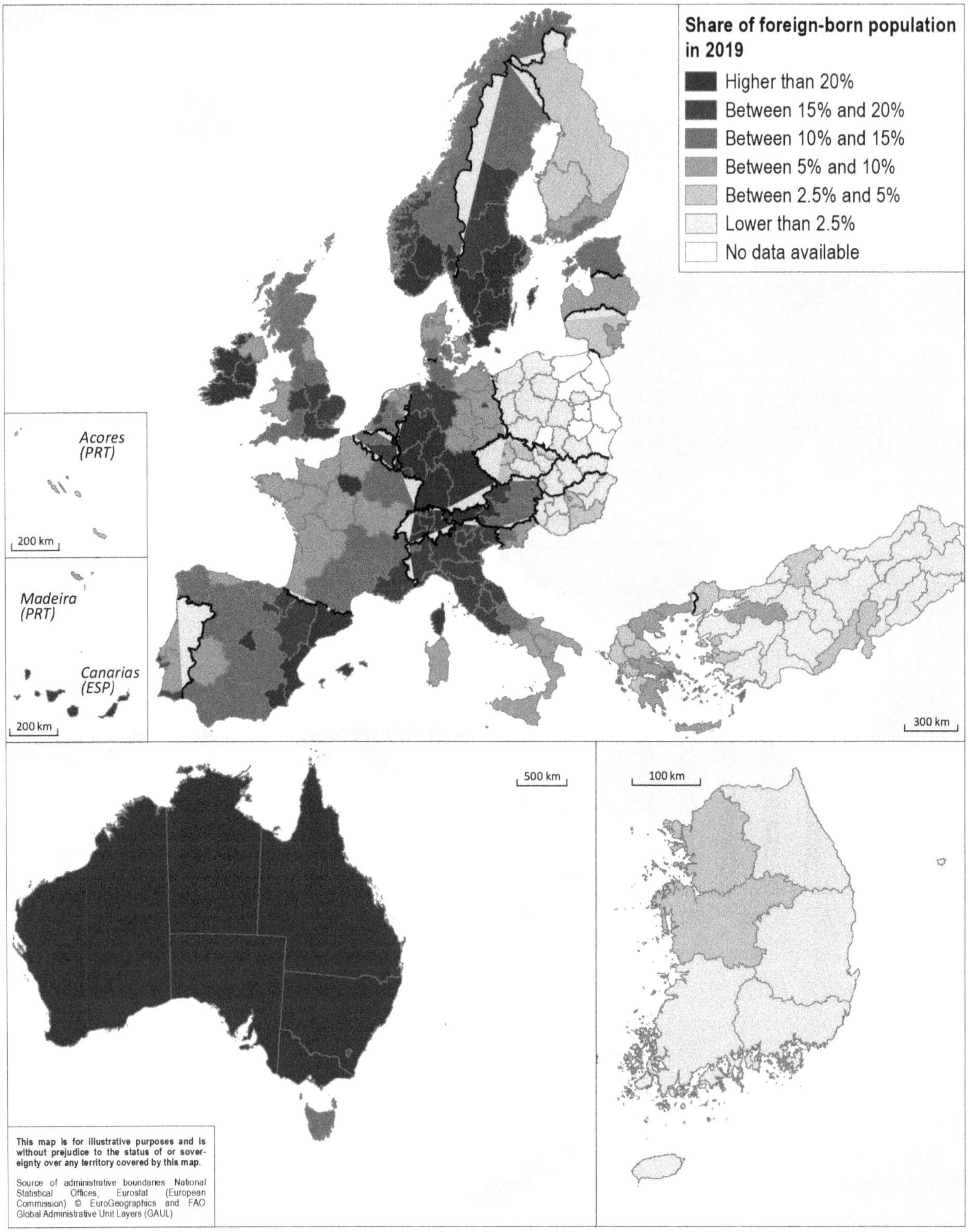

StatLink https://stat.link/a5zrb4

3.16. Migrant population across OECD regions, Chile and Colombia and the US, 2019

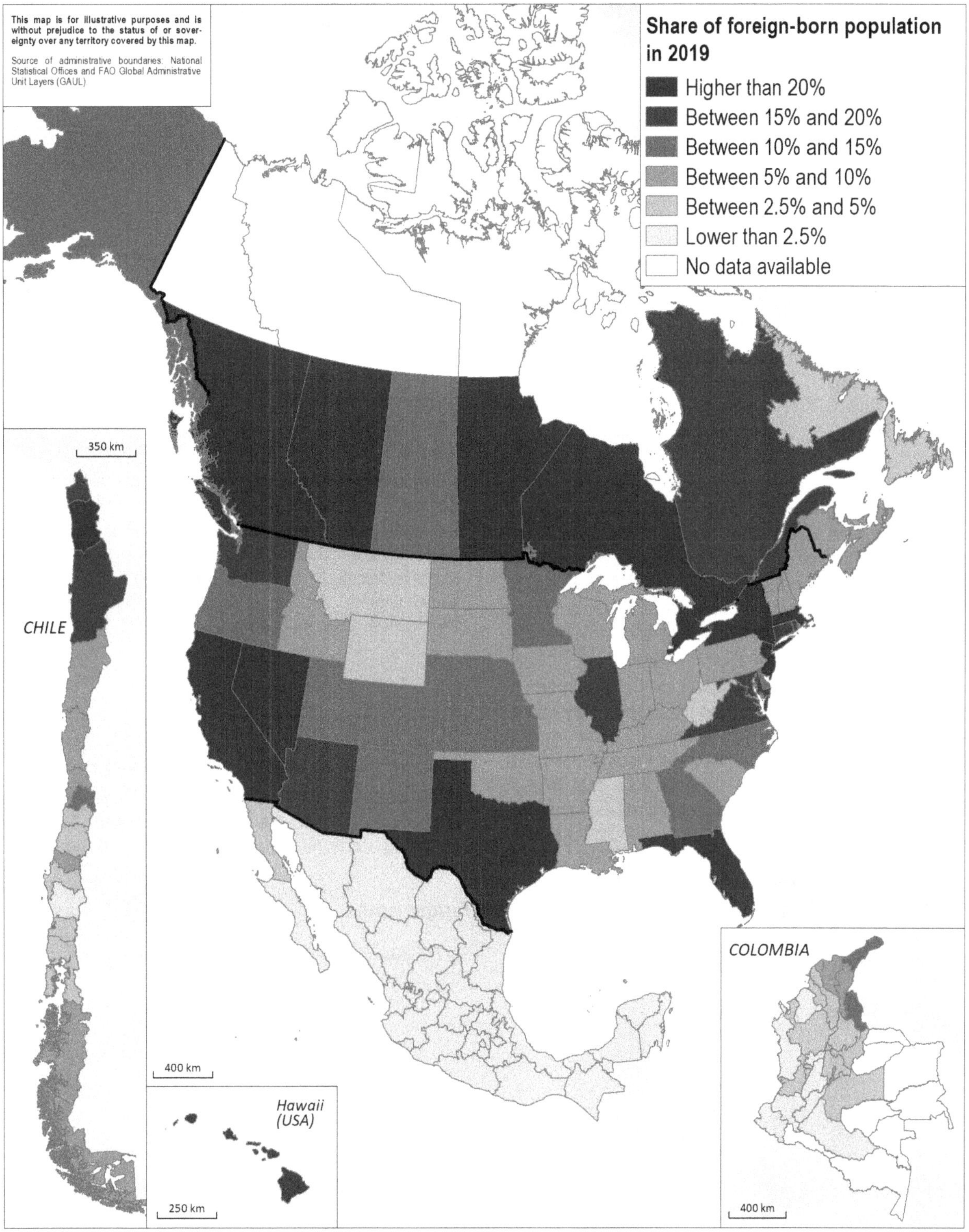

StatLink https://stat.link/dp73cz

Integration of international migrants into regional labour markets

The labour market integration of international migrants has been improving across OECD regions but significant challenges remain.

The integration of migrants into the labour market is of fundamental importance as it offers economic support and facilitates social and cultural integration. While migrant integration remains a significant challenge, with visible geographical variation across and especially within countries, most regions across OECD countries show significant improvements in migrant labour market integration during the last decade.

Despite the progress since 2015, migrant employment rates remain below that of native-born. On average, the employment rate of migrants increased by around 4 pp in OECD countries and by 3 pp in EU27 countries. Overall, the employment rate of migrants has improved, in almost three-quarters of regions (OECD, 2022). However, regional differences in employment rates persist within OECD countries (Figure 3.17), mainly driven by the low female employment rate, as discussed in the next section.

In general, OECD countries with low national employment rates for migrants also document the largest regional variations in migrants' employment rates. For example, in Mexico and Türkiye, employment rates of migrants differ across regions by 36 and 33 pp respectively (Figures 3.19 and 3.20). However, there are also exceptions such as Germany and Hungary, with migrants' national employment rates of 71% and 77%, that also report regional gaps of more than 20 pp or more.

Gender gaps are a significant obstacle to the integration of migrants across OECD regions. While the employment rate of male migrants and native-born is similar in most regions, differences for women are substantial. For instance, in 2019, the employment rate for female migrants was only 57% in OECD regions, compared to 74% for male migrants. Moreover, while the gender gap also exists for the native-born population (9 pp), that gap doubles for migrants (17 pp). While these differences result from complex factors, they may be explained by lower formal education or language proficiency for female migrants, cultural norms and restrictive work visa rules for spouses.

Sources

OECD (2022), *OECD Regional Statistics (database)*, OECD Publishing, Paris, *http://dx.doi.org/10.1787/region-data-en.*

Reference years and territorial level

2019; TL2.

Definitions

International migrants: The terms "migrants" and "foreign-born" are used interchangeably. Migrants are defined by their place of birth. The migrant population is defined as the population born in a country different from the one of residence. Unlike citizenship, this criterion does not change over time, is not subject to country differences in legislation and is thus adequate for international comparisons.

Employment rate: Employed people are all persons who, during the reference week, worked at least one hour for pay or profit or were temporarily absent from such work. Family workers are included. The native-born/migrant employment rate is calculated as the ratio between native-born/migrant employment and the native-born/migrant working-age population (15 to 64 years).

Further information

Territorial grids and regional typology (Annex B).

OECD (2022a), *The Contribution of Migration to Regional Development*, OECD Regional Development Studies, OECD Publishing, Paris, https://doi.org/10.1787/57046df4-en.

Figure notes

3.17-3.20: 2019 or the latest available year.

3.17. Regional differences in the employment gap of the foreign- and native-born population

Large regions (TL2), 2019

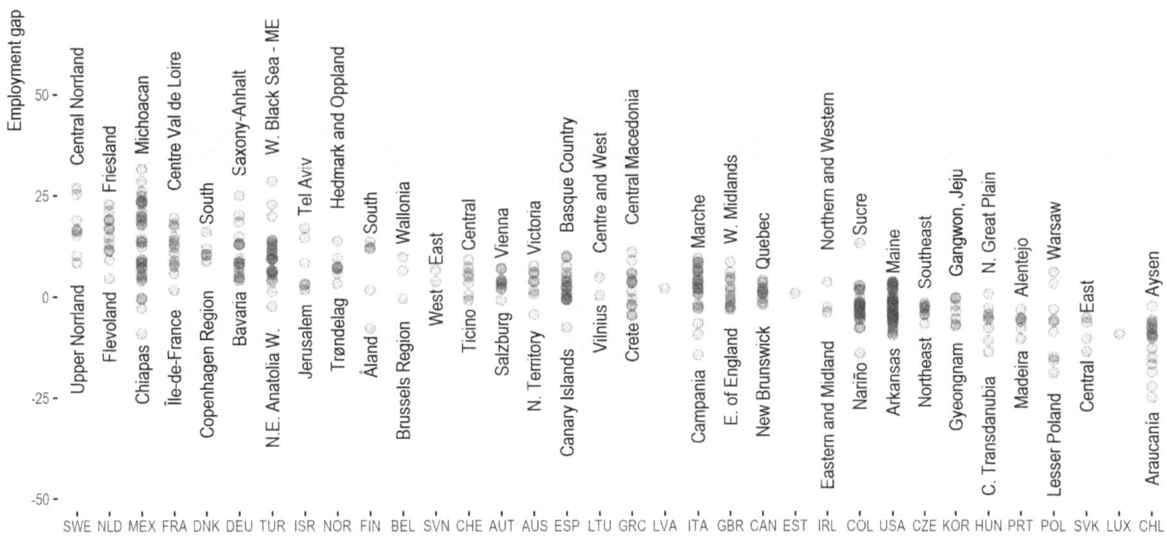

StatLink https://stat.link/kars0v

3.18. Gender employment gap of the foreign- and native-born population

Difference between male and female employment rates; large regions (TL2), 2019

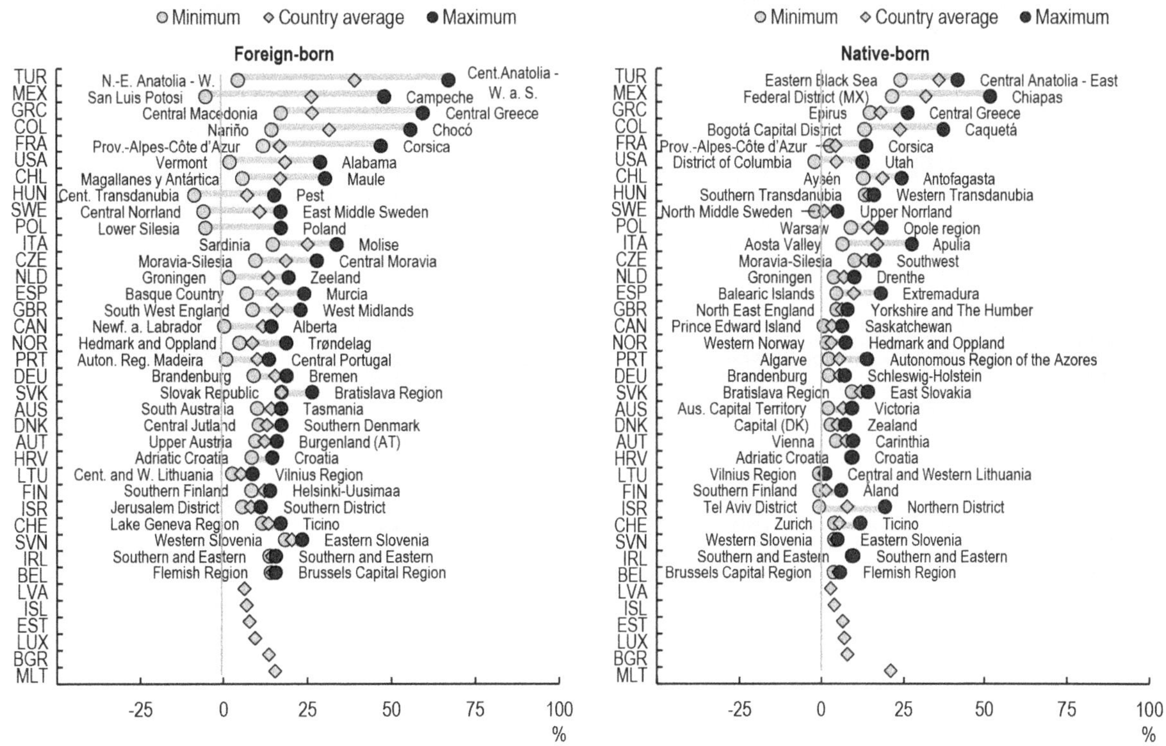

StatLink https://stat.link/sh035u

3.19. Employment rate of foreign-born, Europe, Asia and Oceania, 2019

Employment rate of foreign-born across TL 2 regions, 2019 or latest available year

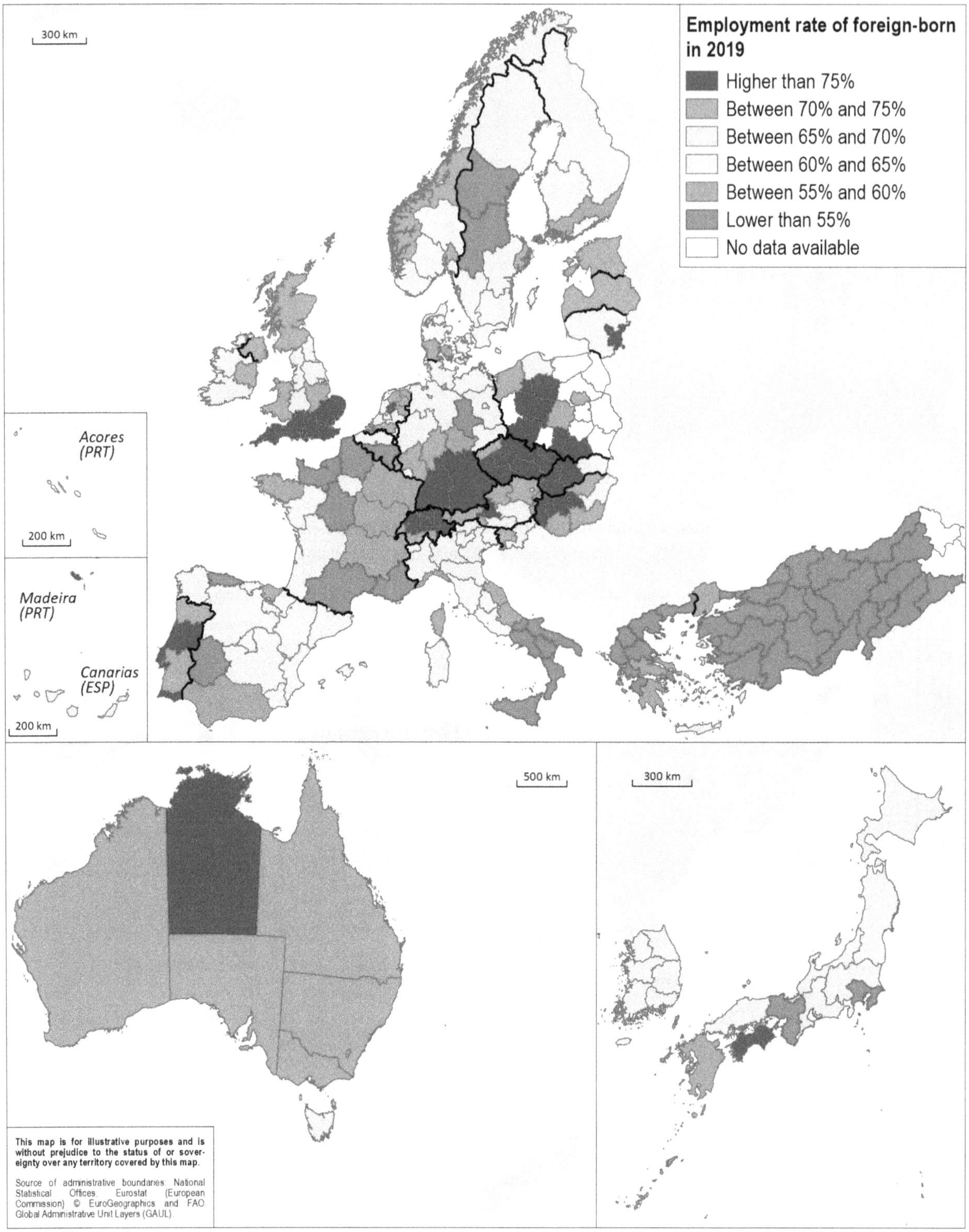

StatLink https://stat.link/h4unto

3.20. Employment rate of foreign-born, Chile, Colombia and the United States, 2019

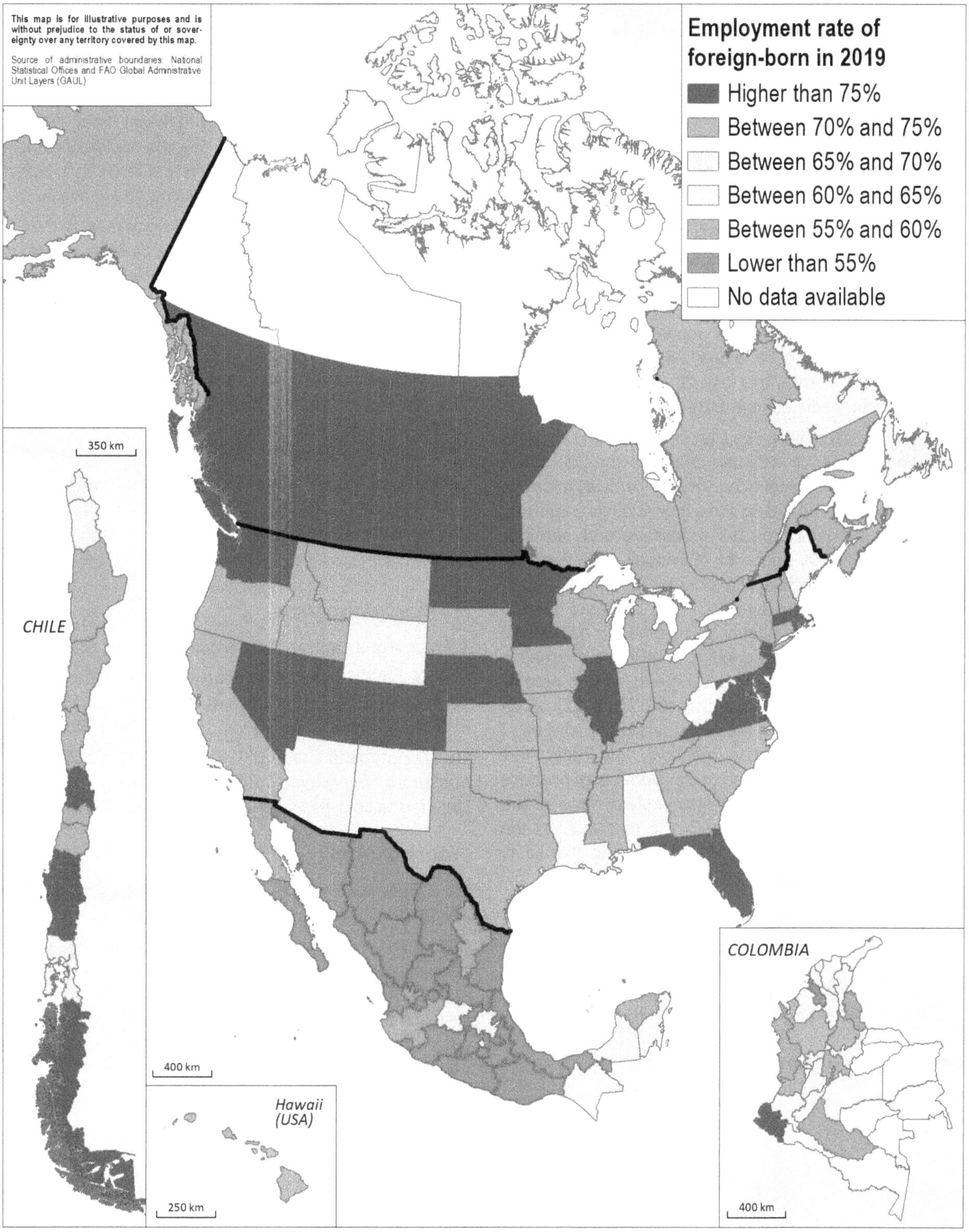

StatLink https://stat.link/aoz4lh

Educational attainment of migrants

Migrants are more likely to be overqualified, especially in lower-density and rural areas.

Educational attainment is a crucial factor in obtaining high-quality jobs. Levels of education of migrants can partially reveal the extent to which migrants struggle to enter and thrive in the regional labour markets of some regions more than in others.

Migrants are highly educated, especially in some OECD countries and regions. In Australia, Canada, Ireland, Norway, Sweden and the UK, most regions show larger shares of highly educated among the foreign-born than among the native-born population, on average (Figures 3.23 and 3.24). In most countries, capital regions house the highest share of both highly educated foreign-born and native-born in their respective country. The share of highly educated migrants represents more than 60% of the foreign-born population in the capital regions of Australia, Mexico and the US. In contrast, in all regions of Italy and Slovenia, less than 20% of the foreign-born population has tertiary education (Figure 3.21).

The labour market, especially jobs that match a worker's skills and occupation, is one of the main channels through which migrants contribute to regional economies. However, migrants often work in occupations below their qualifications, implying that many will not exploit their full productive and earnings potential. In Europe, the share of individuals who work in occupations below their qualifications tends to be higher outside of cities, for both native-born and migrants (Figure 3.22). Although data on educational achievement is not always available for immigrants, it appears that, in all types of areas in Europe, migrants are more likely to be overqualified, notably when their origin is from non-EU countries (OECD, 2022). While the drivers of the differences in the overqualification shares of native-born and foreigners are manifold, the difficulties associated with recognising foreign professional qualifications are an important factor. This could also explain some of the differences between EU-28 and non-EU-28 migrants, as the recognition process is easier for EU-28 migrants thanks to policies that harmonised diplomas obtained across EU countries.

Sources

OECD (2022), *OECD Regional Statistics (database)*, OECD Pu blishing, Paris, *http://dx.doi.org/10.1787/region-data-en*.

Reference years and territorial level

2017-19; TL2.

Definitions

International migrants: The terms "migrants" and "foreign-born" are used interchangeably. Migrants are defined by their place of birth. The migrant population is defined as the population born in a country different from the one of residence. Unlike citizenship, this criterion does not change over time, it is not subject to country differences in legislation and it is thus adequate for international comparisons.

Degree of urbanisation: This typology reflects the urban-rural continuum and proposes three classes instead of the dichotomy of urban or rural. The three classes are: i) cities (or densely populated areas); ii) towns and semi-dense areas (or intermediate density areas); and iii) rural areas (or thinly populated areas).

Overqualification: The overqualification share is calculated as the share of tertiary-educated workers (ISCED Levels 5-8) employed in low- or medium-skilled jobs (ISCO Levels 4-9) following the definition in OECD/European Union (2018).

Share of highly educated: The proportion of men and women who have a degree in tertiary education (ISCED 5 to 8) over the population of the respective gender.

Further information

Territorial grids and regional typology (Annex B).

OECD (2022), *The Contribution of Migration to Regional Development*, OECD Regional Development Studies, OECD Publishing, Paris, *https://doi.org/10.1787/57046df4-en*.

OECD/European Union (2018), *Settling In 2018: Indicators of Immigrant Integration*, OECD Publishing, Paris/European Union, Brussels, *https://doi.org/10.1787/9789264307216-en*.

Figure notes

3.21: Two-year averages are calculated using data for 2018 and 2019.

3.22: The sample includes the employed working-age population (15-64 years old) in Europe. Employees of the public service, international organisations and armed forces (ISCO Level 0) are excluded. This definition follows previous OECD calculations (OECD/EU, 2018). The analysis builds on a pooled sample of observations of the years 2017-19.

3.23-3.24: Data for 2019 or the latest available year.

3.21. Regional disparities in the shares of foreign- and native-born with tertiary education

Large regions (TL2), 2018-19 (2-year average)

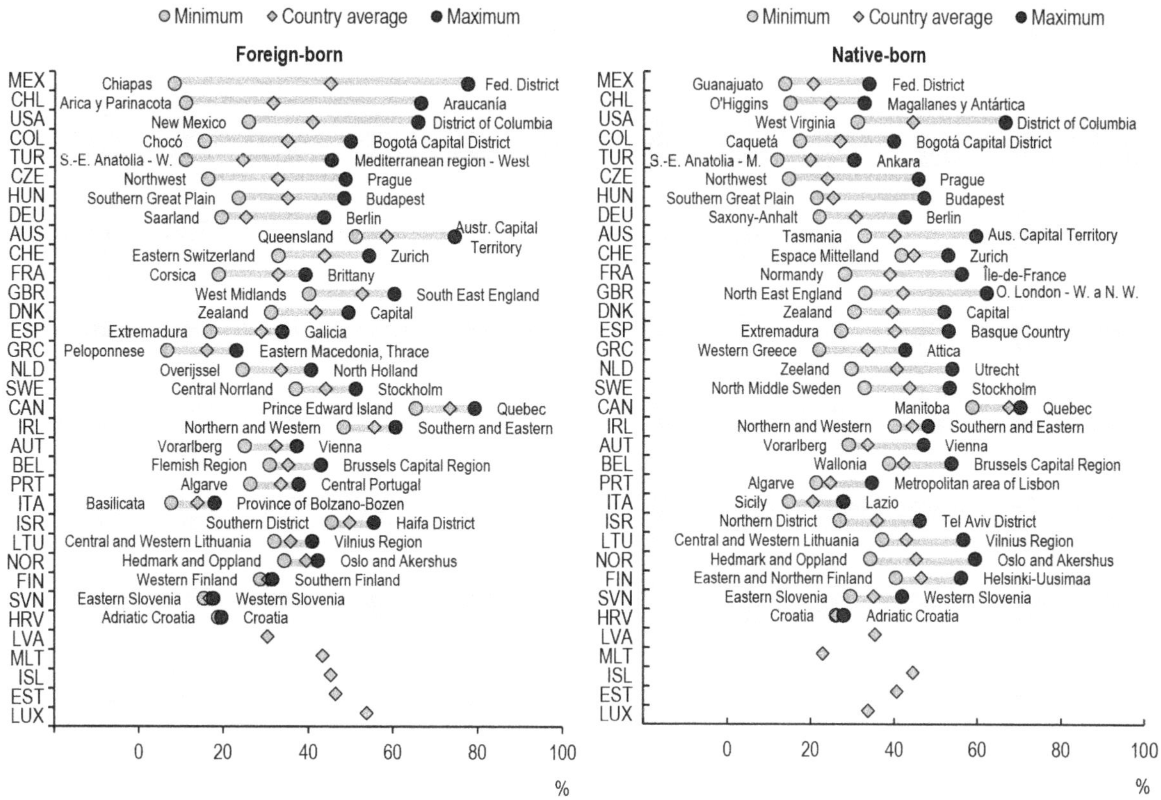

StatLink https://stat.link/tyhko2

3.22. Migrant overqualification by the degree of urbanisation and country of origin, 2017-19

Share of high-skilled workers employed in medium- and low-skilled jobs in Europe

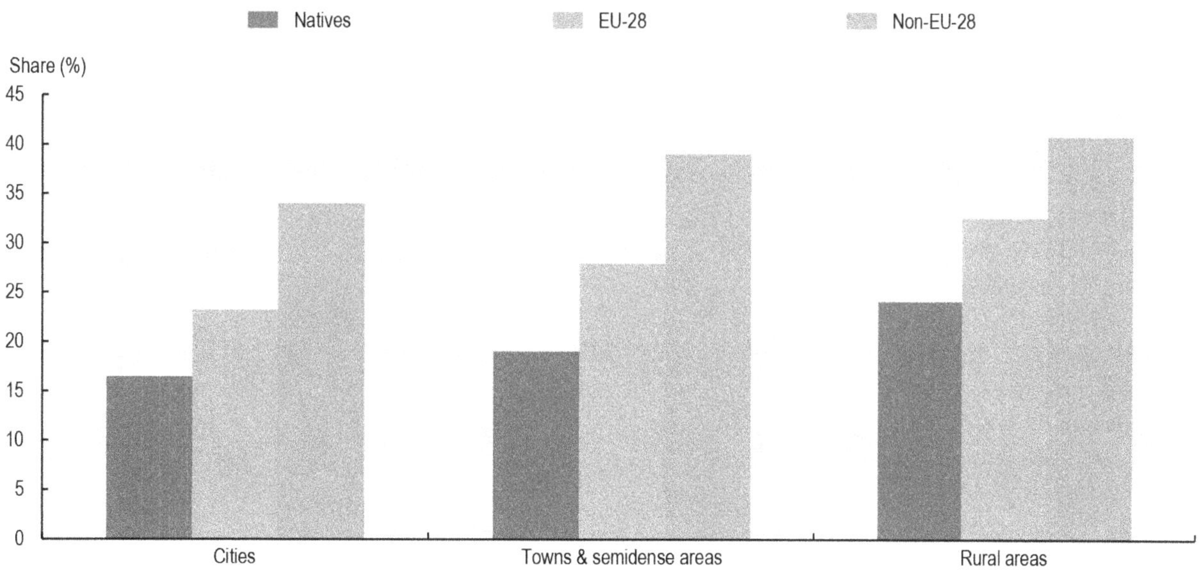

StatLink https://stat.link/tpfzg0

3.23. Educational attainment of migrants across OECD regions, selected European and OECD countries, 2019

Share of tertiary-educated migrants by TL2 regions

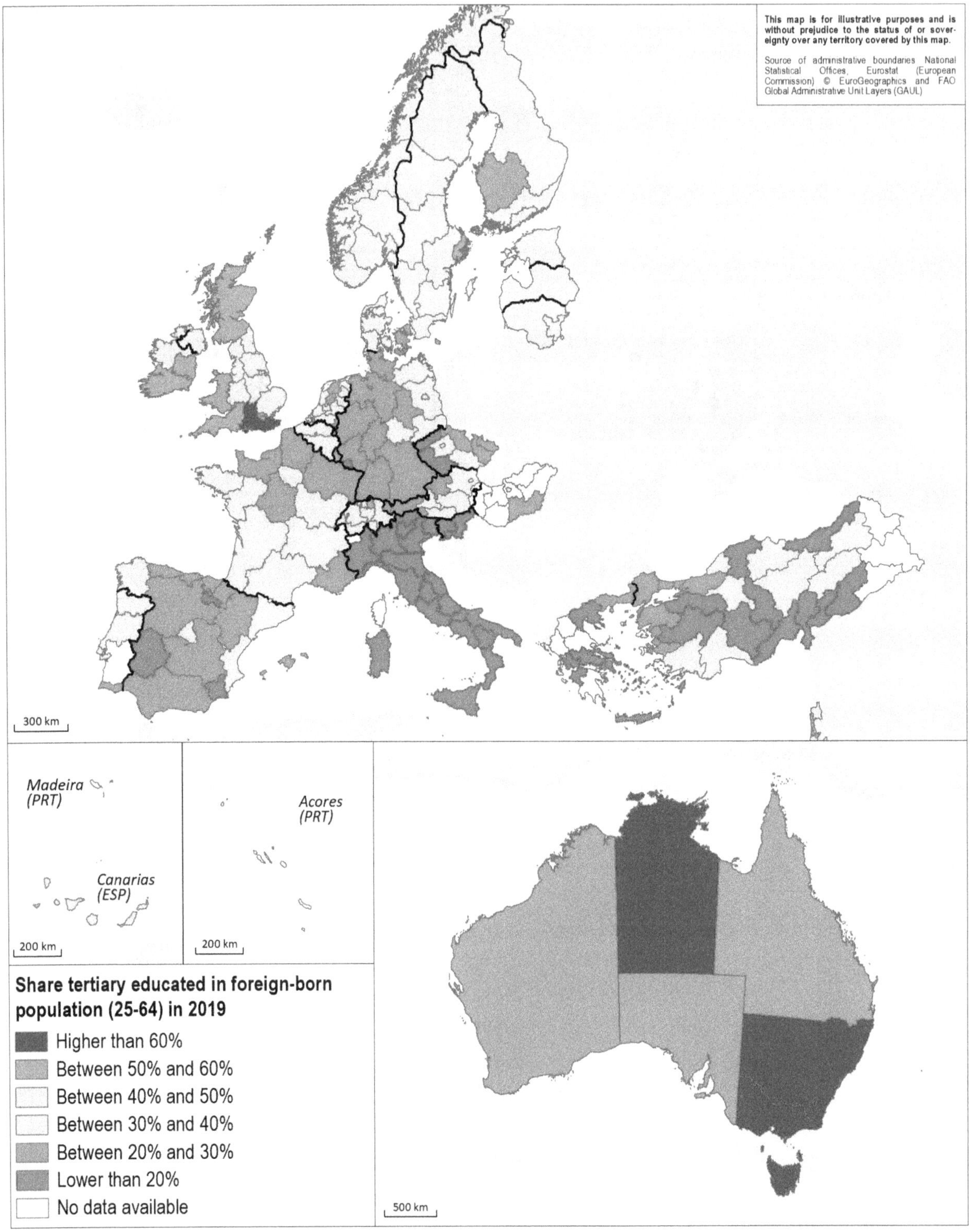

StatLink https://stat.link/ev5tsz

3.24. Educational attainment of migrants across OECD regions, Chile, Colombia and the United States, 2019

Share of tertiary-educated migrants by TL2 regions

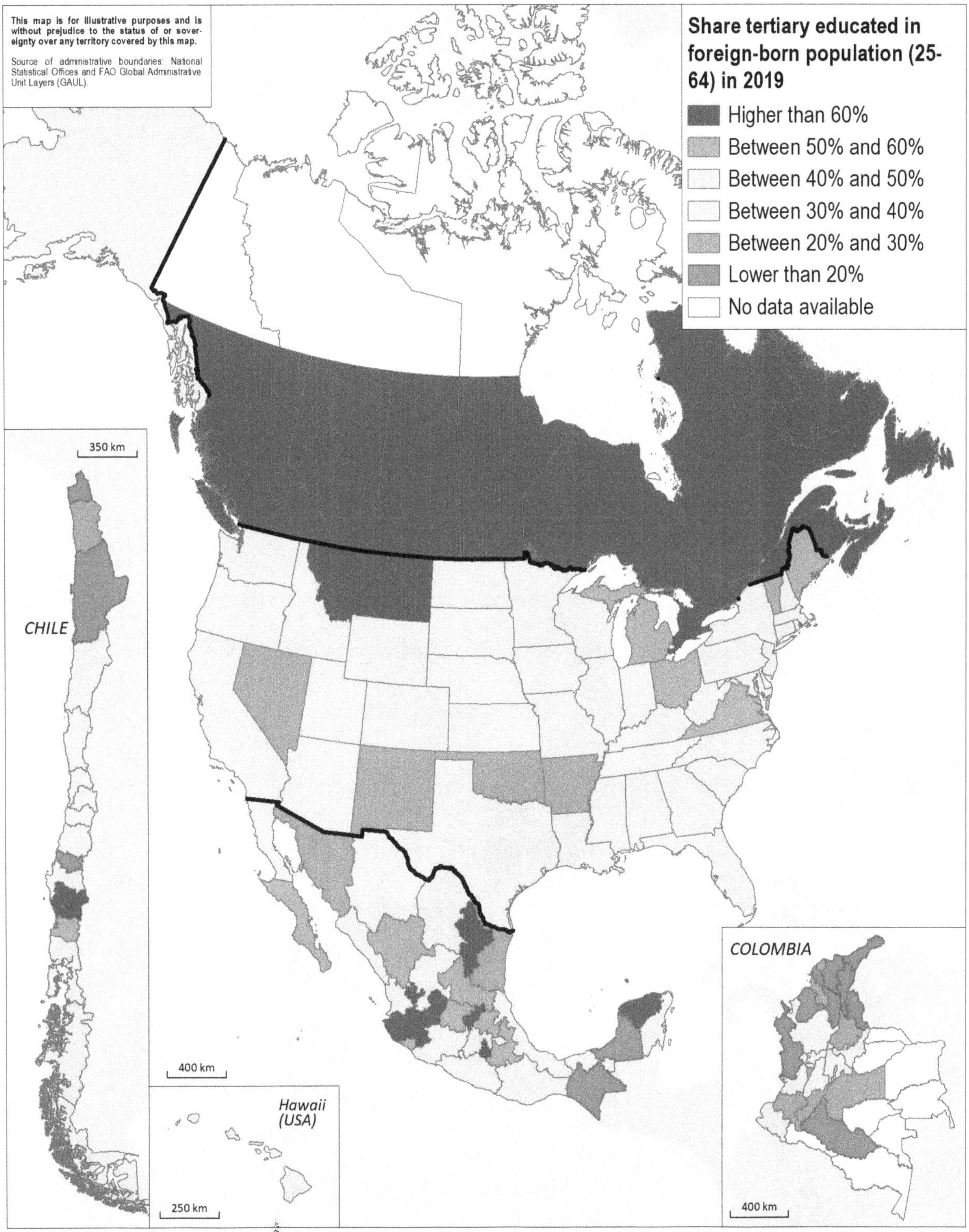

StatLink https://stat.link/mtgav1

4. BUILDING INCLUSIVE AND LIVEABLE REGIONS AND CITIES

Resilient health systems in regions

Income inequality and poverty in regions

Remote work in European regions and cities

Housing affordability in regions and cities

Digitalisation trends in regions

This chapter presents key aspects of inclusion and liveability in regions and cities, such as health system capacity, income conditions, housing affordability and access to services. It also assesses the impact of the COVID-19 pandemic across regions and cities with respect to health outcomes, remote working, digitalisation and housing demand.

Resilient health systems in regions

Although metropolitan regions have been the hardest hit by COVID-19, they are the most prepared with higher access to healthcare facilities and hospital beds.

The health impact of the COVID-19 pandemic has been very unequal across regions within the same country. In the first year of the pandemic, excess mortality in the hardest-hit region (TL2) was 17 percentage points (pp) higher than in the least affected region of the same country, on average. A common characteristic of many hardest-hit regions is that they contain large cities. This pattern is consistent with excess mortality by type of small region (TL3). In 2020, excess mortality was 18% in metropolitan regions compared to 14% in remote regions (Díaz Ramírez, Veneri and Lembcke, 2022).

Differentiated increases in excess mortality in 2020 drove unequal decreases in life expectancy across regions. From 2018 to 2020, life expectancy at birth decreased in more than half of OECD regions (TL2), which – at least temporarily – reversed the pre-pandemic long trend of six decades of growing life expectancy (OECD, 2021). Capitals and large metropolitan regions experienced the largest decreases. For example, in Brussels (Belgium), Lombardy (Italy) and Madrid (Spain), life expectancy fell by more than 2% (1.6 years) in 2020.

Despite the strongest impact of COVID-19 in places that had better health outcomes before the crisis (such as capitals and metropolitan regions), regional disparities in life expectancy remain high in several countries. After the COVID-19 outbreak, the average regional gap in life expectancy slightly declined from 3.3 years in 2018 to 2.8 years in 2020. Nevertheless, this average masks important country-specific inequalities. In Colombia and France, for example, the difference in life expectancy between the better-off and worse-off regions is of 15 and 10 years respectively. Those stark inequalities are due to a substantially low life expectancy in some regions characterised by being far from metropolitan areas (Figure 4.1).

Health system capacity is key to managing sanitary crises, such as the COVID-19 pandemic, and to improving health outcomes in low-performing regions. Yet, it differs significantly across regions. Hospital beds per inhabitant is an indicator that captures the readiness of regions to deliver health services to inpatients (OECD, 2021) and that was strongly associated with lower excess mortality during the pandemic (Díaz Ramírez, Veneri and Lembcke, 2022). In 2020, OECD regions had on average 4 hospital beds per 1 000 inhabitants but, within countries, provisions of beds differed by 3 beds per 1 000 inhabitants, on average. In Japan and Korea, regional gaps in this indicator were the highest due to some regions with very high provision levels (with more than 15 hospital beds per 1 000 inhabitants). In contrast, one-fifth of OECD regions had less than 2 hospital beds per 1 000 inhabitants – including some regions in Chile, Colombia, Greece, Mexico and the United Kingdom (UK) (Figure 4.2). Regional gaps in hospital beds are also significant across types of regions. For 21 OECD countries with available data for small regions (TL3), hospital bed rates were almost 50% higher in metropolitan regions compared to regions far from metropolitan areas.

Good access to healthcare facilities is also crucial for inclusive and resilient health systems. Across OECD regions, on average, three-quarters of the population had good access to a hospital (within a 20-minute drive) in 2022. Nevertheless, only two-thirds of the population in regions far from a metropolitan area had good physical accessibility to a hospital, driving the observed disparities across types of regions. Indeed, in 2022, metropolitan regions had on average 20 pp more population with good access to a hospital compared to regions far from a metropolitan area. Regional differences in access to hospitals were the highest in Belgium, Colombia, Greece and Mexico, with gaps of around 30 percentage points (Figure 4.3).

Definitions

Excess mortality refers to the percentage increase in the number of deaths (all causes) in 2020 with respect to the average number of deaths in the two previous years (2018 and 2019).

Life expectancy at birth estimates the number of years a new born can expect to live if current death rates by age group were to remain the same during her or his lifetime.

Sources

See country metadata in Annex B.

Díaz Ramírez, M., P. Veneri and A. Lembcke (2022), "Where did it hit harder? Understanding the geography of excess mortality during the COVID-19 pandemic", Journal of Regional Science, Vol. 62, pp. 889-908, *https://doi.org/10.1111/jors.12595.*

OECD (2021), *Health at a Glance 2021: OECD Indicators*, OECD Publishing, Paris, *https://doi.org/10.1787/ae3016b9-en.*

Figure notes

4.1: 2020 or latest available year.

4.2: 2020 data or latest available year; 2019 for CYP, DEU, EST, GRC, and LVA; 2018 for MLT and USA; 2021 only for BEL, CHL and DNK.

4.1. Regional differences in life expectancy at birth, 2020

Regional gaps in life expectancy of total population, large regions (TL2)

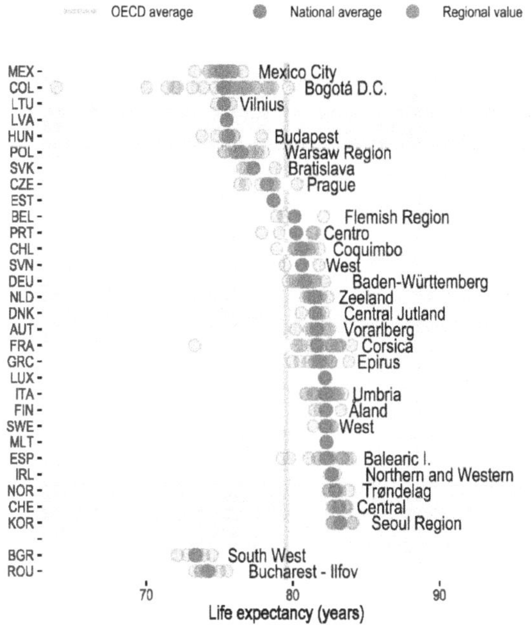

StatLink https://stat.link/r1vapz

4.2. Regional differences in hospital beds per inhabitant, 2020

Beds per 1 000 inhabitants (TL2), large regions (TL2)

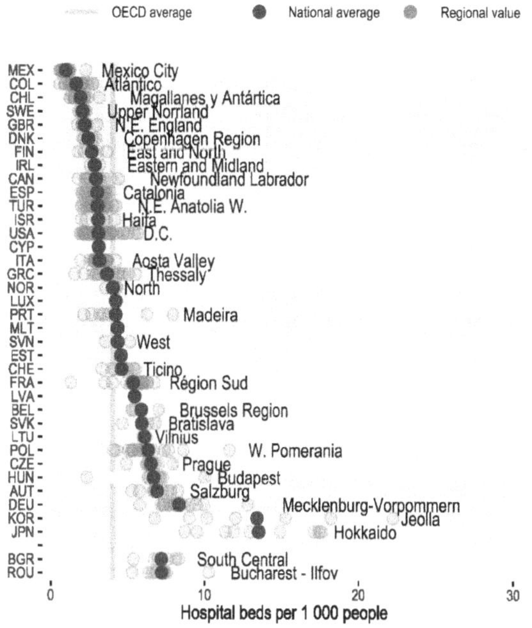

StatLink https://stat.link/4laz89

4.3. Accessibility to hospitals by type of region, 2022

Percentage of population within a 20-minute drive from a hospital, by type of region, small regions (TL3)

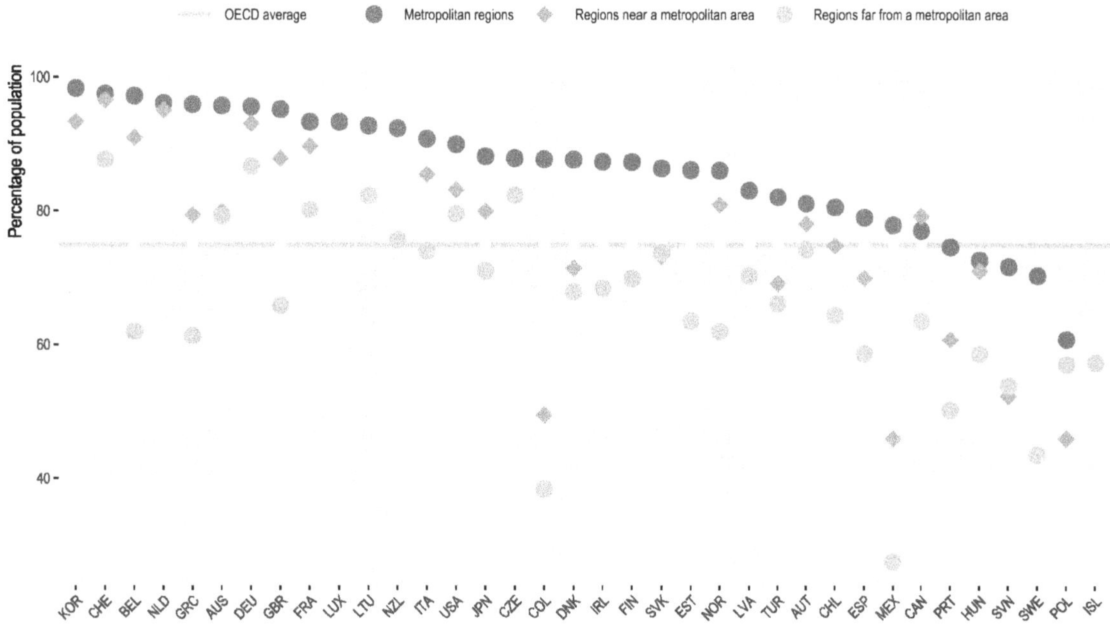

StatLink https://stat.link/180nkp

Income inequality and poverty in regions

Income inequalities are the highest in capitals and less developed regions. In those places, the disposable income of the richest 20% is around 7 times higher than that of the poorest 20%.

Highly unequal societies can stifle opportunities for people and make places more vulnerable to crises. At the individual level, low incomes deteriorate quality of life, long-term economic prospects and the capacity to prevent and respond to risks. At the regional level, stark inequality generates discontent and mistrust, which undermines social cohesion (Rodríguez-Pose, 2018) and limits the capacity to cope with shocks. During the outbreak of COVID-19, higher income inequality and deprivation were associated with higher COVID-19 mortality within regions and cities (Brandily et al., 2021; Iacobucci, 2020).

Income inequalities are stark and persistent within regions. In 2020, capital-city regions and some less developed regions (based on gross domestic product [GDP] per capita) exhibited the highest income inequalities, as measured in terms of the ratio between the 20% richest and 20% poorest population's disposable income (an indicator also known as the S80/S20 ratio for disposable income). In half of the 26 OECD countries with available data, capital-city regions presented among the highest S80/S20 ratios for disposable income. In Santiago (Chile), Warsaw (Poland) and Greater London (UK), the disposable income of the richest 20% of the population ranged from 7 to 13 times that of the poorest 20% of the population. However, in other countries such as Colombia, the Czech Republic, Lithuania and Mexico, the relatively less developed regions are the ones with the highest inequalities (Figure 4.4). Although inequality levels (S80/S20 ratios) can be similar between capital regions and less developed regions, average incomes – especially those of the bottom 20% – are higher in capital regions.

Regional disparities are also large and persistent in terms of poverty rates. The relative poverty rate across OECD regions was around 21% in 2020. The average gap in poverty rates between the worst- and best-performing regions in the same country amounted to 18 pp. The largest differences were in Colombia and Mexico (50 pp or more). In Europe, differences were largest in Belgium, Italy and Spain (20 pp or more) (Figure 4.5).

Within OECD regions, top-to-bottom income inequality has slightly increased during the last decade, while relative poverty rates have remained the same. In most regions, the increase in S80/S20 ratios is due to faster growth in the average incomes of the richest population (15% increase) compared to the poorest (12.5% increase). On the other hand, relative poverty rates (the share of the population with an income below 60% of the national median income) have remained at 21%, on average, in the same period (due to a similar growth between bottom and median incomes). However, in 42 out of 306 OECD regions, relative poverty rates increased by 4 pp or more, including some regions in Colombia, France, Lithuania, Spain and the United States (US).

In 2020, taxes and transfers contributed to significant reductions in inequalities in gross income. They reduced regional S80/S20 ratios for gross income by 36% and regional relative poverty rates for gross income by 21%, on average across OECD regions. Yet, regional differences in this indicator suggest that some places are still not exploiting the full potential of redistributive policies. In 15% of OECD regions, taxes and transfers did not lead to significant reductions in S80/S20 ratios and poverty rates (Figure 4.6).

Definitions

S80/S20 ratio: The total income received by the 20% of people with the highest income in a region divided by the total income received by the 20% of people with the lowest income in the same region.

Relative poverty rate: The share of people – as a % of the regional population – with an income below the relative poverty line (60% of the national median income).

Gross income: Income before taxes and transfers.

Disposable income: Income after taxes and transfers.

Sources

See country metadata in Annex B.

Brandily, P. et al. (2021), "A poorly understood disease? The unequal distribution of excess mortality due to COVID-19 across French municipalities", medRxiv, *https://doi.org/10.1101/2020.07.09.20149955*.

Iacobucci, G. (2020), "Covid-19: Deprived areas have the highest death rates in England and Wales", *The BMJ*, Vol. 369, p. m1810, *https://doi.org/10.1136/bmj.m1810*.

Rodríguez-Pose, A. (2018), "The revenge of the places that don't matter (and what to do about it)", *Cambridge Journal of Regions, Economy and Society*, Vol. 11/1, pp. 189-209, *http://dx.doi.org/10.1093/cjres/rsx024*.

Figure notes

4.4-4.6: Large regions (TL2), except for GRC, HUN, ITA and SWE.

4.4. Regional differences in income inequality

S80/S20 ratios for disposable income

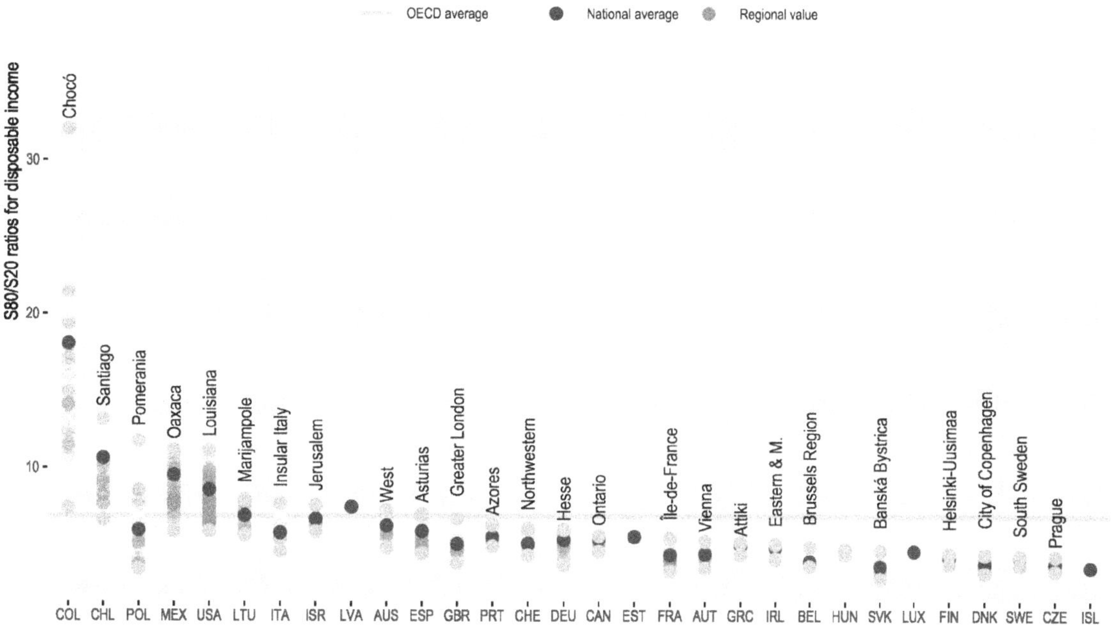

StatLink https://stat.link/p6n5h1

4.5. Regional differences in poverty rates, 2020

Relative poverty rates (disposable income), % of population

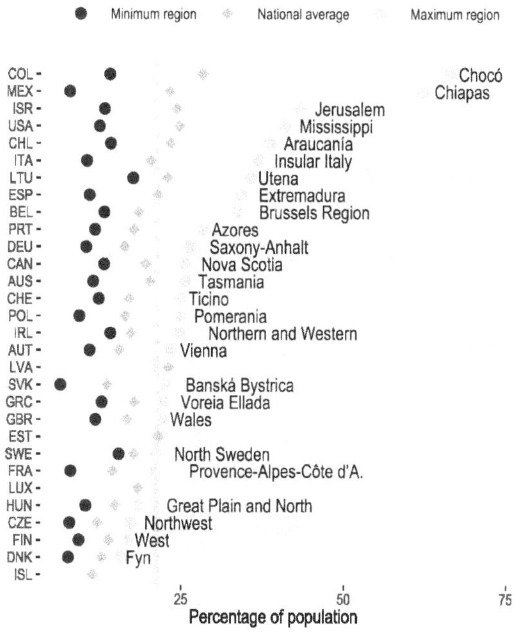

StatLink https://stat.link/w8gmsh

4.6. Decreases in regional poverty rates due to taxes and transfers, 2020

Change in relative poverty after taxes and transfers, percentage points

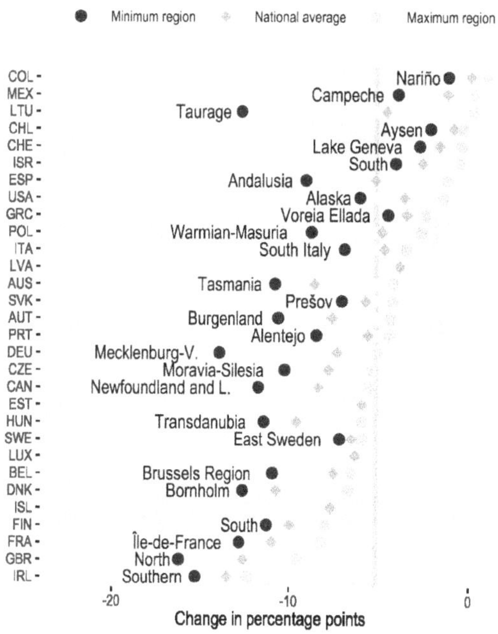

StatLink https://stat.link/u6d1tz

Remote work in European regions and cities

Cities and capital regions experienced the largest increase in remote work.

The COVID-19 pandemic has changed how and where people work. Measures taken to contain the spread of the virus, such as social distancing and mandatory lockdowns, forced firms and workers to rapidly implement remote work by adopting new technologies and changing typical work practices. Although those changes were in response to the initial shock of the pandemic, it now seems clear that remote working will remain much more widespread than in pre-pandemic times (Aksoy et al., 2022).

Throughout 2020, over 12% of employees in European countries worked remotely most of the time (50% of the time or more) and another 10% worked remotely from time to time (less than 50% of the time). However, the share of remote work uptake was not homogenous across or within European countries. For example, while 25% of employed people worked from home in Finland, only 3% did so in Latvia (Figure 4.7, Panel A). Within countries, the average gap between the regions (TL2) with the highest and lowest shares of individuals working remotely was close to 10 percentage points. Regional gaps reached more than 15 pp in Belgium, Finland and Poland, driven by the much higher remote work uptake in those countries' capitals. Overall, in all European countries, cities and capitals had the highest share of remote workers in 2020 (Figure 4.7, Panel B). On average, 20% of workers in capital regions worked remotely most of the time in 2020 compared to only 10% in all European regions.

Cities and capital regions were the faster adopters of remote working during the first year of the pandemic (from 2019 to 2020). Across European regions, on average, the share of remote workers more than doubled, while it tripled in capital regions. Changes in remote work uptake are also significant by degree of urbanisation. Between 2019 and 2020, the share of remote workers almost tripled in cities and doubled in towns and semi dense-areas, whereas it increased by only 70% in rural areas. In 2020, Finland, Ireland, Italy and Portugal displayed the largest within-country differences in remote work uptake by degree of urbanisation. In those countries, cities had around 10 pp more remote workers than rural areas.

The observed spatial differences in remote working uptake confirm previous evidence suggesting that cities had a higher concentration of jobs amenable to remote working compared to other types of areas (OECD, 2020). Consistently, regions with higher shares of workers employed in occupations amenable to remote work also tend to have higher rates of remote working uptake. Figure 4.8 shows this relationship by plotting regions' remote work potential based on occupational composition (horizontal axis) against actual remote work uptake in these regions (vertical axis). The trend line shows a positive correlation between the remote work potential and the remote work uptake in 2020. However, the relationship is not one-to-one and actual remote work uptake (i.e. the share of workers who worked remotely most of the time) appears much lower than expected, given the remote work potential in these regions. Existing evidence suggests that local and country-specific factors such as the sectoral composition of regional economies, the severity of the lockdown measures and other cultural attributes drive the observed regional differences in remote work uptake (Luca, Özgüzel and Wei, forthcoming). While there is some evidence that the prevalence of remote working has receded since 2020 and has not reached its full potential, the percentage of workers who are working fully or partially remote remains much higher than in the pre-pandemic period (Aksoy et al., 2022).

Definitions

Remote work uptake: The number of individuals, as a share of all workers, who reported having "usually worked from home" (i.e. more than 50% of the time in the survey reference month).

Potential for remote working: An assessment of regions' capacity to adapt to remote working based on the diversity of tasks performed in different types of occupations. The estimate is structured in two steps.

Sources

See country metadata in Annex B.

Aksoy, C. et al. (2022), "Working from home around the world", *Brookings Papers on Economic Activity*.

Luca, D., C. Özgüzel and Z. Wei, (forthcoming), "What factors enabled individuals to work remotely during the pandemic?", *OECD Regional Development Papers*, OECD Publishing, Paris.

OECD (2020), "Capacity for remote working can affect lockdown costs differently across places", *OECD Policy Responses to Coronavirus (COVID-19)*, OECD, Paris, *https://www.oecd.org/coronavirus/policy-responses/capacity-for-remote-working-can-affect-lockdown-costs-differently-across-places-0e85740e/*.

Figure notes

4.7-4.8: Data for 2019 and 2020.

4.7. Remote work uptake in European regions and cities, 2020

A: Share of remote workers (%), large regions (TL2) | B: Share of remote workers (%), by degree of urbanisation

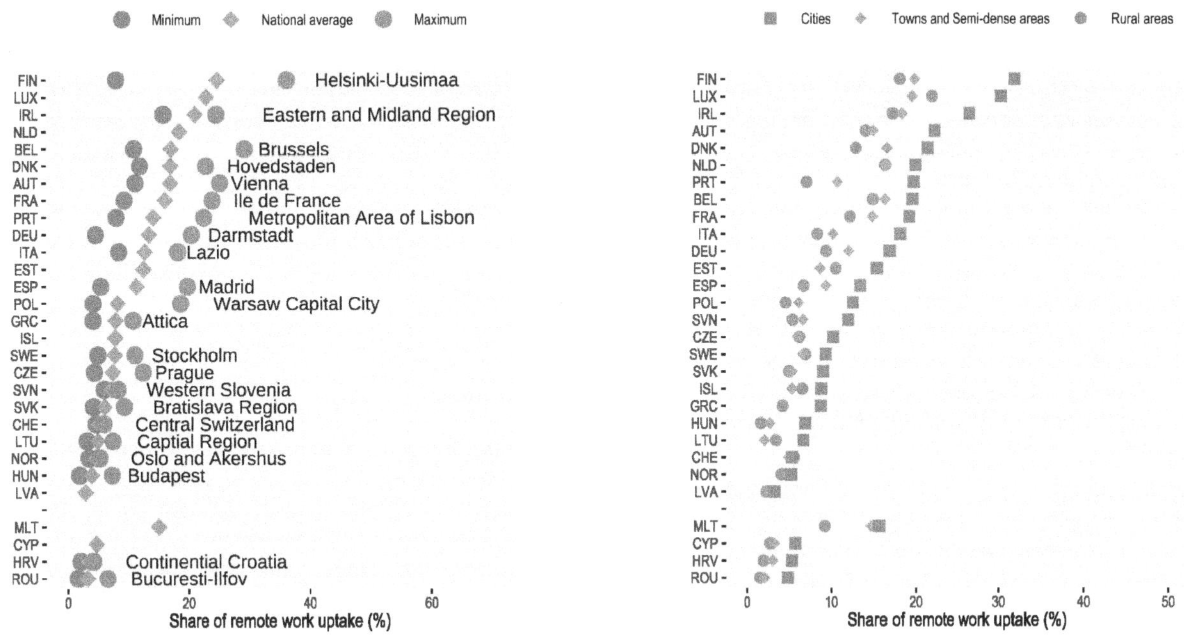

StatLink https://stat.link/up5cnl

4.8. Remote work potential vs. remote work uptake, 2020

Share of jobs amenable to remote work (%) vs. share of remote workers (%), European large regions (TL2)

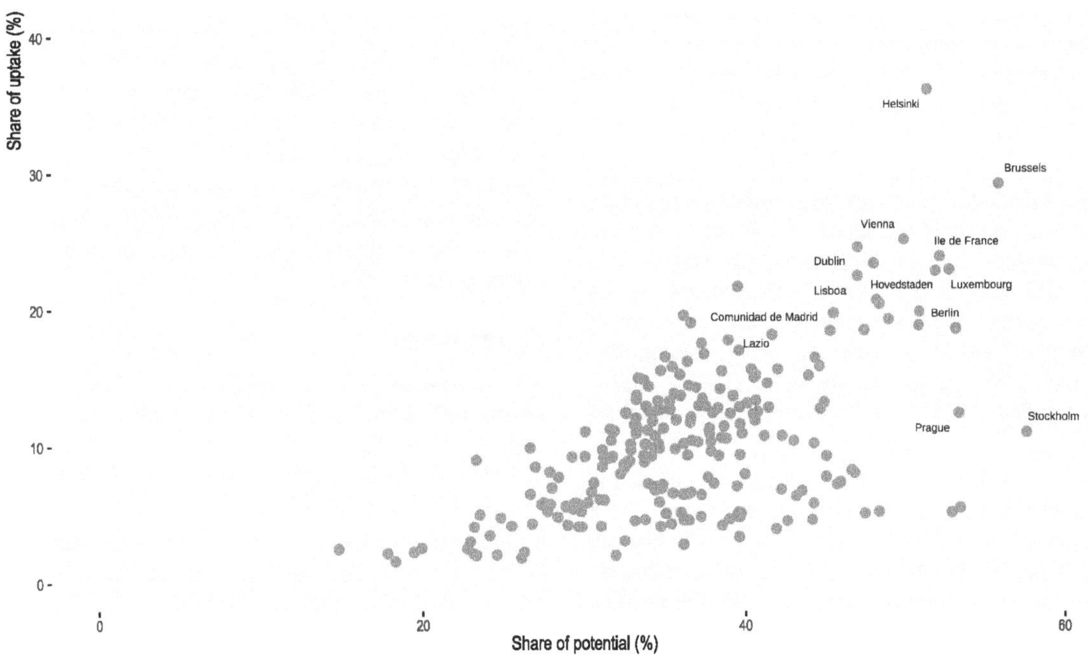

StatLink https://stat.link/cifpos

Housing affordability in regions and cities

In metropolitan areas, buying a house in the city centre is 30% more expensive than in the suburbs, on average. However, after the COVID-19 outbreak and the rise of teleworking, house prices have been growing faster in the suburbs relative to the central neighbourhoods.

Adequate and affordable housing is key for well-being and inclusive and resilient societies. A lack of affordable housing can also limit economic opportunities linked to residential mobility and contribute to labour shortages in some places. In the 15 years before the COVID-19 pandemic, house prices increased dramatically in most OECD countries. Such a trend makes it hard for people, especially those living in large and dense agglomerations, to access sufficient-size and good-quality housing. Fast-growing house prices and overall housing costs also put extra pressure on the budgets and quality of life of people. Housing costs have increased constantly since 2005 and they account for the largest share of household expenditure (OECD, 2021).

Households spend from one-tenth to one-third of their disposable income on housing (including rent and maintenance), depending on the region and country where they live. Differences within countries suggest that households living in capital regions and, more generally, in metropolitan regions struggle the most to afford housing. Indeed, in half of the OECD countries with available data, capital-city regions are the most expensive in terms of housing. In those regions, households spend on average one-fifth of their disposable income on housing. Regional gaps in housing affordability are the highest in Austria, Belgium, Germany and the UK, where the share of household income spent on housing is 7 pp higher in the most expensive regions than in the least expensive ones (Figure 4.9).

Stark differences in house prices across types of regions can also limit home ownership. The lack of possibility of buying a dwelling is associated with lower economic security and social mobility for households, as well as higher wealth inequality for societies (OECD, 2021). In 2021, for 17 OECD countries with available data, buying a house in a metropolitan region was 40 pp more expensive than in a region far from a metropolitan area, on average. The largest gaps between types of regions were in Denmark, Estonia, Hungary and Ireland (above 50 pp) (Figure 4.10).

Beyond the type of regions, house prices are also very unequal between and within cities (functional urban areas, FUAs, of 100 thousand people or more). House prices increase with city size and proximity to the city centre. On average, house prices per square metre in large metropolitan areas are twice the prices in small- or medium-sized cities. In addition, within large metropolitan areas (FUAs of 1.5 million people or more), house prices are 30% higher in the city centre compared to suburban neighbourhoods (Figure 4.11).

Nevertheless, the COVID-19 pandemic and the rise of teleworking might be reshaping the demand for housing in metropolitan areas (Ahrend, et al., 2022). Based on new and granular data from 14 OECD countries, house price inflation within metropolitan areas was lower in central neighbourhoods, relative to the suburbs, after the COVID-19 outbreak. From 2020 Q1 to 2021 Q2, house prices increased by 7% in central neighbourhoods, while they increased by more than 12% in areas farther away from the city centres (60 km and more) (Figure 4.12).

Definition

Housing costs as a percentage of disposable income considers the expenditure of households in housing and maintenance of the house, as defined in the SNA (P31CP040: Housing, water, electricity, gas and other fuels; P31CP050: Furnishings, households' equipment and routine maintenance of the house).

Sources

See country metadata in Annex B.

Ahrend, R. et al. (2022), "Changes in the geography housing demand after the onset of COVID-19: First results from large metropolitan areas in 13 OECD countries", *OECD Economics Department Working Papers*, No. 1713, OECD Publishing, Paris, *https://doi.org/10.1787/9a99131f-en*.

OECD (2021), "Building for a better tomorrow: Policies to make housing more affordable", Employment, Labour and Social Affairs Policy Briefs, OECD, Paris. *http://oe.cd/affordable-housing-2021*.

Figure notes

4.11: Prices were first normalised (from 0 to 100) by country, where 100 is the most expensive small area units (SAUs) in country. Only 16 OECD countries with data available are included: AUT, BEL, DEU, DNK, ESP, FIN, FRA, GBR, HUN, IRL, KOR, MEX, NOR, PRT, SWE and USA.

4.12: For visualisation purposes, the lines are smoothed using a LOESS method. Only 14 OECD countries with data available are included: AUT, BEL, DEU, DNK, ESP, FRA, GBR, HUN, IRL, KOR, MEX, PRT, SWE and USA.

4.9. Regional disparities in housing costs, 2020

Cost of housing as a share of disposable income, large regions (TL2)

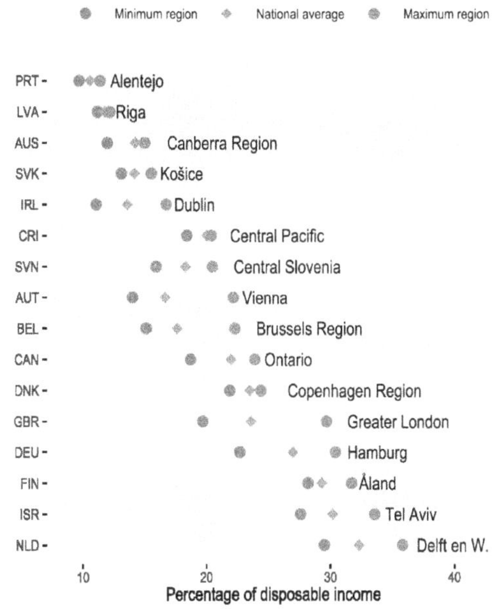

StatLink https://stat.link/ofmxrq

4.10. Difference in house prices by type of region, 2021 H1

Small regions (TL3)

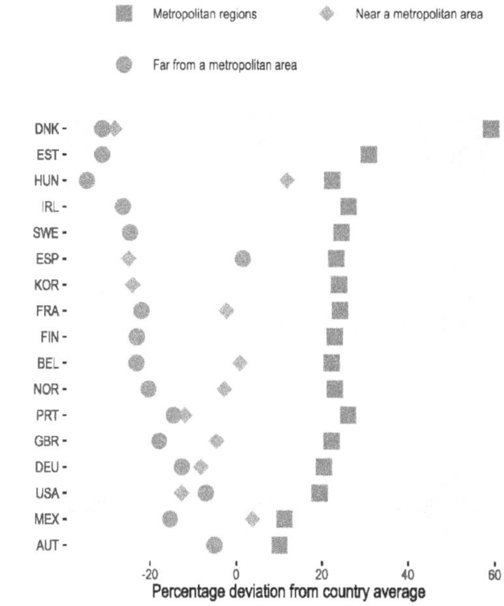

StatLink https://stat.link/yz3epa

4.11. House prices in cities, 2021 H1

Small area units in FUAs of at least 100 000 inhabitants

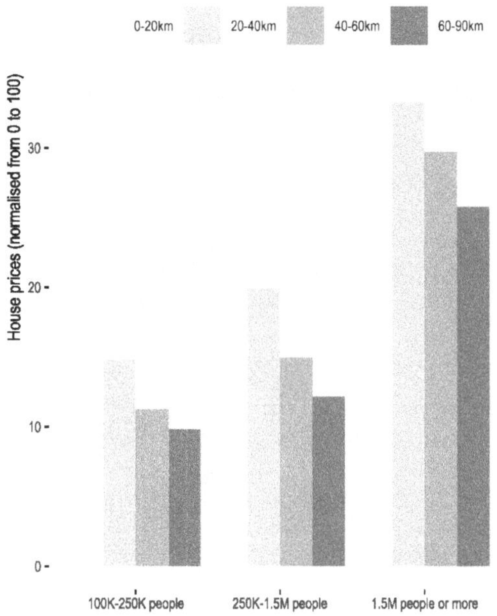

StatLink https://stat.link/jcwbvi

4.12. Evolution of house prices within metropolitan areas, 2018 Q1-2021 Q2

Small area units in FUAs of at least 1.5 million inhabitants

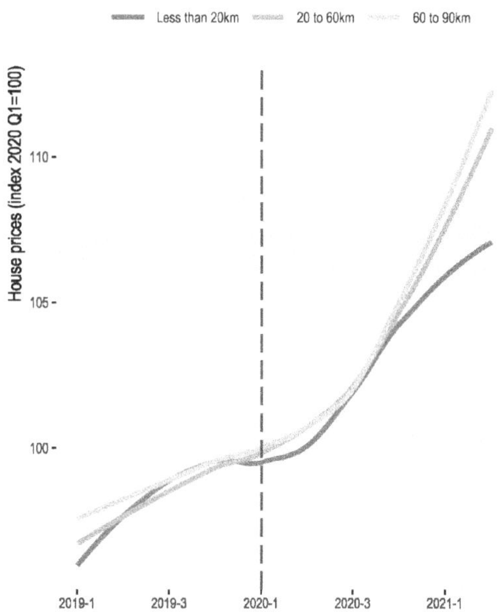

StatLink https://stat.link/xgfpqv

Digitalisation trends in regions

Although the digital gap has been narrowing since the COVID-19 outbreak, people in metropolitan regions experience 40% faster Internet than those in regions far from metropolitan areas.

Internet access and quality are becoming increasingly important in people's lives as many jobs, learning opportunities and public services transition or emerge in the digital world. The demand for communications infrastructure, already growing strong pre-pandemic, accelerated with the mobility restrictions and social distancing measures imposed in the wake of COVID-19. In December 2020, the OECD area saw a record increase of 21 million new high-speed broadband subscriptions. Similarly, businesses have increased demand for communications networks to support new digital applications and businesses (OECD, 2022). While the increased demand for digital infrastructure is contributing to closing some of the regional digital divides, regions and cities are still unequally equipped to make the most of digitalisation.

On average across OECD regions, 85% of households benefitted from access to broadband Internet in 2021. Nevertheless, in countries with overall low levels of broadband access, regional gaps were stark. While the average gap in access to broadband Internet between the better-off and worse-off regions in the same country was around 10 pp, in countries such as Chile, Israel, Japan and Mexico, regional gaps were above 20 pp (Figure 4.13). In those countries, some regions with one-third of the population or more lacking access to basic Internet are driving the digital gap.

Beyond access to basic digital infrastructure, high-speed Internet is also crucial to leveraging social and economic opportunities of digitalisation such as teleworking and new business processes and models. In the first quarter of 2022, people living in metropolitan areas experienced, on average, 40% faster fixed Internet connections than those in regions far from metropolitan areas. Differences by type of region were the highest in Canada and Switzerland (above 40 pp) – although, in the regions of those countries, Internet speed was similar to or higher than the OECD average. Conversely, regions in Greece, Mexico and Türkiye, with relatively small gaps across types of regions, experienced speeds between 60% and 80% slower than the OECD average (Figure 4.14). Overall, a metropolitan vs. non-metropolitan digital divide is present in all OECD countries. However, the quality of connection in non-metropolitan regions (both regions near metropolitan areas and regions far from metropolitan areas) has been improving over the past 3 years as average speeds increased by around 110% in those regions, approximately 18 pp above the rate of metropolitan regions.

In 2021 Q1, Internet speed was also very unequal across cities (FUAs of 50 000 people or more) of OECD countries. Cities with Internet speed 50% above the OECD average are concentrated in Canada, Chile, France, Spain and the US, while many cities with underperforming Internet (50% below the OECD average) are located in Australia, Colombia, Germany, Greece, Mexico and Türkiye. Inequalities across cities can be stark also within the same country. In Chile, France, Italy, New Zealand and the US, the digital gap between the better-off and worse-off city was at least 80 pp (Figures 4.16-4.17).

Digitalisation also affects the labour market, where digital skills are becoming a prerequisite for many jobs. Employers' demands for general and advanced information and communication technology (ICT) skills are high in most OECD countries. In three-quarters of OECD regions, more than 15% of posted job vacancies require advanced ICT proficiency (e.g. programming and related skills) and a further 15% require general ICT proficiency (e.g. word processing, spreadsheet and Internet skills). Belgium, Portugal and the US have some regions with the highest demand for advanced ICT skills but also some regions with very low demand for advanced ICT skills, leading to large within-country differences. In the majority of OECD countries with multiple regions (16 out of 24), capital regions have the highest demand for advanced ICT skills (Figure 4.15).

Definitions

Broadband Internet refers to a download speed of at least 256 kilobits per second.

High-speed Internet corresponds to a download speed of at least 30 megabits per second (Mbps).

Internet download speed estimates, measured in Mbps, are based on user-performed tests from Speedtest by Ookla (Ookla, 2021). As such, data may be subject to testing biases (e.g. fast connections being tested more frequently) or to strategic testing by Internet service providers in specific markets. As speed-testing methodologies can vary across test providers (OECD, 2022), indicators at the regional level are presented as deviations from the OECD average (in %) or as changes over time (in %).

The percentage of vacancies that require ICT skills is based on job posting data provided by Emsi Burning Glass (Emsi Burning Glass, 2021). Advertised jobs with advanced ICT skills have ad keywords related to programming languages or database manipulation whereas those with general ICT skills have ad keywords related to the general Internet, spreadsheet or word processing software.

Sources

See country metadata in Annex B.

Emsi Burning Glass (2021), *Emsi Burning Glass Data Basic Overview https://kb.emsidata.com/methodology/emsi-data-basic-overview/.*

OECD (2022), "Broadband networks of the future", *OECD Digital Economy Papers*, No. 327, OECD Publishing, Paris, *https://doi.org/10.1787/755e2d0c-en.*

Ookla (2021), *Speedtest by Ookla Global Fixed and Mobile Network Performance Map Tiles, https://registry.opendata.aws/speedtest-global-performance/.*

Figure notes

4.14, 4.16-4.17: Average download peak speed tests, weighted by the number of tests, as the percentage deviation from the regional average across 36 OECD countries (Costa Rica and Israel excluded).

4.13. Regional difference in access to broadband Internet, 2021

Large regions (TL2)

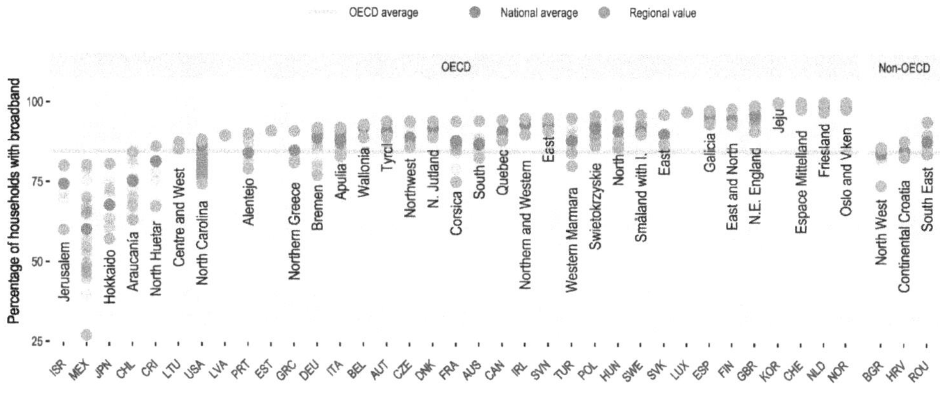

StatLink https://stat.link/kwhi4m

4.14. Disparities in fixed download speeds, 2022 Q1

Percentage deviation from OECD average, by type of region, weighted averages of small regions (TL3)

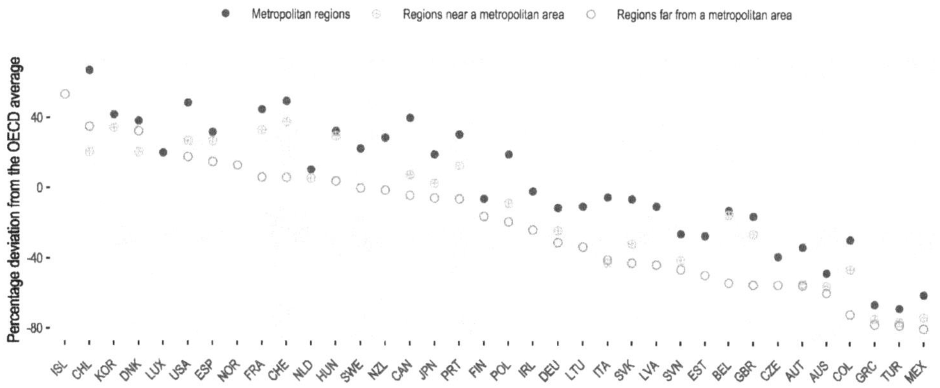

StatLink https://stat.link/761u9h

4.15. Employer demands for advanced ICT skills, 2021 Q3

ICT vacancies as a percentage of all job vacancies posted on line, large regions (TL2)

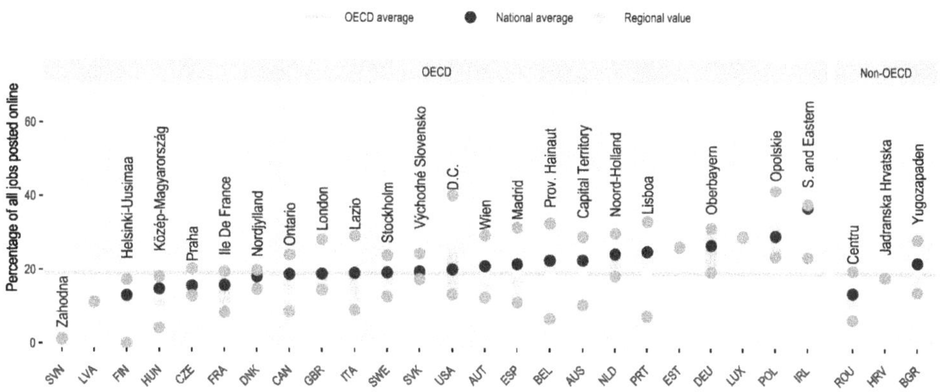

StatLink https://stat.link/stx4gc

4.16. Internet speed in cities, 2021 Q1 – Americas

Percentage deviation relative to OECD average (weighted), FUAs of 50 000 inhabitants or more

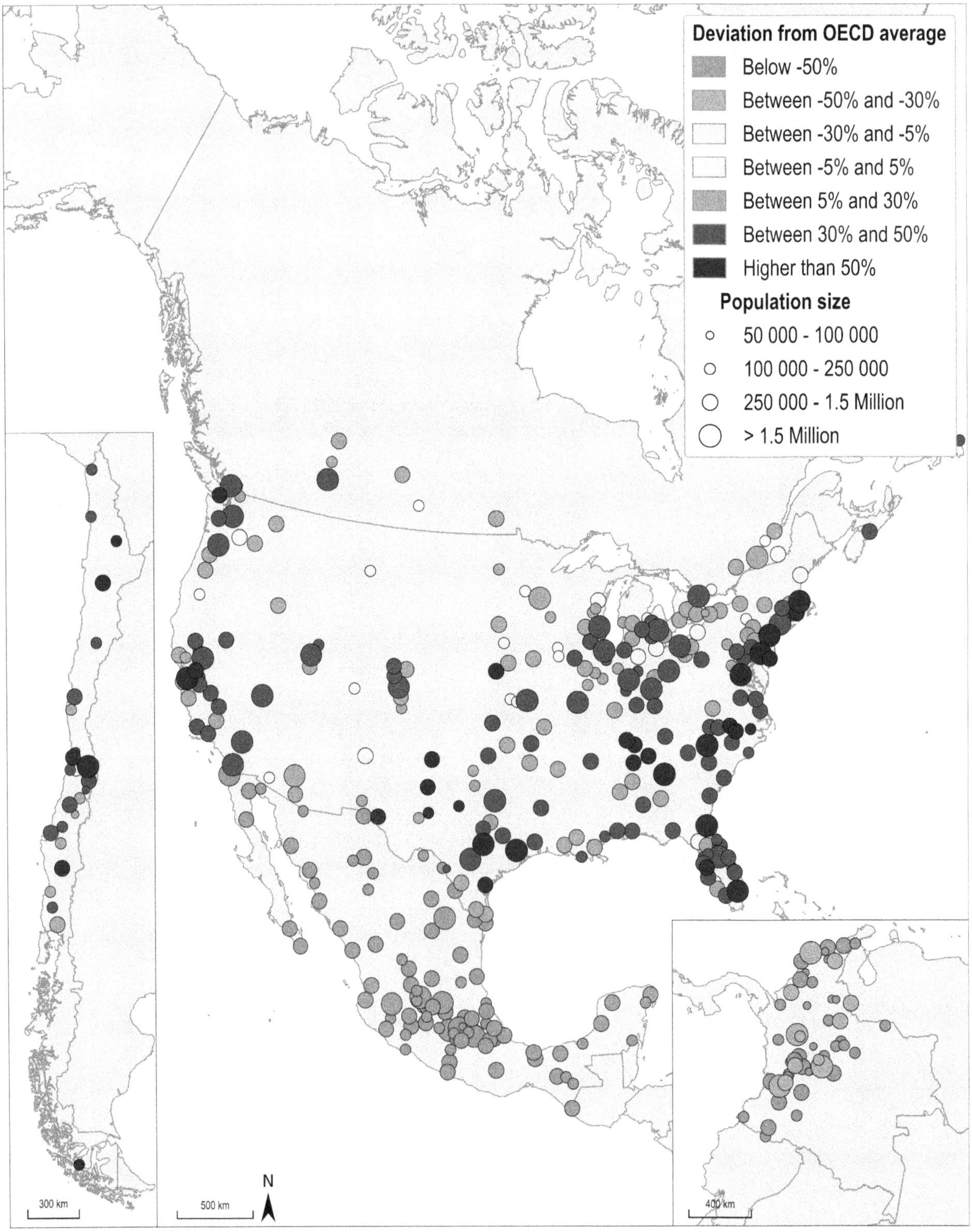

StatLink https://stat.link/8c4mil

4.17. Internet speed in cities, 2021 Q1 – Europe and Asia-Pacific

Percentage deviation relative to OECD average (weighted), FUAs of 50 000 inhabitants or more

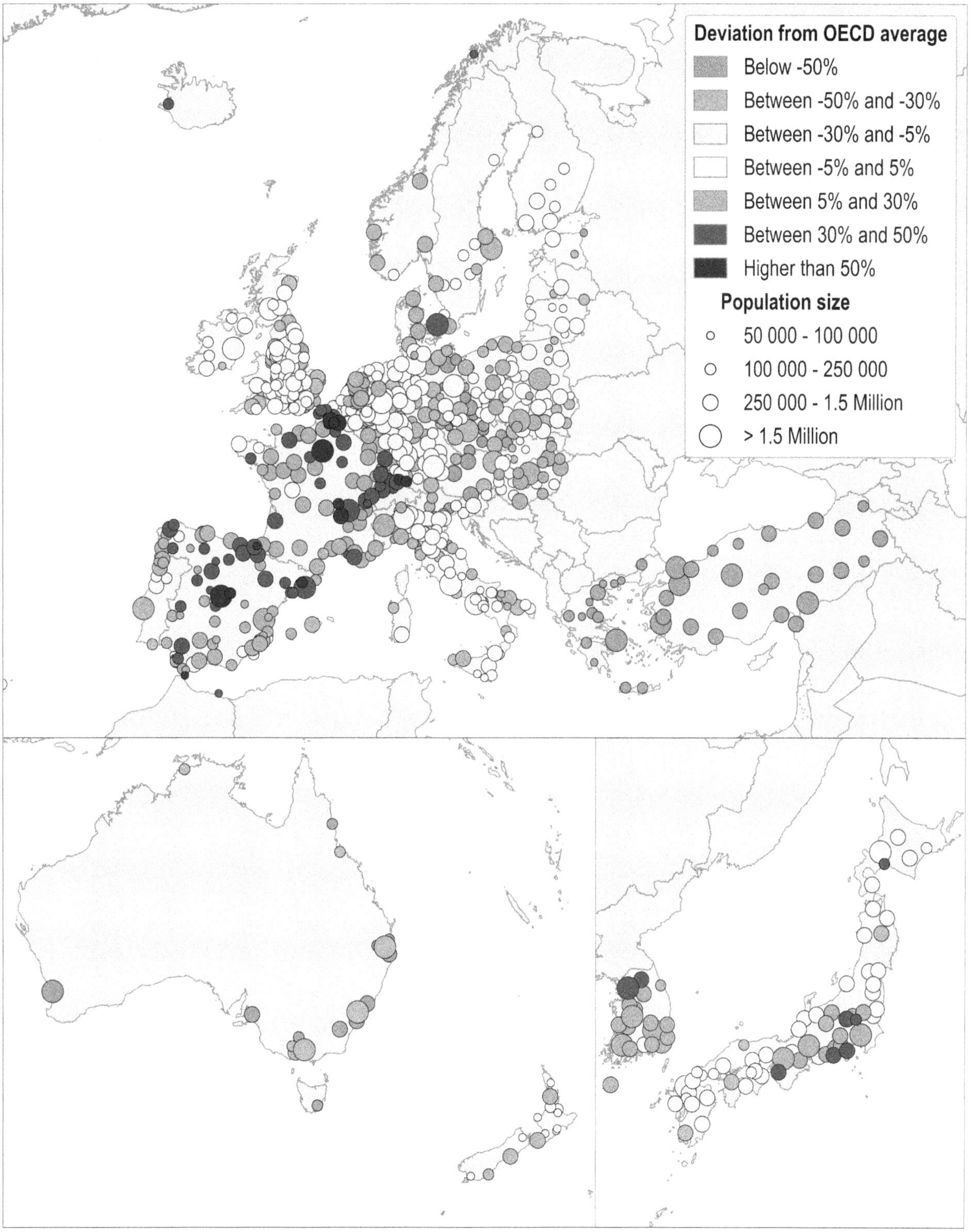

StatLink https://stat.link/4i2gln

ANNEX A

Defining regions, cities and metropolitan areas

Table A.1. **Territorial grid of OECD member countries**

Country	Territorial Level 2 (TL2)	Territorial Level 3 (TL3)
Australia	States/territories (8)	Statistical Areas Level 4 and Greater Capital City Statistical Area (50)
Austria	*Bundesländer* (9)	*Gruppen von Politischen Bezirken* (35)
Belgium	*Régions* (3)	*Arrondissements* (44)
Canada	Provinces and territories (13)	Census divisions (293)
Chile	Regions (16)	*Provincias* (56)
Colombia	*Departamentos* + Capital District (33)	Subregions (158)
Costa Rica	Planning regions (6)	Planning regions (6)
Czech Republic	*Oblasti* (8)	*Kraje* (14)
Denmark	*Regioner* (5)	*Landsdeler* (11)
Estonia	Region (1)	Groups of *maakond* (5)
Finland	*Suuralueet* (5)	*Maakunnat* (19)
France	*Régions* (13) + *Régions d'outre-mer* (5)	*Départements* (96) + *Départements d'outre-mer* (5)
Germany	*Länder* (16)	*Kreise* (401)
Greece	Regions (13)	Regional units and combination of regional units (52)
Hungary	Planning statistical regions (8)	Counties and Budapest (20)
Iceland	Regions (2)	*Landsvaedi* (8)
Ireland	Groups Regional Authority Regions (3)	Regional Authority Regions (8)
Israel	Districts (6)	Districts (6)
Italy	*Regioni* (21)	*Province* (107)
Japan	Groups of prefectures (10)	Prefectures (47)
Korea	Regions (7)	Special city, metropolitan area and province (17)
Latvia	Region (1)	Statistical regions (6)
Lithuania	Group of counties (2)	Counties (10)
Luxembourg	State (1)	State (1)
Mexico	*Estados* (32)	*Grupos de municipios* (209)
Netherlands	Provinces (12)	COROP regions (40)
New Zealand	Regional councils (14)	Regional councils (14)
Norway	*Landsdeler* (7)	*Fylker* (13)
Poland	*Vojewodztwa* (17)	*Podregiony* (73)
Portugal	*Comissaoes de coordenaçao e desenvolvimento regional e regioes autonomas* (7)	*Grupos de municipios* (25)
Slovak Republic	*Zoskupenia krajov* (4)	*Kraj* (8)
Slovenia	*Kohezijske regije* (2)	*Statisticne regije* (12)
Spain	*Comunidades autonomas* (17)/*Ciudades autónomas* (2)	*Provincias* (59)
Sweden	*Riksomraden* (8)	*Län* (21)
Switzerland	*Grandes régions* (7)	*Cantons* (26)
Türkiye	Regions (26)	Provinces (81)
United Kingdom	Regions and countries (12)	Upper-tier authorities or groups of lower-tier authorities or groups of unitary authorities or LECs or groups of districts (179)
United States	States and the District of Columbia (51)	Economic areas (179)

Table A.2. **Territorial grid of selected emerging economies**

Region	Territorial Level 2 (TL2)	Territorial Level 3 (TL3)
Brazil	*Estados + districto federal* (27)	*Mesoregiao* (137)
Bulgaria	Planning regions/*Rayoni za planirane* (6)	*Oblasts/Podregioni* (28)
China	31 provinces; special administrative region of Hong Kong (China), special administrative region of Macao (China) and Chinese Taipei (33)	-
India	States and union territories (36)	-
Malta	State (1)	Islands/*Gzejjer* (2)
Peru	*Departamentos + Provincia Constitucional del Callao* (25)	-
Romania	Regions/*Regiuni* (8)	Counties + Bucharest/*Județe + București* (42)
South Africa	Provinces (9)	-
Tunisia	*Grandes régions* (7)	*Régions* (24)

Table A.3. **Smallest and largest regional population and surface by country, 2021**

Country	Number of TL3 regions	Region with the highest		Region with the lowest		Number of TL2 regions	Region with the highest		Region with the lowest	
		Population	Density	Population	Density		Population	Density	Population	Density
Australia	50	5 361 466	510.1	40 547	0.1	8	8 188 651	183.7	245 909	0.2
Austria	35	1 920 949	4 850.9	20 118	19.9	9	1 920 949	4 850.9	296 010	60.0
Belgium	44	1 229 583	7 590.0	50 476	47.7	3	6 669 426	7 590.0	1 229 583	217.5
Canada	293	2 974 293	4 721.1	708	0.01	13	14 826 276	28.9	39 403	0.02
Chile	56	6 075 403	2 992.8	2 124	0.1	16	8 242 459	538.4	107 737	1.1
Colombia	158	7 834 167	4 794.5	10 409	0.7	33	7 834 167	4 936.5	46 808	0.7
Costa Rica	6	3 189 862	349.2	307 357	39.0	6	3 189 862	349.2	307 357	39.0
Czech Republic	14	1 397 997	2 752.8	293 311	66.9	8	1 704 179	2 752.8	1 110 315	72.0
Denmark	11	903 974	4 592.1	39 660	61.0	5	1 855 084	761.8	590 439	76.5
Estonia	5	613 158	143.4	121 335	13.3	1	1 330 068	30.9	1 330 068	30.9
Finland	19	1 702 678	187.2	30 129	1.9	5	1 702 678	187.2	30 129	6.3
France	101	2 607 879	20 851.6	76 604	3.5	18	12 348 605	1 033.2	288 348	3.5
Germany	401	3 664 088	4 800.7	34 001	35.9	16	17 925 570	4 331.1	680 130	71.4
Greece	52	1 096 665	10 399.0	18 360	10.1	13	3 736 737	986.5	202 371	28.4
Hungary	20	1 723 836	3 380.1	187 574	52.4	8	1 723 836	3 380.1	871 105	63.3
Iceland	8	236 528	226.8	7 108	0.5	2	236 528	228.8	132 264	1.3
Ireland	8	1 423 957	1 541.1	306 702	34.5	3	2 467 483	172.5	884 580	35.4
Israel	6	2 250 600	8 485.5	1 062 600	94.8	6	2 250 600	8 485.5	1 062 600	94.8
Italy	107	4 231 451	2 544.1	81 415	35.8	21	9 981 554	433.1	124 089	38.2
Japan	47	14 010 000	7 315.9	549 000	62.1	10	36 861 000	2 811.2	3 659 000	62.1
Korea	17	13 554 031	15 747.8	365 128	91.3	7	26 054 097	2 225.9	679 882	91.3
Latvia	6	614 618	2 382.2	183 399	12.2	1	1 893 223	29.9	1 893 223	29.9
Lithuania	10	829 983	88.1	90 129	18.6	2	1 965 697	88.1	829 983	36.9
Luxembourg	1	634 730	245.5	634 730	245.5	1	634 730	245.5	634 730	245.5
Mexico	209	8 664 946	7 909.5	8 834	0.7	32	16 992 418	6 298.4	731 391	10.8
Netherlands	40	1 461 412	3 428.0	45 587	142.0	12	3 726 050	1 292.0	385 400	185.2
New Zealand	14	1 715 600	383.3	32 700	1.4	14	1 715 600	383.3	32 700	1.4
Norway	13	1 252 384	1 636.2	0	0.0	7	1 949 394	84.1	0	0.0
Poland	73	1 792 120	3 541.7	184 826	41.1	17	4 450 220	514.7	936 000	57.2
Portugal	25	2 869 033	1 021.0	80 047	13.7	7	3 566 374	1 021.0	242 201	22.5
Slovak Republic	8	827 028	335.0	565 324	68.1	4	1 819 399	335.0	677 024	82.4
Slovenia	12	555 948	238.8	53 254	37.2	2	1 105 046	128.5	1 003 931	89.6
Spain	59	6 755 828	6 001.6	11 475	8.7	19	8 502 216	6 001.6	83 517	25.4
Sweden	21	2 391 990	366.6	60 124	2.6	8	2 391 990	366.6	375 709	3.4
Switzerland	26	1 553 423	5 464.9	16 293	28.3	7	1 895 693	939.2	350 986	105.8
Türkiye	81	15 462 452	2 979.9	81 910	11.3	26	15 462 452	2 979.9	785 265	26.4
United Kingdom	179	1 196 000	17 093.5	22 300	5.7	12	9 217 200	5 774.6	1 895 500	70.4
United States	179	24 161 801	626.7	79 466	0.5	51	39 237 836	4 214.2	578 803	0.5
OECD average	64	3 966 891	4 276.8	151 449	34.4	11	7 567 772	2 026.2	667 223	52.3

Figure A.1. **Extended regional typology**

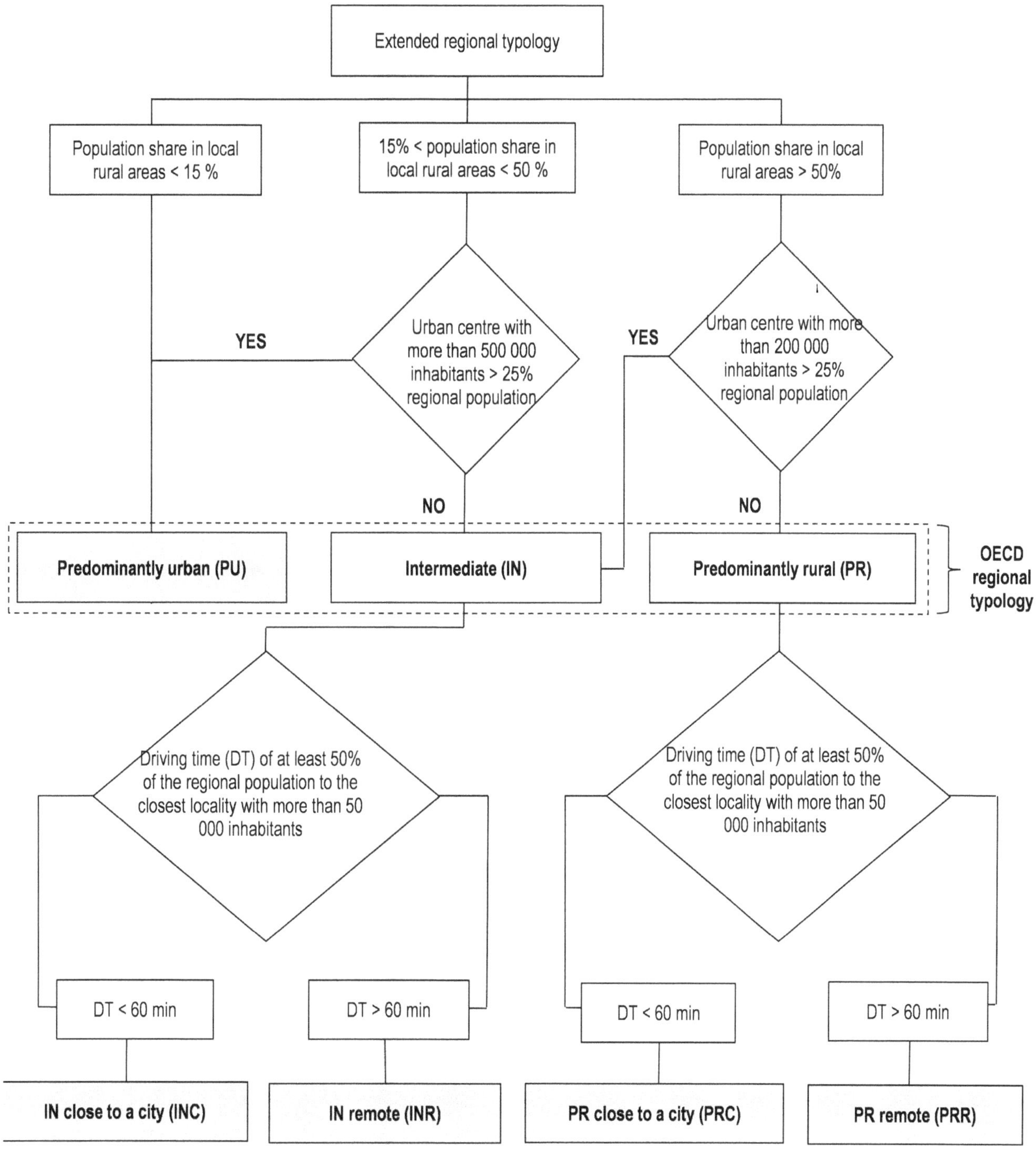

Source: Source: Brezzi, M., L. Dijkstra and V. Ruiz (2011), “OECD Extended Regional Typology: The Economic Performance of Remote Rural Regions”, OECD Regional Development Working Papers, 2011/06, OECD Publishing. *http://dx.doi.org/10.1787/5kg6z83tw7f4-en*.

Figure A.2. **Methodology to define the functional urban areas (FUAs)**

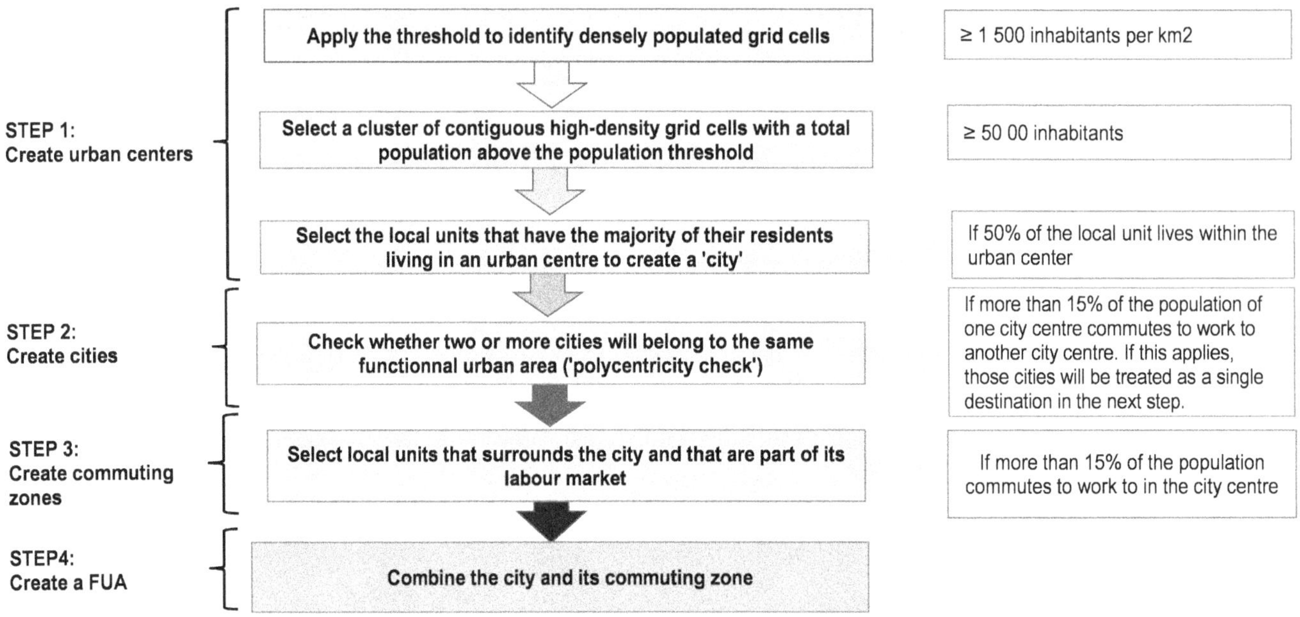

Source: Dijkstra, L., H. Poelman and P. Veneri (2019), "The EU-OECD definition of a functional urban area", OECD Regional Development Working Papers, No. 2019/11, OECD Publishing, Paris, *https://doi.org/10.1787/d58cb34d-en*.

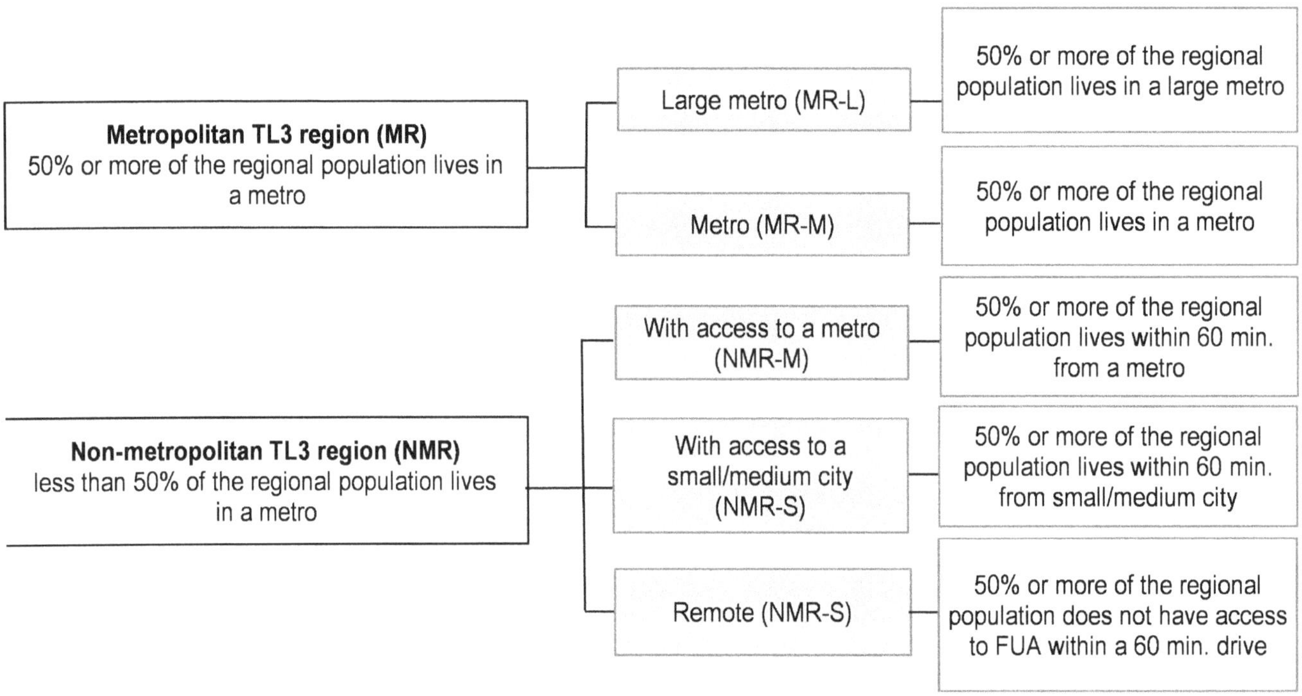

Source: Fadic, M., et al. (2019), "Classifying small (TL3) regions based on metropolitan population, low density and remoteness", OECD Regional Development Working Papers, No. 2019/06, OECD Publishing, Paris, https://doi.org/10.1787/b902cc00-en.

Table A.4. **Number of metropolitan areas and share of the national population in metropolitan areas, 2022**

Metropolitan areas (FUAs with a population above 250 000 inhabitants)

	Total metropolitan areas		Population between 250 000 and 500 000		Population between 500 000 and 1.5 million		Population above 1.5 million		Rest (non-metropolitan)
Country	Number	% of national population	Number	% of national population	Number	% of national population	Number	% of national population	% of national population
Australia	11	74	5	7	2	7.9	4	59.1	26
Austria	6	59.7	3	11.1	2	14.8	1	33.8	40.3
Belgium	7	60	2	4.5	4	26.8	1	28.7	40
Canada	16	66.5	4	3.7	7	15.1	5	47.7	33.5
Chile	10	65.5	6	10.9	3	13.4	1	41.2	34.5
Colombia	22	56.8	8	5.4	10	14.9	4	36.5	43.2
Czech Republic	4	37.3	1	3.2	2	13.4	1	20.7	62.7
Germany	67	68.2	39	16.8	20	20.3	8	31	31.8
Denmark	4	54.7	2	12.1	1	9.1	1	33.5	45.3
Spain	26	55.4	13	9.7	9	13.3	4	32.4	44.6
Estonia	1	30.1	1	30.1	0	0	0	0	69.9
Finland	4	47.8	3	19.7	0	0	1	28	52.2
France	46	56.5	29	14.7	14	17.3	3	24.5	43.5
United Kingdom	46	69	25	13.7	15	18	6	37.3	31
Greece	2	42.7	0	0	1	9.8	1	33	57.3
Hungary	5	42.4	4	11.6	0	0	1	30.8	57.6
Ireland	2	49.3	1	8.9	0	0	1	40.4	50.7
Italy	24	40.8	11	6.3	9	10.5	4	24	59.2
Japan	54	78.9	18	5.2	30	19	6	54.6	21.1
Korea	20	80	8	4.9	8	13	4	62	20
Lithuania	2	29.8	1	10.4	1	19.4	0	0	70.2
Luxembourg	1	100	0	0	1	100	0	0	0
Latvia	1	48.5	0	0	1	48.5	0	0	51.5
Mexico	64	61.3	27	7.5	27	18.2	10	35.6	38.7
Netherlands	16	66	11	22.6	3	16.2	2	27.2	34
Norway	4	46.7	3	19.9	1	26.8	0	0	53.3
New Zealand	3	51.5	1	8.8	1	9.8	1	32.9	48.5
Poland	19	42.1	10	9.7	7	17.3	2	15	57.9
Portugal	3	44.3	1	2.6	1	12.4	1	29.3	55.7
Slovak Republic	1	8.3	1	8.3	0	0	0	0	91.7
Slovenia	1	14	1	14	0	0	0	0	86
Sweden	5	45.8	2	5.5	2	17.1	1	23.3	54.2
Switzerland	5	39.6	2	9.9	3	29.7	0	0	60.4
Türkiye	20	43.5	4	1.7	11	11.5	5	30.3	56.5
United States	165	71.9	70	7.5	60	15.4	35	49	28.1

ANNEX B

Sources and data description

List of variables

Variables used	Chapter(s)
Agricultural droughts	2
Cultural employment	1
Cultural services spending by subnational government	1
Electricity indicators	2
Forest fires	2
Greenhouse gas (GHG) emissions	2
Green areas	2
Gross domestic product (GDP) per capita	2
Hospital beds	1
Hospital accessibility	4
Housing expenditure as a share of household disposable income	4
Housing prices	4
Income distribution: relative poverty rates and S80/S20 ratios	4
Internet: broadband connections in households	4
Internet: download speed from fixed devices	4
Information and communication technology (ICT) jobs vacancies	4
Labour productivity: gross value added (GVA) and employment at place of work	1
Life expectancy at birth	4
Municipal waste	3
Population by degree of urbanisation	3
Population: exposure to floods	2
Population: migrants	3
Population: mobility among regions	3
Population projections	3
Private motor vehicles	3
Quarterly labour force	1
Remote work uptake	4
Tourism: flight passengers	1
Tourism: overnight stays	1
Trade openness	1

Agricultural droughts

Country	Source	Year	Territorial level
All countries	Copernicus Climate Data Store ERA5-Land monthly average data product. See methodology in Annex C	1981-2021	2, 3, FUA

Cultural employment

Country	Source	Year	Territorial Level
EU countries	Eurostat, Cultural employment by NUTS regions, main job, table CULT_EMP_REG	2020	2
Australia	Australian Census, 2016	2016	2
Canada	Mexican National Survey of Occupation and Employment, 2019 Quarter 4	2019	2
United States	OECD calculations on Census Bureau, American Community Survey (ACS)	2019	2

Cultural services spending by subnational government

Country	Source	Year	Territorial Level
OECD countries	OECD National Accounts, General Governments Accounts – Government expenditure by function (COFOG)	2019	1

Electricity indicators

Country	Source	Year	Territorial level
All countries	Byers, L. et al. (2021), *A Global Database of Power Plants*, *https://datasets.wri.org/dataset/globalpowerplantdatabase*. Dunnett, S. et al. (2020), "Harmonised global datasets of wind and solar farm locations and power", *Scientific Data*, Vol. 7/130, *https://doi.org/10.1038/s41597-020-0469-8*.	2019	2, 3

Forest fires

Country	Source	Year	Territorial level
All countries	Joint Research Centre's (JRC) Global wildfire dataset for the analysis of fire regimes and fire behaviours, based on MODIS burned area product Collection 6. See methodology in Annex C	2001-20	2

Greenhouse gas (GHG) emissions

Country	Source	Year	Territorial level
All countries	Emissions Database for Global Atmospheric Research (EDGAR), version 6.0 of the European Commission (EC) JRC. See methodology in Annex C	1998-2018	2, 3

Green areas

Country	Source	Year	Territorial level
All countries	ESA Worldcover data, which provides worldwide landcover data for 2020. See methodology in Annex C	2020	FUA

GDP per capita

Country	Source	Territorial level (last available year)
EU countries[1,2]	Eurostat, Regional economic accounts	2 (2020), 3 (2020)
Australia	Australian Bureau of Statistics, 5220.0. Gross state product, figures based on fiscal year (July-June)	2 (2020)
Canada	Statistics Canada, Provincial economic accounts	2 (2020)
Chile	Banco central de Chile. Cuentas nacionales de Chile	2 (2021)
Colombia	DANE, Directorate of Synthesis and National Accounts	2 (2020)
Costa Rica[2]	n.a.	-
Iceland[2]	n.a.	-
Israel[2]	n.a.	-
Japan	Economic and Social Research Institute, Cabinet Office, data are based on fiscal year (April-March)	2 and 3 (2018)
Korea	Korean National Statistical Office	2 and 3 (2020)
Mexico	INEGI, System of national accounts of Mexico	2 (2020)
New Zealand	Statistics New Zealand	2 and 3 (2020)
Norway	Norwegian Regional Accounts	2 and 3 (2019)
Switzerland	Swiss Federal Statistical Office, Statweb	2 and 3 (2019)
Türkiye	Turkish Statistical Institute (TurkStat)	2 and 3 (2020)
United States	Bureau of Economic Analysis	2 (2021), 3 (2020)

1. EU countries: TL3 last available year 2019 for AUT, DEU, ESP, FIN, GRC, IRL, ITA, LTU, LVA and POL.
2. Costa Rica, Iceland and Israel: data not available at the regional level.

Hospital accessibility

Country	Source	Year	Territorial level
EU countries,[1] Norway and Switzerland	Eurostat, Locations of Healthcare Services in Europe data, *https://ec.europa.eu/eurostat/web/gisco/geodata/reference-data/healthcare-services*	2020	3
Australia	Australia Institute of Health and Welfare (AIHW), *https://www.aihw.gov.au/reports-data/myhospitals/themes/hospital-access#more-data*	2022	3
Canada	Statistic Canada - The Open Database of Healthcare Facilities (ODHF), *https://www.statcan.gc.ca/en/lode/databases/odhf*	2020	3
Chile	Open Street Map, 'hospital' amenities (extracted in March 2022)	2022	3
Colombia	Open Street Map, 'hospital' amenities (extracted in March 2022)	2022	3
Costa Rica	Open Street Map, 'hospital' amenities (extracted in March 2022)	2022	3
Iceland	Open Street Map, 'hospital' amenities (extracted in March 2022)	2022	3
Israel	Open Street Map, 'hospital' amenities (extracted in March 2022)	2022	3
Japan	Open Street Map, 'hospital' amenities (extracted in March 2022)	2022	3
Korea	Data was sent to the OECD by the Ministry of Land, Infrastructure and Transport (MOLIT)	2021	3
Mexico	Open Street Map, 'hospital' amenities (extracted in March 2022)	2022	3
New Zealand	Open Street Map, 'hospital' amenities (extracted in March 2022)	2022	3
Türkiye	Open Street Map, 'hospital' amenities (extracted in March 2022)	2022	3
United Kingdom	Open Street Map, 'hospital' amenities (extracted in March 2022)	2022	3
United States	Homeland Infrastructure Foundation-Level Data (HIFLD)	2022	3

1. EU countries: Data collected from Eurostat except for EST and GRC (Open Street Map).

Hospital beds

Country	Source	Year	Territorial level
EU27, Norway and Switzerland[1]	Eurostat, table EU-hlth_rs_bdsrg	2020	2
Australia[2]	Australian Institute of Health and Welfare (AIHW), for Public Hospitals: Australia Hospital Statistics (cat. no. 4390.0)	2016	2
Canada[3]	Canadian Institute for Health Information, Hospital Beds Staffed and In Operation	2020	2
Chile	INE, Chile; Department of health statistics and information (DEIS), Ministry of health (MINSAL)	2021	2
Colombia	Special Register of Health Services Providers (REPS), Ministry of Health and Social Protection	2020	2
Costa Rica	n.a.	-	-
Iceland	n.a.	-	-
Israel	Central Bureau of Statistics Israel. Ministry of Health of Israel, Health Information Department	2020	2
Japan	Statistics Bureau, Survey of Medical Institutions, MHLW Japan	2020	2
Korea	Statistics Korea. Data provided by the country delegate of the WPTI	2020	2 and 3
Mexico	INEGI; Departamento de Estadísticas de Salud; Estadísticas de Salud en Establecimientos Particulares. Ministry of health	2020	2
New Zealand	n.a.	-	-
Norway	Statistics Norway, Geir Hjemas	2020	2 and 3
Switzerland	Federal Statistical Office (FSO), Neuchâtel; Swiss Medical Association (FMH), Bern; Medical Statistics of Physicians, yearly census	2017	2 and 3
Türkiye	Ministry of Health, General Directorate of Health Research, Health Statistics Yearbook	2018	2
United Kingdom	NHS UK; Beds open overnight and day, Welsh Government, Northern Ireland Health department, ISD Scotland	2020	2
United States	Area Health Resources Files, AHA Annual Survey	2018	2

1. EU27 countries: Latest available year 2021 for BEL and IRL; 2019 for DEU, DNK, LUX and LVA; 2018 for BGR, EST, FIN, GRC, HRV, ROU. 2. Australia: Average available beds count from public hospital and private hospital. Private hospital includes both private acute and/or psychiatric hospitals and free-standing day hospital facilities. Available beds are those immediately available (occupied and unoccupied) for the care of admitted patients as required. In the case of free-standing day hospital facilities, they include chairs, trolleys, recliners and cots and are used mainly for post-surgery recovery purposes only.
2. Canada: Beds and cribs available and staffed to provide services to inpatients at the required type and level of service at the beginning of the fiscal year. When the number of hospital beds staffed and in operation is not available, calculations are made based on other methods, such as rated bed capacity. Bassinets set up outside the nursery and used for infants other than new borns are included.

Housing expenditure as a share of household disposable income

Country	Source	Year	Territorial level
Australia	Australia Bureau Statistics; Table 4130.0	2017	2
Austria	Statistics Austria, EU-SILC	2019	2
Belgium	Household Budget Survey (HBS). Calculation based on data from the Institute of National Accounts	2019	2
Canada	Statistics Canada; CANSIM, Table 203-0022	2016	2
Costa Rica	INEC	2018	2
Denmark	Statistics Denmark; Household Budget Survey, Tables FU51 and FU6	2016	2
Finland	Statistics Finland; Table ktutk_003_201600	2016	2
Germany	Statistical Offices of the Federal States, Spatial Monitoring System of the BBSR	2018	2
Ireland	Household Budget Survey, Tables HS067 and HS068	2015	2
Israel	Central Bureau of Statistics Israel, Household Expenditure survey	2015	2
Latvia	CSB Official statistics *https://data.stat.gov.lv/pxweb/en/OSP_PUB/START__POP__MA__MAI/MAI010/*	2020	2
Netherlands	Statistics Netherlands	2018	2
Portugal	Statistics Portugal, Household Budget Survey	2020	2
Slovak Republic	Statistical Office of the SR, Household Budget Survey	2020	2
Slovenia	SURS (EU-SILC)	2020	2
United Kingdom	Office for National Statistics; Table A35	2016	2

Housing prices

Country	Source	Period covered	Geographical units
Austria	Statistik Austria	2019 Q1-2021 Q2	955 municipalities
Belgium	National Bank of Belgium, *https://www.nbb.be/en*	2019 Q1-2021 Q2	532 municipalities
Denmark	Statistics Denmark	2019 Q1-2021 Q2	582 postal codes
Estonia	Estonian Land Board transactions database	2019 Q1-2021 Q2	45 Towns + 13 District
Finland	Statistics Finland	2019 Q1-2021 Q2	225 municipalities
France	*Demande de valeurs foncières* (data.gouv.fr)	2019 Q1-2021 Q2	1 571 communes + 273 districts
Germany	Vdp Research	2019 Q1-2021 Q2	4 413 postal codes + 121 districts
Hungary	Hungarian Central Statistics Office	2019 Q1-2021 Q2	2 889 Settlements + 23 Districts
Ireland	Property Services Regulatory Authority	2019 Q1-2021 Q2	119 local electoral areas + 331 communes
Korea	MOLIT	2019 Q1-2021 Q2	250 municipalities
Mexico	Sociedad Hipotecária Federal (SHF)	2019 Q1-2021 Q2	10705 zip codes
Norway	Statistics Norway	2019 Q1-2021 Q2	56 large municipalities + 11 counties
Portugal	Confidencial Imobiliário	2019 Q1-2021 Q2	1 222 parishes
Spain	Spain municipal data (Source: INE); Spanish District data for Barcelona and Madrid (Source: Centro de information estadistica del notariado)	2019 Q1-2021 Q2	5 400 municipalities (+31 districts)
Sweden	Svensk Mäklarstatistik	2019 Q1-2021 Q2	275 municipalities
United Kingdom	UK Government Price Paid data	2019 Q1-2021 Q2	8 382 postcode sectors
United States	Zillow Research Institute	2019 Q1-2021 Q2	29 827 zip codes

ICT jobs vacancies

Country	Source	Year	Territorial level
All countries	OECD calculation based on EMSI Burning Glass	2021 Q1	2

Income distribution: relative poverty rates and S80/S20 ratios

Country	Source	Year	Territorial Level
Australia	Luxembourg Income Study Database (LIS), based on Australian Bureau of Statistics (ABS) - Survey of Income and Housing (SIH)	2018	2
Austria	Luxembourg Income Study Database (LIS), based on Statistics Austria - Survey on Income and Living Conditions (SILC)	2019	2
Belgium	Eurostat, at-risk-of-poverty rate by NUTS regions table ilc_li41, and LIS	2021	2
Canada	Statistics Canada - Canadian Income Survey (CIS)	2017	2
Chile	Luxembourg Income Study Database (LIS), based on Ministry of Social Development - National Socio-Economic Characterization Survey (CASEN)	2017	2
Colombia	Luxembourg Income Study Database (LIS), based on National Administrative Department of Statistics (DANE) - Great Integrated Household Survey (GEIH)	2020	2
Costa Rica	n.a.	-	-
Czech Republic	Eurostat, at-risk-of-poverty rate by NUTS regions table ilc_li41, and EU-SILC	2021	2
Denmark	Eurostat, at-risk-of-poverty rate by NUTS regions table ilc_li41, and LIS	2021	2
Estonia	Eurostat, at-risk-of-poverty rate by NUTS regions table ilc_li41, and EU-SILC	2021	2
Finland	EU-SILC based on Statistics Finland - Income Distribution Survey (IDS); Survey on Income and Living Conditions (SILC)	2020	2
France	EU-SILC based on Centre Maurice Halbwachs; National Institute of Statistics and Economic Studies - Household Budget Survey (BdF)	2019	2
Germany	Luxembourg Income Study Database (LIS), based on German Institute for Economic Research (DIW) - German Socio-Economic Panel (GSOEP)	2017	2
Greece	Eurostat, at-risk-of-poverty rate by NUTS regions table ilc_li41, and EU-SILC	2021	2
Hungary	Eurostat, at-risk-of-poverty rate by NUTS regions table ilc_li41, and EU-SILC	2015	2
Iceland	Eurostat, at-risk-of-poverty rate by NUTS regions table ilc_li41, and EU-SILC	2018	1
Ireland	Eurostat, at-risk-of-poverty rate by NUTS regions table ilc_li41, and LIS	2021	2
Israel	Luxembourg Income Study Database (LIS), based on National Insurance Institute of Israel; Central Bureau of Statistics - Household Expenditure Survey	2018	2
Italy	Eurostat, at-risk-of-poverty rate by NUTS regions table ilc_li41, and EU-SILC	2016	2
Japan[1]	n.a.	-	-
Korea[1]	n.a.	-	-
Latvia	Eurostat, at-risk-of-poverty rate by NUTS regions table ilc_li41, and EU-SILC	2021	1
Lithuania	Eurostat, at-risk-of-poverty rate by NUTS regions table ilc_li41, and LIS	2021	2
Luxembourg	Eurostat, at-risk-of-poverty rate by NUTS regions table ilc_li41, and EU-SILC	2020	1
Mexico	Luxembourg Income Study Database (LIS), based on National Statistical Institute (INEGI) - Household Income and Expenditure Survey (ENIGH)	2018	2
Netherlands	Eurostat, at-risk-of-poverty rate by NUTS regions table ilc_li41	2021	2
New Zealand	n.a.	-	-
Norway[1]	n.a.	-	-
Poland	Eurostat, at-risk-of-poverty rate by NUTS regions table ilc_li41, and LIS	2021	NUTS2
Portugal	Eurostat, at-risk-of-poverty rate by NUTS regions table ilc_li41, and EU-SILC	2020	2
Slovak Republic	Eurostat, at-risk-of-poverty rate by NUTS regions table ilc_li41, and LIS	2020	2
Slovenia	Eurostat, at-risk-of-poverty rate by NUTS regions table ilc_li41	2021	2
Spain	Eurostat, at-risk-of-poverty rate by NUTS regions table ilc_li41, and EU-SILC	2021	2
Sweden	Eurostat, at-risk-of-poverty rate by NUTS regions table ilc_li41, and EU-SILC	2021	2
Switzerland	Eurostat, at-risk-of-poverty rate by NUTS regions table ilc_li41, and LIS	2020	2
Türkiye	TurkStats - Income Distribution and Living Conditions Statistics	2021	2
United Kingdom	Luxembourg Income Study Database (LIS), based on Department for Work and Pensions (DWP); Office for National Statistics (ONS) - Family Resources Survey (FRS)	2018	NUTS1
United States	Luxembourg Income Study Database (LIS), based on Bureau of Labor Statistics (BLS); U.S Census Bureau - Current Population Survey (CPS) - Annual Social and Economic Supplement (ASEC)	2019	TL2

1. JPN, KOR and NOR: No recent subnational data.

Internet: Broadband connections in households

Country	Source	Year	Territorial Level
EU20 countries	Eurostat, Regional information society statistics, table isoc_r_broad_h	2021	2
Australia	Australian Bureau of Statistics (ABS), Household Use of Information Technology, Australia, 2012-13 (cat. no. 8146.0), Financial year	2017	2
Canada	Statistics Canada. CANSIM (database), Table 11-10-0228-01 - Survey of household spending (SHS)	2019	2
Chile	Ministerio de Educación from National Socioeconomic Characterization Survey	2017	2
Colombia	DANE - Survey on Technologies and Communications ENTIC	2020	2
Costa Rica	INEC	2021	2
Iceland	n.a.	..	..
Israel	Central Bureau of Statistics Israel, Household expenditure survey, Table 16	2018	2
Japan	Statistics Bureau, Ministry of Internal Affairs and Communications, Japan	2020	2
Korea	Korean Ministry of Science, ICT and Future Planning - Survey on the Internet Usage (MSIP, KISA)	2021	2
Mexico	INEGI-Módulo, Availability and Use of Information Technologies in Households (MODUTIH)	2021	2
New Zealand	n.a	..	..
Switzerland	Federal Statistical Office of Switzerland (FSO). enquête sur l'utilisation d'Internet par la population	2021	2
Türkiye	Eurostat, Regional information society statistics, table isoc_r_broad_h	2021	2
United Kingdom	Eurostat, Regional information society statistics, table isoc_r_broad_h	2019	2
United States	Census Bureau, American Community Survey (ACS), 1-year estimates, table S1501	2019	2

Internet: Download speed from fixed devices

Country	Source	Year	Territorial level
All countries	OECD calculation based on Speedtest by Ookla Global Fixed and Mobile Network Performance Map Tiles, *https://registry.opendata.aws/speedtest-global-performance*	2019 Q1 - 2021 Q1	3, FUA

Labour productivity: Gross value added (GVA) and employment at place of work

Country	Source	Territorial level (last available year)
EU countries[1, 2]	Eurostat, Regional economic accounts	2 (2020), 3 (2020)
Australia	Australian Bureau of Statistics, cat. no. 5220.0 - Australian National Accounts: State Accounts, and Table 6291.0.55.003 Labour Force	2 (2020)
Canada	Statistics Canada. CANSIM database, Tables 379-0028 Gross domestic product (GDP) at basic prices and 282-0008 Labour force survey estimates (LFS), by North American Industry Classification System	2 (2020)
Chile	Banco central de Chile. Cuentas nacionales de Chile	2 (2021)
Colombia	DANE, Directorate of Synthesis and National Accounts	2 (2020)
Costa Rica[2]	n.a.	-
Iceland[2]	n.a.	-
Israel[2]	n.a.	-
Japan	Economic and Social Research Institute, Cabinet Office, data are based on fiscal year (April-March)	2 and 3 (2016)
Korea	Korean National Statistical Office	2 and 3 (2020)
Mexico	INEGI, System of national accounts of Mexico	2 (2020)
New Zealand	Statistics New Zealand. GDP by industry, per region	2 and 3 (2019)
Norway	Norwegian Regional Accounts	2 and 3 (2019)
Switzerland	Federal Statistical Office (FSO). Gross value added (GVA) by canton and industries (je-e-04.06.02) and Swiss Labour Force Survey - SLFS	2 and 3 (2019)
Türkiye	Turkish Statistical Institute (TurkStat). Employment data from the Household Labour Force Survey	2 and 3 (2020)
United States	Bureau of Economic Analysis. GVA by State and employment by industry (SA25, SA25N)	2 (2020), 3 (2019)

1. EU countries: TL3 last available year 2019 for AUT, DEU, ESP, FIN, GRC, IRL, ITA, LTU, LVA, NLD, POL, PRT and SWE.
2. Costa Rica, Iceland and Israel: Data not available at the regional level.

Life expectancy at birth

Country	Source	Year	Territorial level
EU27, Norway and Switzerland[1]	Eurostat, Regional Demographic Statistics	2020	2
Australia	Australian Bureau of Statistics; Table 3302.0	2019	2
Canada	Statistics Canada; CANSIM, Table 053-0003	2019	2
Chile	INE	2021	2
Colombia	DANE	2021	2
Costa Rica	n.a	-	-
Iceland	n.a.	-	-
Israel	Central Bureau of Statistics	2019	2
Japan	Statistics Bureau of Japan, MIC, Population Census	2015	2
Korea	Statistics Korea; Kosis, Life tables by Provinces	2020	2
Mexico	National Institute of Statistics and Geography (INEGI)	2021	2
New Zealand	Statistics New Zealand	2018	2
Türkiye	Eurostat, Regional Demographic Statistics	2019	2
United States	Measure of America	2019	2

1. EU27 countries: Latest available year 2021 for SWE; 2019 for HRV.

Municipal waste

Country	Source	Last year	Territorial level
Australia	National Waste report	2018	2
Austria	Environment Agency Austria (UBA) - Austrian Federal Waste Management Plan and related Status Reports	2019	2
Belgium	Statbel (Bruxelles data collected from Brussels Environment, Flemish Region data collected from OVAM)	2020	2
Chile	INE, Chile. Pollutant Release and Transfer Register (PRTR) - Registro de Emisiones y Transferencias de Contaminantes (RETC)	2017	2
Colombia	DANE	2019	2
Costa Rica	INEC	2020	2
Czech Republic	Czech Statistical Office CZSO, Annual statistical survey	2020	2
Estonia	Eurostat, Municipal waste (env_rwas_gen)	2013	2
France	Odd-numbered years: Ademe survey data; Even-numbered years: SDES estimates	2019	2
Germany	Waste Statistics of the Federal Statistical Office and the Statistical Offices of the Federal States, Spatial Monitoring System of the BBSR	2020	2
Hungary	HCSO, Hungarian Central Statistical Office	2019	2
Israel	Central Bureau of Statistics Israel	2017	2
Italy	ISPRA (Italian Institute for Environmental Protection and Research)	2020	2
Japan	Ministry of Internal Affairs and Communications	2020	2
Korea	Korean Ministry of Environment	2020	2
Latvia	Official statistics "2-Waste" by Latvian Environment, Geology and Meteorology Agency	2020	2
Luxembourg	Eurostat, Municipal waste (env_rwas_gen)	2013	2
Mexico	INEGI. Censo Nacional de Gobiernos Municipales y Delegacionales 2017	2020	2
Netherlands	Statistics Netherlands	2020	2
Norway	Statistics Norway	2020	2
Poland	Central Statistical Office	2020	2
Portugal	Statistics Portugal, Urban waste statistics	2020	2
Slovak Republic	Statistical Office of the SR statistical survey	2020	2
Slovenia	SURS, Generated amounts	2020	2
Sweden	Swedish Environmental Protection Agency	2020	2
Türkiye	Municipal Waste Statistics Survey	2014	2
United Kingdom	Department for Environment, Food and Rural Affairs, Local Authority Collected Waste Statistics	2020	2
United States	n.a.	-	-

Population by degree of urbanisation

Country	Source	Year	Territorial level
All countries	OECD computation based on Florczyk A.J. et al. (2019), GHSL Data Package 2019, EUR 29788 EN, Publications Office of the European Union, Luxembourg, 2019, ISBN 978-92-76-13186-1, doi:10.2760/290498, JRC 117104.	2000-15	Degree of urbanisation

Population: Exposure to floods

Country	Source	Territorial level
All countries	River Flood Hazard Maps at European and Global Scale, 100-year return period. See methodology in Annex C	2

Population: Migrants

Country	Source	Year	Territorial level
OECD countries	OECD Migrant Municipal Database. OECD (2022), *The Contribution of Migration to Regional Development*, OECD Regional Development Studies, OECD Publishing, Paris, *https://doi.org/10.1787/57046df4-en.*	2017-20	2, 3, degree of urbanisation

Population: Mobility among regions

Country	Source	Year	Territorial level
Australia[1]	Australian Bureau of Statistics (ABS), ABS.Stat	2016-19	3
Austria	Statistics Austria, Migration statistics	2016-19	3
Belgium	FPS Economie/Statistics Belgium	2016-19	3
Canada	Statistics Canada. Cansim table 17-10-0015-01	2016-19	3
Chile	INE, Population and Housing Census	2015-17	3
Colombia	n.a.	-	-
Costa Rica	n.a.	-	-
Czech Republic	Czech Statistical Office CZSO - Immigrants table Code: DEMD130062-6-1/8	2016-19	3
Denmark	Statistics Denmark, StatBank, table FLY66	2016-19	3
Estonia	Statistics Estonia, Statistical database, table RVR07	2016-19	3
Finland	Statistics Finland, Population Statistics, Migration	2016-19	3
France	INSEE, Recensement de la Population	2018	3
Germany	Spatial Monitoring System of the BBSR. Periodic update of population statistics by the Federal Office of Germany and the Statistical Offices of the Federal States	2016-19	3
Greece[2]	n.a.	-	-
Hungary	HCSO, Hungarian Central Statistical Office, Internal migration statistics based on the registration system of home addresses	2016-19	3
Iceland	Statistics Iceland, Internal migration	2016-19	3
Ireland[2]	n.a.	-	-
Israel	Central Bureau of Statistics Israel	2018	3
Italy	Istat, Iscrizioni e cancellazioni anagrafiche (changes of residence from/to Italian municipalities)	2016-19	3
Japan	Statistics Bureau, Migrants by prefecture derived from the Basic Resident Registers	2016-19	3
Korea	Statistics Korea, KOSIS database - Internal Migration Statistics	2016-19	3
Latvia	Central Statistical Bureau of Latvia	2016-19	3
Lithuania	Statistics Lithuania, Data sources – the State Enterprise Centre of Registers, the Population Register; the Ministry of the Interior	2016-19	3
Luxembourg	n.a.	-	-
Mexico	INEGI. Censo de población y vivienda	2015	3
Netherlands	Statistics Netherlands on Statline	2016-19	2
New Zealand[2]	n.a.	-	-
Norway	Statistics Norway. Statbank, table 01222: Population change (M)	2016-19	3
Poland	Central Statistical Office of Poland, PESEL register	2016-19	3
Portugal[2]	n.a.	-	-
Slovak Republic	Statistical Office of the SR	2016-19	3
Slovenia	Statistical Office of the Republic of Slovenia, Ministry of the Interior - Central Population Register, Ministry of the Interior - Administrative Internal Affairs Directorate	2016-19	3
Spain	INE - Data provided by the delegate of the OECD Working Party on Territorial Indicators	2016-19	3
Sweden	Statistics Sweden, Central Office for Administrative and Electronic Public Services registration system	2016-19	3
Switzerland	Swiss Federal Statistical Office, 1990 to 2010: Annual Population Statistics (ESPOP), from 2011 onwards: Population and Households Statistics (STATPOP)	2016-19	3

Population: Mobility among regions *(cont.)*

Country	Source	Year	Territorial level
Türkiye	Turkish Statistical Institute (TurkStat), Address-Based Population Registration System	2016-19	3
United Kingdom[3]	National Statistical Office, Population Estimates	2016-19	3
United States	Census Bureau. County-to-County Migration Flows, 5-year ACS datasets	2017	3

Note: Data refer to domestic migration: inflows and outflows of population from one region to another region of the same country. They do not include international immigration and outmigration.

1. Australia: Regional internal migration covers the movement of people from one location to another within Australia. Regional internal migration estimates (RIME) are prepared for sub-state regions and capture moves over each financial year on an annual basis.
2. Greece, Ireland, New Zealand and Portugal: Recent data not available at the regional level.
3. United Kingdom: Data do not include Northern Ireland and Scotland.

Population projections in regions

Country	Source	Year	Territorial level
EU countries	Eurostat, Population on 1st January by age, sex, type of projection and NUTS 3 region (proj_19rp3)	2020-40	3
Japan	National Institute of Population and Social Security Research; Regional Population Projections for Japan: 2015-2045 (2018)	2020-40	3
Korea	Statistics Korea, KOSIS database	2020-40	3

Population projections in functional urban areas

Country	Source	Year	Territorial level
All countries	Schiavina M., S. Freire and K. MacManus (2022), *GHS-POP R2022A - GHS Population Grid Multitemporal (1975-2030)*, Joint Research Centre (JRC), European Commission	2020-30	FUA

Private motor vehicles

Country	Source	Year	Territorial Level
Australia	Australian Bureau of Statistics (ABS), Motor Vehicle Census (cat. no. 9309.0)	2021	2
Austria	Statistics Austria, Transport statistics	2021	2
Belgium	Statbel and IWEPS computation. *https://statbel.fgov.be/fr/themes/mobilite/circulation/parc-de-vehicules*	2021	2
Canada	Statistics Canada. CANSIM database: Table 23-10-0067-01 Vehicle registrations, by type of vehicle; Electric vehicles OECD estimates based on table 20-10-0025-01 Zero-emission vehicle registrations, quarterly	2019	2
Chile	INE	2020	2
Colombia	DANE -RUNT 2021	2021	2
Costa Rica	n.a.	-	-
Czech Republic	Czech Statistical Office CZSO, Ministry of Transport of the Czech Republic. *www.mdcr.cz*	2020	2
Denmark	Statistics Denmark, StatBank Table BIL707: Stock of vehicles per 1 January by region, passenger cars (for private use, taxis and rental)	2021	2
Estonia	Statistics Estonia	2011	2
Finland	Statistics Finland, Transport and tourism statistics	2020	2
France	MEDDTL (CGDD/SOeS) Fichier central des automobiles. *https://www.statistiques.developpement-durable.gouv.fr/*	2021	2
Germany	Motorist's Federal Office (Kraftfahrt-Bundesamt), Spatial Monitoring System of the BBSR. Private cars	2019	2
Greece	Hellenic Statistical Authority	2020	2

Private motor vehicles *(cont.)*

Country	Source	Year	Territorial Level
Hungary	Hungarian Central Statistical Office. Until 2017: Central Office for Administrative and Electronic Public Services, from 2017 Ministry of Interior - stock of road vehicles	2021	2
Iceland	Iceland road traffic directorate (*www.us.is/umferdarstofa*). Private vehicles, *http://bifreidatolur.samgongustofa.is/?nid=1233*	2014	2
Ireland	CSO Department of Transport, Tourism and Sport. Irish Bulletin of vehicle and driver statistics, Table 5a. Number of Private Cars by CO_2 Emission Band in each Licensing Authority Area, *http://www.dttas.ie*	2020	2
Israel	Central Bureau of Statistics Israel	2019	2
Italy	Automobile club d'Italia	2020	2
Japan	Ministry of Internal Affairs and Communications	2013	2
Korea	Ministry of Land, Infrastructure and Transport	2021	2
Latvia	CSB Directorate of Road Traffic Safety	2021	2
Lithuania	State Enterprise Regitra, Register of Road Motor Vehicles of the Republic of Lithuania	2020	2
Luxembourg	..	2012	2
Mexico	INEGI. Statistics of Motor Vehicles Registered in Circulation; Administrative record of the light vehicle automotive industry	2020	2
Netherlands	CBS, datasets 70072ned and 71405ned	2020	2
New Zealand	n.a.	-	-
Norway	Statistics Norway: Tables 07849 and 11823	2020	2
Poland	Ministry of Interior of Poland, Central Register of Vehicles	2020	2
Portugal	Institute of Registries and Notaries	2020	2
Slovak Republic	Ministry of Interior of the SR	2021	2
Slovenia	Statistical Office of the Republic of Slovenia (SURS), the Central Register of Vehicles and Traffic Documents (MRVL) by the Ministry of Infrastructure (MZI)	2020	2
Spain	Govierno de España, Ministerio del Interior, Direción General de Tráfico. Parque de vehículos por provincias y tipos. *http://www.dgt.es/portal/ca/seguridad_vial/estadistica/parque_vehiculos/por_provincia_y_tipo_parque/*	2005	2
Sweden	Statistics Sweden, Registered vehicles, table START__TK__TK1001__TK1001A	2021	2
Switzerland	Federal Statistical Office (FSO), Federal Roads Office (FEDRO): Stock of road vehicles (MFZ)	2021	2
Türkiye	Data sent by the Türkiye delegate of the OECD Working Party on Territorial Indicators	2014	2
United Kingdom	Office for National Statistics, United Kingdom Ministerial Department for Transport statistics	2020	2
United States	Federal Highway Administration. State Motor-Vehicle Registrations. Private and commercial automobiles (including taxicabs), *http://www.fhwa.dot.gov/policyinformation/statistics.cfm*	2020	2

Quarterly labour force

Country	Source	Last available quarter	Territorial Level
Australia	ABS 6291.0.55.001 Labour Force, Australia, Detailed. Table 02 and Table 03 (youth data); ages 15+ and 15-24	2022 Q2	2
Austria	Austrian Micro census - Labour Force Survey Quarterly Data N, Q, Smetadata; ages 15+ and 15-24	2022 Q2	2
Belgium	StatBel. Active (working and unemployed) population since 2017 based on the reformed Labour Force Survey, by quarter, region, age class and level of education; ages 15-64 and 15-24	2022 Q1	2
Canada	Statistics Canada. Table 14-10-0017-01 Labour force characteristics by sex and detailed age group, monthly, unadjusted for seasonality (x 1 000); ages 15+ and 15-24	2022 Q2	2

Quarterly labour force *(cont.)*

Country	Source	Last available quarter	Territorial Level
Chile	Chilean National Statistical Institute. National Labour Force Survey (ENE). Unemployment rate; ages 15+.	2022 Q2	2
Colombia	DANE Gran encuesta integrada de hogares - Ciudades (23) data; ages 15+	2022 Q2	2
Costa Rica	INEC-Costa Rica. Encuesta Continua de Empleo (ECE). Temas especiales de empleo. Sinopsis de la condición de actividad de las regiones de planificación; ages 15+	2022 Q2	2
Czech Republic	Source: LFS - labour force survey. Table Code: ZAM01-A/13; ages 15+	2022 Q1	2
Denmark	Statistics Denmark. AKU120K and AKU121K: Labour force status by employment status and region; ages 15-64	2022 Q2	2
Estonia	Statistika andmebaas – tables: TT467 - Labour status of population aged 15-74 by region (quarters); TT497 - Youth employment rate; TT468 - Youth participation rate	2022 Q2	2
Finland	137i -- Population aged 15-74 by labour force status, sex and major region, quarterly data, 2012Q1-2022Q2 - 11c9 -- Population aged 15-74 by labour force status, sex and major region, quarterly data	2022 Q2	2
France	Localised unemployment rates ; ages 15+	2022 Q1	2
Germany	n.a.		-
Greece	Hellenic Statistical Authority. Labour force (Quarterly data) - Table 02B. Population 15+ (employment status, region)	2022 Q2	2
Hungary	Economic Activity Measures of Population Aged 15-74 by Sex Non-institutional population. Table LD4F04	2022 Q2	2
Iceland	Statistics Iceland; ages 16-74	2022 Q2	2
Ireland	CSO - QLF08 - Persons aged 15 years and over; QLF07 - Persons aged 15-89 years in Employment	2022 Q2	2
Israel	CBS; ages 15+	2022 Q2	2
Italy	ISTAT Unemployment rate: Regional data - age; ages 15+ and 15-24	2022 Q2	2
Japan	Labour Force Survey/Basic Tabulation Historical data; ages 15+	2022 Q2	2
Korea	Statistics Korea, Economically Active Population Survey - Summary of economically active pop. by city & province/gender (table DT_1ES3B01S); ages 15+ and 15-24	2022 Q2	2
Latvia	DotStat Short Term Labour statistics; ages 15+ and 15-24	2022 Q2	1
Lithuania	DotStat Short Term Labour statistics; ages 15+ and 15-24	2022 Q2	1
Luxembourg	DotStat Short Term Labour statistics; ages 15+ and 15-24	2022 Q2	1
Mexico	INEGI. Encuesta Nacional de Ocupación y Empleo.; ages 15+	2022 Q2	2
Netherlands	CBS - Labour participation; province; ages 15-75	2022 Q1	2
New Zealand	Household Labour Force Survey - HLF - Table: Labour Force Status; ages 15+ and 15-24	2022 Q2	2
Norway	Statistics Norway, table 13497: Population, by labour force status, age and region; ages 15-74	2022 Q2	2
Poland	Statistics Poland//Category K4 Labour Market//Group G623 Economic activity of the 15-89 and 15-24 population (quarterly data)// Subgroup P3969 Economic activity of the population by place of residence	2022 Q2	2
Portugal	Statistics Portugal - Unemployment rate (Series 2011 - %) by Place of residence (NUTS - 2013) and Sex; Quarterly - Statistics Portugal, LFS; ages 16-84 and 16-24	2022 Q2	2
Slovak Republic	Statistical Office of the Slovak Republic, Balance of economic activity of population aged 15+ (since 2021) [pr3102qr]	2022 Q2	2
Slovenia	Working age population by activity and activity rates, age groups, sex and cohesion regions, Slovenia, quarterly; ages 15+	2022 Q2	2
Spain	INE - Economic activity, unemployment and employment rates, by province; ages 15+	2022 Q2	2
Sweden	Statistics Sweden - table AM0401UZ. Population aged 15-74 (LFS) by region, labour status and sex. Quarter 2005K2 - 2020K4; ages 15+	2022 Q2	3
Switzerland	OFS - Swiss Labour Force Survey in 2nd quarter 2022 - table je-f-03.02.00.02.02.01	2022 Q2	2
Türkiye	n.a.		-

Quarterly labour force *(cont.)*

Country	Source	Last available quarter	Territorial Level
United Kingdom	ONS - annual population aged 16+ survey - regional - labour market status by age	2022 Q2	2
United States	Based on US BLS - Local Area Unemployment Statistics ages 16+. Monthly unemployment rates averaged by quarter	2022 Q2	2

Remote work uptake

Country	Source	Year	Territorial level
EU20 countries, Norway, and Switzerland[1]	European Labour Force survey, based on the work presented at the Annual Congress of the European Regional Science Association, Pécs, Hungary, August 2022: "From potential to reality: Regional enablers and inhibitors of telework across European regions" by Zhiwu Wei, Davide Luca, Cem Özüzel	2019-20	Degree of urbanisation

1. The number of individuals, as a share of all workers, who reported having "usually worked from home" (i.e. more than 50% of the time in the survey reference month).

Tourism: Flight passengers

Country	Source	Year	Territorial level
EU20 countries, Norway, and Switzerland	Eurostat, table tran_r_avpa_nm	2020	2
Mexico	Dirección General De Aeronáutica Civil	2020	2
United Kingdom	UK Civil Aviation Authority	2020	2
United States	Federal Aviation Administration	2020	2

Tourism: Overnight stays in tourist accommodations

Country	Source	Year	Territorial level
EU20 countries, Norway, and Switzerland	Eurostat, table tour_occ_nin2	2020	2
Australia	Australian Trade and Investment Commission – Tourism Research Australia	2020	2
Chile	INE, *https://www.ine.cl/estadisticas/economia/comercio-servicios-y-turismo/actividad-del-turismo*	2020	2
Israel	Central Bureau of Statistics Israel	2020	2
Japan	Statistics bureau	2020	2

Trade openness

Country	Source	Year	Territorial level
Australia	Australian Bureau of Statistics, 5368.0 - International Trade in Goods and Services. Table 15a. Merchandise exports, State and Australia, FOB Value and Table 15b. Merchandise imports, State and Australia, Customs Value	2019	2
Austria[1]	Statistics Austria compiles on behalf of the Austrian Chamber of Commerce (WKO) and the nine Austrian federal states regionalised foreign trade data by federal states	2019	2
Belgium	National Bank of Belgium – Foreign trade, national concept	2019	2
Canada	Statistics Canada. CANSIM database. Table 228-0060 Merchandise imports and domestic exports	2019	2
Colombia	National Administrative Department of Statistics - DANE, Directorate of Methodology and Statistical Production	2019	2

Trade openness *(cont.)*

Country	Source	Year	Territorial level
France	Douanes. Statistiques départementales et régionales du commerce extérieur pour l'exportation de marchandises	2019	2
Germany	Spatial Monitoring System of the BBSR	2019	2
Greece	Hellenic Statistical Authority. External Trade Survey	2019	2
Italy	ISTAT, Instrastat System	2019	2
Korea	Statistics Korea	2019	2
Latvia[2]	The External trade database and the Business register information of the Central Statistical Bureau	2019	2
Lithuania[3]	Statistics Lithuania, Lithuanian Customs: extra-EU trade Customs declarations, intra-EU trade (since 2004) Intrastat survey; Statistics Lithuania: Statistical Business Register	2019	2
Portugal[4]	Statistics Portugal, Statistics on external trade of goods	2019	2
Slovenia	SURS	2019	2
Spain	Ministerio de hacienda y funcion publica - Agencia Tributaria	2019	2
Sweden	Statistics Sweden	2019	2
Switzerland[5]	Swiss Federal Customs Administration FCA	2019	2
United Kingdom	HM Revenue and Customs: Trade Statistics, UK Regional Trade in Goods Statistics	2019	2
United States	U.S. Census Bureau: Economic Indicators Division USA Trade Online. U.S. Import and Export Merchandise trade statistics	2019	2
China	National Bureau of Statistics China. Customs statistics	2019	2

1. Austria: Austrian federal states regionalised foreign trade data by federal states. In order to calculate statistically reliable regional foreign trade data in compliance with the principles of the national official statistical institution, individual records are matched and reassigned by resorting to already existing data sources.
2. Latvia: Unspecified data have been adjusted for non-response as well as trade below the threshold related to the trade between the member states. Other unspecified information includes trade figures about the enterprises that are not registered in the business register (foreign enterprises) but which carried out the trade in goods activities in Latvia.
3. Lithuania: Trade data are compiled according to the Special Trade System. Data by region were compiled by linking International Trade in Goods Statistics (ITGS) and Statistical Register of Economic Entities (Statistical Business Register) data. Intrastat adjustments for non-response and trade below exemption thresholds are not included. Data are based on the information of only successfully linked enterprises.
4. Portugal: The value for Portugal may not match the sum of the regions, since the head offices of some economic operators are not identified or are located abroad.
5. Switzerland: Data include gold, silver in bars and coins, electricity, returned goods and outward processing. Data omits two regions considered by FCA (the Principality of Liechtenstein and *canton* not specified); therefore, the sum of CH01-CH07 does not correspond to the official Swiss foreign trade at the total level, *www.swiss-impex.admin.ch*.

ANNEX C

Indexes and estimation techniques

Cultural and creative sectors (CCS) and occupations

Table C.1. **Cultural and creative sectors included in CCS**

NACE Rev. 2 industry code	Industry title
18	Printing and reproduction of recorded media
32.12 and 32.2	Manufacture of jewellery and related articles and manufacture of musical instruments
47.61-63	Retail sale of books, newspapers and stationery, music and video recordings in specialised stores
58.11 and 58.13-14	Book publishing and publishing of newspapers, journals and periodicals
58.21	Publishing of computer games
59	Motion picture, video and television programme production, sound recording and music publishing activities
60 and 63.91	Programming and broadcasting activities and news agency activities
71.11	Architectural activities
74.1-3	Specialised design, photographic, translation and interpretation activities
77.22	Renting of video tapes and disks
90	Creative, arts and entertainment activities
91	Libraries, archives, museums and other cultural activities

Source: Adapted from Eurostat.

Table C.2. **Cultural occupations included in CCS employment statistics**

ISCO-08 occupation code	Occupation title
216	Architects, planners, surveyors and designers
2353-55	Other language, music and arts teachers
262	Librarians, archivists and curators
264	Authors, journalists and linguists
265	Creative and performing artists
3431-32	Photographers and interior designers and decorators
3433	Gallery, museum and library technicians
3435	Other artistic and cultural associate professionals
3521	Broadcasting and audio-visual technicians
4411	Library clerks
7312	Musical instrument makers and tuners
7313-14	Jewellery and precious-metal, potters and related workers
7315	Glass makers, cutters, grinders and finishers
7316	Sign writers, decorative painters, engravers and etchers
7317-19	Handicraft workers in wood, basketry, textile, leather and those not elsewhere classified

Source: Eurostat.

Methodology to estimate the share of green areas in FUA urban centres

The share of green areas in FUAs is estimated at the urban centre level, using ESA Worldcover data (Zanaga et al., 2021[1]), which provides worldwide land cover data for 2020 at a 10 m resolution. Green areas are defined by the following classes: trees, shrublands and grasslands.

Methodology to estimate the urban heat island intensity

The measure for urban heat island intensity in OECD FUAs was adapted from Chakraborty and Lee (Chakraborty and Lee, 2019[2]). The suggested methodology is composed of the following steps:

1. Define for each FUA using MODIS yearly land cover data (Friedl and Sulla-Menashe, 2019[3]) "urban" and "non-urban" lands, where "urban" refers to the "urban and built-up lands" class in the International Geosphere-Biosphere Programme (IGBP) classification, and "non-urban" to the remaining classes except "water bodies".
2. By using the ALOS World 3D (Tadono et al., 2014[4]) digital elevation model (DEM), compute elevation statistics for "urban" and "non-urban" lands to ensure elevation patterns are similar in both contexts.
3. Compute land surface temperature using MODIS Terra (Wan, Hook and Hulley, 2015[5]) and Aqua (Wan, Hook and Hulley, 2021[6]) land surface temperature (LST) daily dataset:
    a. Apply quality filters to remove clouds and ensure an average LST error ≤3K.
    b. Compute mean temperature in both zones described above. For the "non-urban" land, only pixels with similar elevation statistics as the "urban" area were considered, namely in the range $[\bar{z} - 2\sigma_z, \bar{z} + 2\sigma_z]$, where z is the elevation in the "urban" area.
    c. Compute this mean temperature for the whole year, summer and winter. Summer is defined as 1 June to 31 August for the Northern Hemisphere, and 1 December to 28 February for the Southern hemisphere. Winter is defined reciprocally.

4. Finally, the urban heat island intensity is defined as the temperature difference $T\_u - T\_r$.

Methodology to estimate soil moisture anomaly

Water content in the superficial layers of the soil is important for water supply and vegetation health. Soil moisture anomaly is a suitable indicator for monitoring the intensity of agricultural droughts. This publication measures agricultural droughts in terms of cropland soil moisture anomaly using the Copernicus Climate Data Store ERA5-Land monthly average data product (European Centre for Medium-range Weather Forecasts, 2022[7]). It is a global gridded product with a 0.1° spatial resolution (~ 11.1 km) from 1950 to the present and provides land variables related to the energy and water cycles over several decades. It contains per-pixel information of the monthly average volume of water in the surface soil layer of 0 to 7 cm deep, expressed as m^3 of water per m^3 of soil. The Copernicus annual 300 m land cover (CCI-LC) (European Space Agency Climate Change Initiative, 2019[8]) enables to get cropland boundaries. Cropland here includes: cropland, rainfed, irrigated or post-flooding; mosaic cropland (>50%)/ natural vegetation (tree, shrub, herbaceous cover) (<50%); and mosaic natural vegetation (tree, shrub, herbaceous cover) (>50%)/cropland (<50%). Once soil moisture grid cells for each year are selected based on cropland land cover, cropland soil moisture anomaly is obtained by computing the percentage change based on the reference period (1981-2010).

Methodology to estimate public transport accessibility

Public transport accessibility is measured using Open Street Map (OSM) (Haklay and Weber, 2008[9]) to get public transport stops. Because of the lack of reliability of OSM in small cities, this publication only focuses on the largest FUA of each OECD country. The Mapbox isochrone API (Mapbox, 2022[10]) then enables to compute isochrones from these public transport stops to get to all the areas located within 10-min walking distance. The Global Human Settlement Population layer 2015 then enables to get the share of the population in each FUA who has access to public transport in less than a 10-min walk.

Methodology to estimate exposure to wildfires

Burnt area by land cover was obtained using JRC's Global wildfire dataset for the analysis of fire regimes and fire behaviours (Artes Vivancos et al., 2019[11]), based on MODIS burned area product Collection 6. This dataset provides monthly individual fire perimeters for 2001-20. Burnt areas are aggregated at the yearly level and then crossed with Copernicus annual 300 m land cover (CCI-LC) data (European Space Agency Climate Change Initiative, 2019[8]).

Population exposure to wildfires over 2010-20 was computed by merging monthly wildfire perimeters and by then taking a 5 km buffer. The Global Human Settlement Population layer for 2015 (Schiavina, Freire and MacManus, 2019[12]) enabled then to compute the population exposed to at least one fire over 2010-20.

Methodology to estimate exposure to river floods

Population exposure to river floods was estimated using the River Flood Hazard Maps at European and Global Scale (Dottori et al., 2021[13]). For OECD countries located in Europe and the Mediterranean Basin, the regional map was used, as the spatial granularity is 250 m. For the remaining OECD countries, the global map with a spatial granularity of 1 km was used. These datasets identify flooded areas for river flood events of different return periods (10 to 500 years). A return period refers to the estimated time interval between floods of similar intensity. Here a return period of 100 years is considered. The 100-year return period is calculated based on past events but the frequency of such climate-related disasters is likely to increase. Changes in flood risk are unevenly distributed, with the largest increases in America, Asia and Europe but without higher flood protection standards, flood events are projected to rise in all continents. Therefore, 100-year floods are likely to happen more often going forward.

Methodology to estimate population exposure to heat stress

Population exposure to heat stress was estimated using the Universal Thermal Comfort Index (UTCI). The UTCI considers air temperature, wind, radiation and humidity and enables to assess the impact of atmospheric conditions on the human body: 32°C < UTCI < 38°C is considered as strong heat stress, 38°C < UTCI < 46°C as very strong heat stress, and UTCI > 46°C as extreme heat stress.

The Copernicus Climate Data Store provides hourly thermal comfort indices grids derived from ERA5 reanalysis (CDS, 2022[14]). The spatial resolution is 0.25°x0.25°. To obtain the population exposure to strong heat stress, we applied the following steps:

- Compute daily maximum UTCI grids.
- Apply a threshold of 32°C on these daily masks and sum by year to get yearly grids of the number of days of strong heat stress or worse.
- Compute by large region zonal statistics weighted by population by using the GHSL-POP layers.
- Consider 1981-2010 as the reference period to get the reference average number of days of strong heat stress and compare this value with recent years.

Methodology to estimate electricity indicators at the regional level

To estimate the electricity indicators at the regional level, the Global Power Plant Database (GPPD) (Byers et al., 2021[15]), the International Energy Agency (IEA) electricity and heat database (OECD, 2022[16]) and the harmonised global dataset of wind and solar farm (GWS) locations and power (Dunnett et al., 2020[17]) are used.

The GPPD provides information on power plants located in 167 countries all over the world, including the 38 OECD countries. For each power plant, the GPPD provides the geographic co-ordinates and the following attributes:

- The energy source: oil, gas, coal, petroleum coke, cogeneration, hydro, wind, waste, biomass, wave and tidal, geothermal, solar, nuclear and others.
- The generation capacity, which is the maximum power (in megawatts, MW) that the plant can deliver. The capacity is a facility-specific characteristic and does not change over time, unless extension or upgrade of the power station, or a shutdown of a part of it.
- The annual electricity generation, which provides the amount of electricity generated over a year (in GWh). This indicator is reported over the period 2013-19. When no electricity generation was reported, the annual electricity generation was estimated. The annual generation corresponds to the gross generation, i.e. the electricity consumption of the power plant for its operation is not deducted.
- The country where the power plant is registered.

As the coverage of wind and solar power plants in the GPPD was not satisfying, the GWS farm locations and power was used instead to get the locations of wind and solar power sources.

The International Energy Agency (IEA (IEA, 2022[18])) database includes national-level electricity generation data by energy source for most OECD countries. The IEA dataset used to estimate electricity generation indicators at the local level corresponds to the gross electricity production by energy source in 2019. A breakdown of 53 different sources is available.

Electricity generation estimates

In order to remain consistent across countries and energy sources, electricity generation was estimated at the power plant level based on the relative capacity of each power plant (from the GPPD and GWS) and on the total national electricity generation form each energy source (from the IEA). The methodology follows the four steps below:

1. Map energy sources from the IEA to the GPPD classification.
   The IEA electricity production data provides a higher level of detail in terms of breakdown by energy source compared to the GPPD data. For this reason, each energy source type recorded in the IEA database was matched to a source category in the GPPD.
2. Determine the share of national capacity for each power plant.
   For each power plant *p*, located in the country *c* and generating electricity from the energy source *f*, the share of the capacity of the power plant in the national capacity for the source *f* is calculated as:

$$share_{p,c,f} = \frac{capacity_{p,c,f}}{\sum_i capacity_{i,c,f}}$$

where $i \in$ power plants located in the country *c*, and generating electricity from the source f.

3. Allocate a part of the national generation to each power plant.
   For each power plant *p*, generating electricity from source *f*, in the country *c*, the estimated generation is calculated as:
   $generation_{p,c,f} = share_{p,c,f} * national\ generation_{c,f}$

Aggregation at local scales

To compute indicators at different geographical scales, a point shapefile was created from the GPPD and GWS databases using the latitude and longitude provided for each facility – each point representing a power plant. The point shapefile was overlapped with two other shapefiles corresponding to the boundaries of the subnational geographies available in OECD countries (TL2 and TL3 regions). Thus, each power plant can be associated to a TL2 region and a TL3 region. Offshore power plants were assigned to the closest region (of the registered host country) based on the distance to the coast.

Year of reference

All indicators presented in this document refer to the year 2019, which corresponds to the latest year for which capacity data is available in the GPPD.

Breakdown by energy source categories

The GPPD includes 13 different energy sources. These energy sources were aggregated into 6 categories (coal, gas, oil, nuclear, renewables and others). The energy sources within each category are comparable in terms of technology, risks and impacts on the environment.

Electricity generation indicators

For each region *r*, generation data was aggregated into each category *i* as:

$$generation_{r,i} = \sum_{k \in i} power\ plant\ generation_{r,k}$$

where $k \in$ {coal, gas, oil, petroleum coke, cogeneration, nuclear, hydro, wind, waste, biomass, wave, geothermal, solar}, $i \in$ { coal, gas, oil, nuclear, renewables and others}, and $power\ plant\ generation_{r,k}$ is the electricity generation of a power plant located in the region *r*, generating electricity from the source type *k*.

Energy mix indicators

For each region *r*, the share of each energy source category *i* is calculated as:

$$share_{r,i} = \frac{generation_{r,\ i}}{\sum_j generation_{r,\ j}}*100$$

where $j \in$ {coal, gas, oil, nuclear, renewables, others}.

Greenhouse gas (GHG) emissions from electricity generation indicators

GHG emissions indicators are derived from both the electricity generation by energy source and the emission factors for each energy source. Electricity generation was estimated at the power plant level for each energy source included in the GPPD as described above. Emission intensity by energy source comes from the IPPC estimates on GHG emissions of supply technologies.

For each region *r*, the GHG emissions (in tons of CO_2 equivalent) are calculated as:

$$emissions_r = \sum_{k\ \in\ f} generation_{r,\ k}*emission\ intensity_k$$

where the emission intensity corresponds to the median value of the lifecycle emissions (in gCO2eq/kWh), $f \in$ {coal, gas, oil, petroleum coke, cogeneration, nuclear, hydro, wind, waste, biomass, wave, geothermal, solar}.

Emission intensity

For each region *r*, the emission intensity (in tons of CO_2 equivalent per GWh) is calculated as:

$$emission\ intensity_r = \frac{emissions_r}{\sum_i generation_{r,\ i}}$$

where $i \in$ {coal, gas, oil, nuclear, renewables and others}.

Methodology to estimate GHG emissions by sector

GHG emissions at the subnational level were estimated using the Emissions Database for Global Atmospheric Research (EDGAR) (Crippa et al., 2021[19]), version 6.0 of the EC JRC. EDGAR provides annual sector-specific grid maps for the three main GHGs (CO_2, CH_4, and N_2O) at a 0.1° spatial resolution (~11 km). Other GHGs, such as fluorinated gases, are not available at the moment. The different sectors and subsectors covered are:

- **Energy industry**:
  - **Energy production**: Power industry (IPCC 2006: 1A1a).
  - **Energy transformation**: Oil refineries and transformation industry (1A1b, 1A1ci, 1A1cii, 1A5biii; 1B1b, 1B2aiii6, 1B2biii3, 1B1c).
  - **Energy extraction**: Fuel exploitation (oil, coal, natural gas) (1B1a, 1B2aiii2, 1B2aiii3, 1B2bi, 1B2bii).
- **Manufacturing industry**: Combustion for manufacturing (1A2), chemical processes (2B), iron and steel production (2C1, 2C2), non-ferrous metals production (2C3 to 2C7), non-energy use of fuels (2D1, 2D2, 2D4), solvents and products use (2D3, 2E, 2F, 2G), non-metallic minerals production (2A), oil refineries and transformation industry (1A1b, 1A1ci, 1A1cii, 1A5biii; 1B1b, 1B2aiii6, 1B2biii3, 1B1c).
- **Buildings**: Energy for buildings (1A4+1A5).
- **Waste**: waste water handling (4D), solid waste landfills (4A+4B), solid waste incineration (4C).
- **Transport**: Road transportation (1A3b), aviation (1A3a), shipping (1A3d), railways, pipelines, off-road transport (1A3c+1A3e).

- **Agriculture**: Enteric fermentation (3A1), manure management (3A2), agricultural waste burning (3C1b), agricultural soils (3C2+3C3+3C4+3C7), indirect N_2O emissions from agriculture (3C5+3C6).
- **Other**: Fossil fuel fires (5B), indirect emissions from NOx and NH_3 (5A).

Emissions from Land Use and Land Cover Change (LULCC) are not included. National GHG emissions are disaggregated by using subsector-specific geospatial proxies. For example, the road transport emissions estimates are based on different types of road networks extracted from Open Street Map (Haklay and Weber, 2008[9]) (highways, primary and secondary, residential and commercial roads) and different weighting factors for each road type. Road traffic is not directly considered. For more details about the disaggregation methodology, refer to the *OECD Regional Outlook 2021* (OECD, 2021[20]).

GHG emissions are expressed in CO_2 equivalents using 100-year global warming potential from the IPCC 5th Assessment Report (AR5), i.e. 28 for CH_4, and 265 for N_2O.

Methodology to estimate emissions from key manufacturing sectors

European Union Emission Trading System (EU-ETS, 2020[21]) emissions and ORBIS (Pinto Ribeiro, Menghinello and De Backer, 2010[22]) data were used to estimate emissions in key manufacturing sectors. EU-ETS emissions data cover high emissions installations and provide the exact location of each installation. They cover most emissions in refined petroleum and coke, chemicals, basic metals and other non-metallic minerals. However, publicly available ETS emissions data provide limited information on the sectoral origin of emissions within manufacturing and this information does not follow NACE sectors. Most ETS emissions are attributed to fuel combustion with no breakdown. ETS emissions have been mainly attributed to NACE sectors according to the main activity of businesses owning installations using ORBIS business data.

For more details on the methodology, refer to *Regional Industrial Transitions to Climate Neutrality: Identifying vulnerable regions* (OECD, forthcoming[23])

Methodology to estimate regional energy intensity in European large regions

Regional energy intensity estimates were obtained using the following Eurostat datasets:

- Energy supply and use by NACE Rev. 2 activity (env_ac_pefasu) (Eurostat, 2022[24]).
- SBS data by NUTS 2 regions and NACE Rev. 2 (from 2008 onwards) (sbs_r_nuts06_r2) (Eurostat, 2021[25]).

National energy consumption data by NACE sector for European countries provided in env_ac_pefasu were disaggregated using the NUTS-2 employment data by NACE sector given in sbs_r_nuts06_r2.

Methodology to estimate land use in cities

Land use in cities was estimated by using publicly available satellite imagery (Sentinel-1 and -2) and a Deep Learning image segmentation model (U-Net). The model was trained on the Copernicus Urban Atlas (EEA, 2020[26]) to automatically detect land use patterns on satellite images aggregated at the yearly level. Population estimates are obtained using the GHSL-POP layer (2022 release) for 2020

(JRC, 2022[27]). For more details on the methodology, refer to "Monitoring land use in cities using satellite imagery and deep learning" (Banquet et al., 2022[28]).

Methodology to estimate the potential for remote working

The assessment of regions' capacity to adapt to remote working is based on the diversity of tasks performed in different types of occupations and is structured in two steps.

The first step requires classifying each occupation based on the tasks required and according to the degree to which those tasks can be performed remotely. Such a classification is based on a recent study by Dingel and Neiman (2020[29]), which is built from the O*NET surveys conducted in the United States. The second step relies on data from labour force surveys and consists of assessing the geographical distribution of different types of occupations and subsequently matching those occupations with the classification performed in the first step. Combining the two data sets allows for assessing the number of workers who can perform their tasks from home as a share of the total employment in the region.

This assessment does not consider the specific regulations or arrangements that each country applies to remote working and which affect the actual share of people working remotely. For example, limitations in the days of remote working for cross-border workers are not reflected in the estimates presented here.

Theil entropy index

Definition

Regional disparities are also measured by a Theil entropy index, which is defined as:

$$Theil = \sum_{i=1}^{N} \frac{y_i}{\overline{y}} ln\left(\frac{y_i}{\overline{y}}\right)$$

where N is the number of regions in the OECD, y_i is the variable of interest in the i-th region (i.e. household income, life expectancy, homicide rate, etc.) and $\overline{y}$ is the mean of the variable of interest across all regions.

The Theil index can be easily decomposed into two components: i) the disparities within subgroups of regions – where for example a subgroup is identified by a set of regions belonging to a country; ii) the disparities between subgroups of regions (i.e. between countries). The sum of these two components is equal to the Theil index.

In order to decompose the Theil index, let us start by assuming *m* groups of regions (countries). The decomposition will assume the following form:

$$Theil = \sum_{j=1}^{M} \sum_{i=1}^{N} s_j \frac{y_{ij}}{\overline{y}_j} ln\left(\frac{y_{ij}}{\overline{y}_j}\right) + \sum_{j=1}^{M} s_j ln\left(\frac{\overline{y}_j}{\overline{y}}\right)$$

where the first term of the formula is the *within* part of the decomposition equal to the weighted average of the Theil inequality indexes of each country. Weights, s_i, are computed as the ratio between the country average of the variable of interest and the OECD average of the same variable. The second term is the between a component of the Theil index and represents the share of regional disparities that depends on the disparities across countries.

Interpretation

The Theil index ranges between zero and ∞, with zero representing an equal distribution and higher values representing a higher level of inequality.

The index assigns equal weight to each region regardless of its size; therefore, differences in the values of the index among countries may be partially due to differences in the average size of regions in each country.

References

[11] Artes Vivancos, T. et al. (2019), "A global wildfire dataset for the analysis of fire regimes and fire behaviour", *Scientific Data*, Vol. 6, p. 296.

[28] Banquet, A. et al. (2022), "Monitoring land use in cities using satellite imagery and deep learning", *OECD Regional Development Papers*, No. 28, OECD Publishing, Paris, *https://doi.org/10.1787/dc8e85d5-en*.

[15] Byers, L. et al. (2021), *A Global Database of Powerplants*, *https://www.wri.org/publication/global-power-plant-database*.

[14] CDS (2022), *Thermal Comfort Indices Derived from ERA5 Reanalysis*, Copernicus Climate Change Service Climate Data Store, *https://cds.climate.copernicus.eu/cdsapp#!/dataset/derived-utci-historical?tab=overview*.

[2] Chakraborty, T. and X. Lee (2019), "A simplified urban-extent algorithm to characterize surface urban heat islands on a global scale and examine vegetation control on their spatiotemporal variability", *International Journal of Applied Earth Observation and Geoinformation*, Vol. 74, pp. 269-280, *https://doi.org/10.1016/j.jag.2018.09.015*.

[19] Crippa, M. et al. (2021), *EDGAR v6.0 Greenhouse Gas Emissions*, Joint Research Centre (JRC), European Commission, *http://data.europa.eu/89h/97a67d67-c62e-4826-b873-9d972c4f670b*.

[29] Dingel, J. and B. Neiman (2020), "How many jobs can be done at home?", *Becker Friedman Institute White Paper March*, *https://bfi.uchicago.edu/working-paper/how-many-jobs-can-be-done-at-home/*.

[13] Dottori, F. et al. (2021), "River flood hazard maps for Europe and the Mediterranean Basin region", Joint Research Centre (JRC), European Commission.

[17] Dunnett, S. et al. (2020), "Harmonised global datasets of wind and solar farm locations and power", *Scientific Data*, Vol. 7/1, p. 190, *https://doi.org/10.1038/s41597-020-0469-8*.

[26] EEA (2020), *Urban Atlas LCLU 2018*, European Environment Agency, *https://land.copernicus.eu/local/urban-atlas/urban-atlas-2018*.

[21] EU-ETS (2020), *Verified Emissions for 2019*, European Union Emission Trading System, *https://ec.europa.eu/clima/eu-action/eu-emissions-trading-system-eu-ets/union-registry_en#ecl-inpage-1121*.

[7] European Centre for Medium-range Weather Forecasts (2022), *ERA5-Land Monthly Averaged Data from 1950 to Present*, *https://cds.climate.copernicus.eu/cdsapp#!/dataset/reanalysis-era5-land-monthly-means?tab=overview*.

[8] European Space Agency Climate Change Initiative (2019), *Land Cover Classification Gridded Maps from 1992 to Present Derived from Satellite Observations*.

[24] Eurostat (2022), *Energy Supply and Use by NACE Rev. 2 Activity*, *https://ec.europa.eu/eurostat/databrowser/view/env_ac_pefasu/default/table?lang=en*.

[25] Eurostat (2021), *Structural Business Statistics Data by NUTS 2 Regions and NACE Rev. 2 (from 2008 onwards)*, *https://appsso.eurostat.ec.europa.eu/nui/show.do?dataset=sbs_r_nuts06_r2&lang=en*.

[3] Friedl, M. and D. Sulla-Menashe (2019), *MCD12Q1 MODIS/Terra+Aqua Land Cover Type Yearly L3 Global 500m SIN Grid V006. NASA EOSDIS Land Processes DAAC*, NASA EOSDIS Land Processes DAAC.

[9] Haklay, M. and P. Weber (2008), "OpenStreetMap: User-generated street maps", *IEEE Pervasive Computing*, Vol. 7, pp. 12-18.

[18] IEA (n.d.), ""OECD - Electricity and heat generation"", *IEA Electricity Information Statistics*, *https://doi.org/10.1787/data-00457-en* (accessed on 24 October 2022).

[27] JRC (2022), *GHSL Data Package 2022: Public Release GHS P2022*, European Commission Joint Research Centre, *https://data.europa.eu/doi/10.2760/19817*.

[10] Mapbox (2022), *Isochrone API*, *https://docs.mapbox.com/api/navigation/isochrone/*.

[16] OECD (2022), "OECD - Electricity/heat supply and consumption", *IEA Electricity Information Statistics*, OECD, Paris, *https://doi.org/10.1787/e2da2a08-en* (accessed on 13 October 2022).

[23] OECD (2022), *Regional Industrial Transitions to Climate Neutrality: Identifying vulnerable regions*, OECD Publishing, Paris.

[20] OECD (2021), *OECD Regional Outlook 2021: Addressing COVID-19 and Moving to Net Zero Greenhouse Gas Emissions*, OECD Publishing, Paris, *https://doi.org/10.1787/17017efe-en*.

[22] Pinto Ribeiro, S., S. Menghinello and K. De Backer (2010), "The OECD ORBIS Database: Responding to the Need for Firm-Level Micro-Data in the OECD", *OECD Statistics Working Papers*, No. 2010/1, OECD Publishing, Paris, *https://doi.org/10.1787/5kmhds8mzj8w-en*.

[12] Schiavina, M., S. Freire and K. MacManus (2019), "GHS population grid multitemporal (1975, 1990, 2000, 2015)".

[4] Tadono, T. et al. (2014), "Precise Global DEM Generation By ALOS PRISM, ISPRS Annals of the Photogrammetry", *Remote Sensing and Spatial Information Sciences*, Vol. II-4, pp. 71-76.

[6] Wan, Z., S. Hook and G. Hulley (2021), *MODIS/Aqua Land Surface Temperature/Emissivity Daily L3 Global 1km SIN Grid V061*.

[5] Wan, Z., S. Hook and G. Hulley (2015), *MOD11A1 MODIS/Terra Land Surface Temperature/Emissivity Daily L3 Global 1km SIN Grid V006*.

[1] Zanaga, D. et al. (2021), *ESA WorldCover 10 m 2020 v100*, *https://doi.org/10.5281/zenodo.5571936*.

www.ingramcontent.com/pod-product-compliance
Lightning Source LLC
Chambersburg PA
CBHW061220240926
51846CB00006B/1288
9789264778177